SYMBOLS OF THE HOLY COVENANT:

DEEPER SPIRITUAL UNDERSTANDING FOR A COVENANTED LIFE

VOLUME ONE

A Divine Covenant Confirmation Miracle

MARGARETTE C. HUNTTE

A guide to the Holy Covenant, an unrivaled account of a modern-day covenant confirmation miracle, the sacred meaning and consequences of this unprecedented occurrence in our time.

WESTBOW
PRESS
A DIVISION OF THOMAS NELSON

Unless otherwise noted, all Scripture quotations are taken
from the King James Version of the Bible.

WestBow Press books may be ordered through booksellers or by contacting:

WestBow Press
A Division of Thomas Nelson
1663 Liberty Drive
Bloomington, IN 47403
www.westbowpress.com
1-(866) 928-1240

ISBN: 978-1-4497-9504-7 (sc)
ISBN: 978-1-4497-9503-0 (hc)
ISBN: 978-1-4497-9505-4 (e)

Library of Congress Control Number: 2013908844

Printed in the United States of America.

WestBow Press rev. date: 1/30/2014

ACKNOWLEDGEMENTS

COVER PHOTOGRAPH: COVENANT SYMBOLISM

This exquisite and unique bridal creation worn by the author is used to depict some of the symbols of a covenanted life in a manner that is relatable and personal. God guided me to this creation by coincidence, by His providence and intervention, as I pondered how I should introduce, in some small measure, covenant symbols on the cover for the benefit of readers.

Under the holy covenant of grace the bride is a symbol of the redeemed of Jesus Christ. Her "lips are like a thread of scarlet" (Song of Sol.4:3); they speak of redemption by His precious blood. The white silk Swiss dot embroidered blouse portrays the fine twined linen, embroidery and needlework of which the Bible speaks. These are symbols of God's intricate and delicate work of grace. White is the color of His righteousness. Flesh is the symbol of sin. The sheerness says there is no perfect covering for sin to be found in the world, only the righteousness of Jesus Christ. Green is the eternal nature of Christ who gives to us the gift of eternal life. A covenanted life becomes a prayer, greater than words, that worships and glorifies Almighty God in the precious name of Jesus Christ. (To be continued).

Special appreciation is expressed to

Moshe Zusman: Moshe Zusman Photography Studio

Nour Kazoun: Makeup Artist, MadeupArt

Oscar de la Renta: Fashion Designer

The staff of the Bridal Salon at Saks Jandel

CONTENTS

Preface... ix

Part 1:   Ancient Miracle in Modern Times.....................1
Chapter 1:   Divinely Inspired Prayer 3
Chapter 2:   Spiritual Alignment.......................................8
Chapter 3:   Sacred Season of Lent 11
Chapter 4:   The Day That I Was Covenanted:
             The Divine Miracle 13
Chapter 5:   The Divine Symbols.....................................19
Chapter 6:   My Search for Answers.................................22
Chapter 7:   God Would Provide the Interpretation 26
Chapter 8:   Separation unto God.....................................34
Chapter 9:   The Divine Process and Rewards of
             Spiritual Knowledge...................................41
Chapter 10: Visions of the Word of God Facilitate Knowledge....46
Chapter 11: Visions of the Word of God in Ancient Times 51
Chapter 12: Ancient Visions Depicting the Person of God.........60
Chapter 13: The Gift of Prophecy and the Effect
             of Sacred Visions...................................... 64
Chapter 14: The Protection of the Holy Spirit 71
Chapter 15: Divine Wisdom and Deeper
             Spiritual Understanding 83
Chapter 16: Heavenly Symbols...91
Chapter 17: The Impact of Sacred Symbolism 96

Part 2:   The Symbols and Their Interpretation.............103
Chapter 18: The Shield of God....................................... 105
Chapter 19: God, the Deliverer 114
Chapter 20: Preparation for Divine Presence...............119

Chapter 21: Divine Placement, Spaces, and
Movement of Symbols...127
Chapter 22: The Number Three—Symbol of Divine Nature 132
Chapter 23: The Number Two—Symbol of Human Nature 139
Chapter 24: Two Raindrops—Symbol of Water 155
Chapter 25: Scarlet Droplet—Symbol of Blood........................ 166
Chapter 26: The Rainbow 175
Chapter 27: Flames of Fire—Symbol of the Furnace................. 185
Chapter 28: Symbol of the Lamp/Lighted Candle 192
Chapter 29: The Symbols—Numbers Seven and Eight.............201
Chapter 30: The Holy Covenant—An Overview.......................209
Chapter 31: Summary of Divine Declarations in
the Sacred Vision..226
Chapter 32: How Near Is God?...243
Chapter 33: An Immeasurable Mercy.......................................256

Bibliography..261
References..263
Index 265

PREFACE

*S*ymbols of the Holy Covenant: Deeper Spiritual Understanding for a Covenanted Life is the first in a multivolume series that illuminates the spiritual symbolism entrenched within the holy covenant.

The holy covenant is the essential foundation of knowledge of life and creation. As a result, it is imperative that knowledge of it not remain upon the shelves of imposing and intimidating libraries around the world or left to be studied only by theologians and Bible scholars. It should be brought into the availability and access of the masses in a manner that is relatable and personal.

There is no denying the enormous complexity of the scope of this spiritual knowledge, yet the covenant is deeply rooted in the core of who we are and touches each life in ways that range from simple and mundane to the most mysterious. This examination of the covenant through the scope of its symbolism transforms it to the status of familiarity through common denominators and renders it easier to grasp.

The symbols show us how personal the covenant is and how God values each of us and has created us for a personal union with Him, kinship with each other, and harmony with all of nature. Christ Jesus established an agreement on our behalf before we were born, and with the world before it was created. The covenant governs all life and determines the eternal destiny of every human being.

Knowledge of the structure of the holy covenant's guarantees and assurances is the foundation for a spiritually prepared life. This foundation for wisdom and deeper spiritual understanding gives enlightenment regarding the processes of the soul in its return to God for grace.

My reason for writing this book came after God called me into covenant by revealing a covenant-confirmation miracle just as God also confirmed His covenant in ancient time. The symbols God gave me in the course of a sacred vision are uniquely revealed, yet they reaffirm the covenant confirmations made throughout the history of the world. This includes from the beginning of creation to the new covenant of grace in Jesus Christ, which is the overarching covenant. The symbols that constitute this heavenly language particularly evoke those confirmations made with Noah, Abraham, and the New covenant, though they are all-encompassing of the others. For there is one God and one covenant but several confirmations, as the knowledge of grace was progressively revealed. And now, in our time, God is reaffirming the holy covenant. When God confirms His covenant, there are major spiritual consequences, as you will discover in this illumination of the symbols presented in the sacred vision.

Consequently, it became an inevitable mission to share this information that reveals God's immeasurable mercy, particularly since an occurrence such as this is unrivaled in modern time. The ramifications of such an occurrence are beyond the scope of what it means for me, and they have a broader spiritual mission that impacts the world.

As we travel together through the journey of the six volumes in this series, you will discover that by means of symbolism, God speaks to each of us. The first volume introduces the themes of the covenant in a spiritually autobiographical approach. It describes how I became covenanted, as it initiates the illumination of the symbolism in the covenant. The later volumes progressively uncover the deeper interpretation in a manner that is thorough, practical, and relevant to everyday life. And at the same time, they reveal the majesty and profound sacredness that define the holy covenant.

PART 1

ANCIENT MIRACLE IN MODERN TIMES

CHAPTER 1

DIVINELY INSPIRED PRAYER

Then shall ye call upon me, and ye shall go and pray unto
me, and I will hearken unto you. And ye shall seek me, and
find me, when ye shall search for me with all your heart.
Jeremiah 29:12–13

Since my childhood, I have lovingly desired to know of the majesty of God. I knew that God exists, and I wanted to grasp as much knowledge as I could of matters concerning Him. I remember, when I was between the age of six and seven, asking my mother questions about God. I asked, "How did God come into being? When was He formed?"

"Do not question God!" my mother exclaimed.

My mother did not have knowledge of these mysterious answers, of course, and indeed no one does. God is divine, and this means that knowledge of Him is beyond what we are able to comprehend. This is the essence of why God is God. And there is a limited amount that we can expect to know of Him in this mortal life.

Job, in the agony of his afflictions, contended, "By his spirit he hath garnished the heavens; his hand hath formed the crooked serpent. Lo, these are parts of his ways: but how little a portion is heard of him? but the thunder of his power who can understand?" (Job 26:13–14).

As I ponder the greatness and glory of God, I know that God exists in time without end—from eternity past, to present, and to eternity future. He depends on nothing apart from Himself for His own existence. He is omnipresent—present at all places at all times. He is omnipotent—all-powerful, almighty, supreme, and divine. This much I know. But who is able to truly comprehend all of this?

Decades later, identical questions linger in my mind, but at least I am confident of God's constant presence. I am confident that He hears and answers prayers, even the prayers of a little child. And He grants our requests in a measure that is far greater than we can ever imagine.

Jesus said, "Ask, and it shall be given you; seek, and ye shall find; knock, and it shall be opened unto you: For everyone that asketh receiveth; and he that seeketh findeth; and to him that knocketh it shall be opened." (Matthew 7:7–8). Jesus left these words for us, and we can be secure that this is true. If we seek God, God will make Himself known to us in an approach that is personal and understandable.

God-Guided Prayer

I was christened and baptized as a baby in the Anglican Church, attended Sunday school as a child, participated in church youth group, and was a member of the choir. My family often delighted in discussing Bible stories after dinner. As a teenager, my mother instilled in us the importance of prayer and a godly life, and she taught us by her example. I watched my mother set aside times for prayer each day at 8:00 a.m., 12:00 noon, and 9:00 p.m. In the evening, she took pleasure in reading the psalms and a prayer publication called *FAITH Magazine*.

FAITH Magazine is a modest publication with daily scheduled prayers. It has been published for over seventy years and is distributed worldwide by a nondenominational Christian organization called Life-Study Fellowship, which is headquartered in Noroton, Connecticut.

It provides a source of inspiration to its readers, encouraging them to lead a "prayerful and positive way of life." By word of mouth, knowledge of *FAITH Magazine* had spread among a women's group at our church in St. Peter, Barbados.

My mother often mailed the organization small donations, and it responded by sending her the *FAITH Magazine* along with other Christian literature. Occasionally, included with the literature was a list that identified special prayer requests for a variety of life's circumstances. I am in no manner associated with this organization and I do not speak for it or promote any teaching or doctrine on its behalf, but I appreciated the inspiration it offered my mother.

When I was between the age of fifteen and sixteen, at noon one day I watched my mother pray. I decided to review the list. The prayers were thought provoking. I was interested in the prayers that related to special spiritual gifts— perfect faith, the joy of knowing and serving God, that I may walk close to Him, for divine wisdom, deeper spiritual understanding, God's guidance, and that I may know that the light of His presence surrounds me and He is directing every step that I take. On the list, I checked several prayers requesting a variety of spiritual gifts and sent it with my donation to Noroton, Connecticut.

The prayers were stimulating and particularly personal. They included requests that God would give me the ability to know how close He is to me, by revealing that He is hearing me and answering my prayers, and that I would know that everything I say and do is heard and seen by Him. The prayers blessed God. They expressed how wonderful it would be to know Him, and that God would "bless me with deeper spiritual understanding". They expressed an earnest request that my life's purpose may help in doing the work of His kingdom.[i] I asked God for "divine wisdom and guidance in all that I say and all that I do" that I may know what He is saying to me through the opportunities He presents for me to help others.[ii] And I asked God for "perfect faith and trust".[iii] The prayers were written with such sincerity and longing.

Decades later, I still have these prayers—tattered and torn from much use—and they are my most treasured possessions. But looking back to that time, and considering how my life has changed, I can see clearly how God directed me in all of this to the right prayers, and He granted me a prayerful heart. I can perceive God's guidance by the power of His Holy Spirit, and through all the mistakes I have made along the way, that did not prevent God from making me to be in harmony with His will for my life. I have observed how God attended to all the things I had to say and answered the details of my requests.

God's Plan

As I grew into adulthood, I became busy with college and a fledgling career. I neglected the time I needed for worship, prayer, and developing the knowledge of God. Even so, I was convinced that when the time was right, and I had completed certain milestones in my life, I would then devote the time that is required for building a spiritual bond with God.

On completing my studies in May 1994, there was freedom from assignments, group meetings, and all that college requires. A week after graduation, I bought an inexpensive Bible—the King James Version. In it was a modest, topical concordance with no commentary.

Suddenly, I remembered those tattered pages of prayers from Life-Study Fellowship that I had not used for more than twenty years. I had kept them safe through my college years and had taken them with me wherever I had relocated. After an extensive search, I found them crumpled in an old suitcase. I read them each night before proceeding to study the Bible.

Studying the Bible

As I rededicated—developed a regular reading and prayer routine—little did I know of the enormous benefits and blessings that awaited me.

During my childhood, God instilled in me a sense of purpose through prayer. I had sensed that God had a special mission for me—and there was something specific God wanted me to do. However, I had not given it serious thought as I grew up. I never did anything toward realizing this mission, since I never fully understood what my mission was. That is, until now. For it is now that I have made myself available so that God is able to guide the way.

And I have come to realize how God, in His great love, mercy, and patience, had waited for me all those years as I worked on my career. At last, the time had come for Him to answer my prayers for wisdom, guidance, and the knowledge of Him and reveal the plans that He had established for the rest of my life.

CHAPTER 2

SPIRITUAL ALIGNMENT

I was not as knowledgeable in the Bible as I am today, but God nurtured within me a desire to search for knowledge. And without considering where in the Bible I should begin, without any predetermination on my part, I let God guide me through the pages in my quest for knowledge of God.

I benefitted significantly from reading the books of the Old Testament. This gave me insight into attributes of God: how He thinks, His will for mankind, His anger, and His way of manifesting His love and mercy. This laid a good biblical foundation for me—a foundation that gave me the basis for spiritual knowledge and initiated a distinct harmony in the way I think of God.

How God Gave Me Spiritual Awareness

In mid-September 1995, I began to experience an unusually high number and sequence of coincidences. I use the word *coincidences*, which are two similar incidences occurring in a manner and in timing or succession that cannot be easily explained in natural terms. In actuality, I should identify them as God's divine providence and intervention. There was a divine purpose rooted in these coincidences.

Numerous Coincidences and Divine Providences

These instances of divine intervention continued as I went about my daily activities, but they were mostly biblically related. I observed an increasingly harmonious alignment of daily life with my study of the Word of God. An unusual spiritual alignment began to unfold. My Bible study mirrored my thoughts, prayers, and conversations. The knowledge I was gaining gave me direct answers to my prayers and confirmations of prayer. I became increasingly astonished by the way the Scriptures complemented my prayers as God gave me understanding and provided answers to my requests and insights into what I was experiencing in daily life "no matter how small or how important my daily decisions may be."[iv] (These were the words of prayer.)

And as God manifested Himself incrementally, these divine providences—coincidences—also manifested with increasing regularity. I subsequently learned that this is the way God would guide and facilitate me as I grow in spiritual knowledge.

Double Coincidences

Occasionally, a divine providence and intervention would occur, and subsequently the same occurrence—doubled shortly thereafter. Two coincidences occurring in succession. My ponderings of life's circumstances or of biblical knowledge were confirmed, facilitated, and clarified by these coincidences.

There became such an alignment, the product of which were real-time answers to prayers as God gave me knowledge and fed my spirit. I became increasingly confident of the presence of God. I experienced an awakening and illumination as I studied the Bible and such joy in my discovery of the knowledge of God's Word.

As this continued the harmony in my prayers, Bible reading and life's daily activities increased. God applied within my spirit a greater richness of preparation for daily life. There was such a sense of comfort and peace as I became aware of God's guidance, which provided answers to potential prayers before I knew of my need.

I developed a heightened sense of spiritual awareness that I could not fully explain. Upon occasion, strangers unaware of my circumstances brought to my attention coincidences involving me. With much concern, they tried to determine the reasons why. But this mystery was greater than I could put into words; I could only say, peacefully, "I generally have many coincidences."

I continued to read the Bible each night with the confidence that God was guiding me. My heart and mind were uncluttered, open, and available to the communion of His Holy Spirit with my spirit. I learned that this is what spiritual alignment is about. God aligns our spirit with His Holy Spirit in order to impart spiritual knowledge.

Although I did not know where all of these many coincidences would lead, knowing that God was guiding me gave me much peace. And my prayer each night was that God would bless me with understanding.

This was a puzzling period. But imagine the wonder when conclusively I accepted that all I had been experiencing was the answer to my teenage prayers. But I could not imagine where, when, or how I would ever know the entirety of what this meant or anticipated that this would eventually lead to something greater.

But as time progressed, I understood that these experiences constituted the parts of my initial phase of preparation for spiritual knowledge. First, the Holy Spirit heightened my awareness and captivated my attention. Second, God was beginning to give me the divine knowledge and deeper spiritual understanding through the study of His Word. As such, life was becoming into alignment with His guidance as the Spirit of God communed with my spirit.

CHAPTER 3

SACRED SEASON OF LENT

It was the middle of the sacred season of Lent. Since my childhood, I had enjoyed the observance of the Lenten season—a solemn yet joyous time of prayer and worship. For the benefit of readers who are not familiar with Lent, this is a sacred time on the Christian calendar, a period of prayer, meditation, fasting, and repentance. Lent begins on Ash Wednesday, a day of prayer with the imposition of ashes on the forehead during worship. Ashes were used in ancient times as a symbol of repentance and atonement. Lent is a period of forty days when Christians commemorate aspects of the life of Jesus Christ, His many miracles and teachings, His love and forgiveness, and His baptism, suffering, and death on the cross. This leads to Easter Sunday commemorating His resurrection from death.

The week leading up to Easter Sunday is Holy Week. I particularly enjoy these opportunities of worship at Grace Church in northern Virginia. The activities of Holy Week include the holiest days of the Christian year, which are Holy Thursday, Good Friday, Holy Saturday, and Easter. On Holy Thursday, the Last Supper of Jesus with His disciples before His crucifixion is commemorated. On that night, Jesus took bread, blessed it and broke it, and gave it to the disciples. He said, "Take, eat; this is my body. And, he took the cup, and gave thanks, and gave it to them saying, Drink ye all of it; For this is my blood of the new testament, which is shed for many for the remission of sins." (Matthew 26:26–28). The bread and the cup of wine are symbols of Jesus Christ, our Savior and Redeemer, our sacrifice in payment for our sins. On this night, the washing of feet is commemorated, symbolically following Jesus' example of serving others and the washing His disciples' feet. Jesus' sorrow, agony, and prayer in the garden of Gethsemane, and His subsequent arrest, are also commemorated (Matthew 26:36–58).

Good Friday is a day of fasting and prayer commemorating the crucifixion of Jesus. Congregations participate in a three-hour reading of the Passion of Jesus and symbolic retracing of the route to Calvary that Jesus took to the place of His crucifixion. This worship is called the Stations of the Cross. I looked forward to attending the Stations of the Cross with my mother. I watched as she prepared for worship, how she prepared us— making sure that everything was ready the night before—and how she read the Scripture in preparation for worship. This is a beautiful memory that I will always cherish greatly.

Holy Saturday is a quiet day of prayer. Easter Day is a beautiful celebration of the resurrection of Jesus from death. It proclaims that Jesus has won for us victory over sin and death for those that believe, and He has perfected forever all that is required for our redemption. Baptism, confirmation, and reaffirmation of faith are celebrated, followed by a service of light that heralds Easter Day. The service of light is a festive celebration that is rich in symbolism with burning firepots, a candle-lit sanctuary, and the lighting of the Easter candle, which is a symbol of Jesus Christ, "the light of the world" (John 9:5).

It was during this sacred season of Lent in 1996 that the many coincidences—divine providence and intervention—I had been experiencing would assume a new significance and reach a greater height. And it is not at all surprising that this would occur during such a holy and blessed time of the year.

CHAPTER 4

THE DAY THAT I WAS
COVENANTED:
THE DIVINE MIRACLE

On the night of Thursday, March 7, 1996, after prayer and Bible reading, I became overcome by sleep, so I put my Bible beside me and closed my eyes. I was not yet fully asleep when suddenly and clearly coming into view was an image. The image was a head of gold wearing a king's golden helmet—shiny armor to shield the head and face. The clarity of this symbol as it glistened, and the sudden appearance of it, caused me to become fully awake. The image was more vivid than a dream, but looking back to that moment, I would assume that I had been in a trance. This was different from anything I had ever experienced, and I recall being mystified as to why and what this could mean.

I must admit that though the unusual frequency and nature of divine interventions had raised my level of awareness, and had caused me to believe that I might be in the initial stages of a divine purpose, I was puzzled. At this stage, I was unfamiliar with sacred dreams or visions. I was not yet knowledgeable in the Scripture and was in my early stages of a heightened awareness and the beginning of knowledge. And though I discerned that it was special, with no meaningful understanding of what had occurred I did not regard this experience as needing further inquiry. I received it peacefully and continued to settle into a restful night.

The following evening, preceded by prayer, as I had done so many times before, I opened the Bible to answered prayer by divine intervention. Unexpectedly, as I searched for the passage I would read that night, my eyes wandered upon confirmation and explanation of what I had seen in the sacred dream the previous night. The first words I saw were "head of gold." I was astounded—unaware that this could be found in Scripture. I certainly had not thought of looking to the Bible regarding this and had not expected that the Bible could explain what I had seen. But, of all the divine interventions I had experienced leading up to this sacred day, this was the most astonishing.

By divine providence, the prayer God gave me was Daniel's prayer of thanksgiving for the details of a dream, and also the interpretation. In this Scripture, Daniel is blessing God and thanking Him for revealing the secrets of Nebuchadnezzar's dream in a night vision.

> He revealeth the deep and secret things; He knoweth what is in the darkness, and the light dwellest with Him ... Thy thoughts came into thy mind upon thy bed, what should come to pass thereafter: and He that revealeth secrets maketh known to thee what shall come to pass ... This image's head was of fine gold ... Thou art this head of gold. (Daniel 2:22–38)

It was particularly astonishing that upon my first opportunity to open the Bible, after the dream, God gave me this prayer of thanksgiving for a dream but also confirmed the image that I had seen—that it was a "head of gold." But, as I read this, I did not understand the deep significance and profound importance this would have for my life. Nevertheless, I realized that it had a direct connection to the sacred dream and that it confirmed it by the fact that it related to the "head of gold."

It would later become clearer why God, by the power of His Holy Spirit, guided me to read this prayer of thanksgiving. God was speaking to me by the use of this sacred symbol, and I was fascinated when I was able to grapple with that fact. As I mulled over what had occurred, I thought of God transcending time and space, yet it was at that appointed time that God gave the command for this miraculous event. And I shuddered at the reality of the closeness of God. The continuous interventions that were bringing me into spiritual alignment and heightening my awareness had now advanced to a new level as God gave me the dream, confirmed it in Scripture, and by so doing, also led me in prayer to give Him thanks.

In the days following, I reread the same prayer—Daniel's prayer of thanksgiving—each night as I tried to understand it. I would later discover that a greater divine providence and intervention was yet to come and that this would be the first part of two interrelated sacred events—interconnected by this prayer, divinely chosen.

This was where the numerous coincidences and divine providences I had been experiencing for such an extended period were taking me. The coincidences led me to heightened awareness. Heightened awareness led me to spiritual alignment. And having spiritual alignment, God was able to give me the sacred dream.

Thus, in these three stages of this divine process, first God captured my attention, second He heightened my awareness, and third, now God is ready to give me greater understanding and truth.

Divinely Inspired Conversation about Violence

On Friday, March 15, 1996, I had been watching the popular television magazine program *20/20*. The host, Barbara Walters, was interviewing Christopher Darden, the Los Angeles County prosecutor, about the O. J. Simpson murder trial. It was an uncanny period during the years of the trial. It had captivated national as well as international attention and was full of twists, turns, drama, mystery, and anticipation. The manner in which the trial had galvanized worldwide interest seemed extraordinary, a turning point, a milestone in history, and a poignant moment in the world.

As I sat watching the program, I felt that as the world's collective interest concentrated upon this violent story, our attention turned away from God. But as I would later learn, there was also a spiritual purpose correlating with all of this.

On this day in March, the trial had been concluded and it was now time to look back at the proceedings, which Barbara Walters did as she interviewed her guests. At the conclusion of the program, I made a telephone call to discuss some of the details. The discussion expanded sequentially, advancing to troubled areas around the world where there was violence, primarily the Israeli-Palestinian conflict that we discussed at length.

In the early to mid-1990s, the world was a hotbed of bloodshed and violence with many areas of trouble, conflict, unrest, and wars. *Genocide* and *ethnic cleansing* were the popular words of the time. We discussed the ethnic war in Bosnia with neighbor at war with neighbor. As we discussed the violence, the scope of our conversation spread from country to country and from continent to continent. There were high death tolls and great suffering in many countries. Some of the other countries we mentioned include Croatia and Serbia, Congo, Ethiopia, Haiti, Ireland/Britain (religious conflict), India, Iraq, Mozambique, Rwanda, Sierra Leone, South Africa, Sudan, and Uganda. And here, in the United States of America, there was, and continues to be, much violence in the streets of our cities, communities, churches, and schools.

I compared the violence and corruption of our day to that of Noah's day. The evil that comes from deep within the human heart is much more severe, imaginative, and creative in our time. God is now also watching from heaven the display of violence and corruption, manipulation, distortion, and deceit for power and control. If you scratch the surface of any issue in the world, you realize that nothing is as it is being portrayed but is based upon ulterior motives and cannot stand up to scrutiny because it is corrupted. And God is watching the deceit of religion.

I remarked how the violence in Noah's time had resulted in God's anger, and the consequence was the great flood. Weeks earlier, by divine providence, I had been reading Genesis 6–9, which describes the details of the great flood. These chapters speak of how God grieved in His heart over the level of corruption and violence in the earth. "And God saw the wickedness of man was great in the earth, and that every imagination of the thoughts of his heart was only evil continually. And it repented the LORD that he had made man on the earth, and it grieved him in his heart" (Genesis 6:5–6). The fact that God grieved in His heart made such an impression on me when I read it for the first time that I never forgot it.

Having this recent knowledge, I was able to make the comparison. To briefly summarize my conversation, I said that there was so much violence in the world. Compared to Noah's time, we have much more violence and corruption today, and it's more creative and imaginative. God's heart is grieving over us just as in the time of Noah. Likewise, God's wrath will follow this level of violence. But God sent the rainbow because He promised that He would never again destroy the earth with a flood; the next time it will be by fire.

At the time of making this comparison, I did not know then that the Bible says, "But as the days of Noah were, so shall also the coming of the Son of man be" (Matthew 24:37).

The Sacred Vision

I ended my conversation, immediately turned off the television, and grabbed my Bible that lay on the bed beside me. As I had been doing for the past week, I proceeded to read the same verses of Daniel's prayer of thanksgiving. It was then that the divine purpose for this prayer would be revealed. I read from the top of the page to the last verse. In an instant, as my eyes were affixed upon the last verse, there appeared by the power of the Holy Spirit three sets of sacred symbols across the pages of my Bible.

It was absolutely astonishing! It occurred so suddenly! I was dumbfounded as I sat quietly, but I was not afraid. And as I now know with surety, God had prepared me so well—by all the many coincidences—as I was brought into spiritual alignment. These experiences gave me a heightened awareness but also enabled the impartation of so much more than I am aware of.

Looking back at the events leading up to this sacred night, it became clearer that God was around me, constantly guiding my life, preparing me for this sacred moment, and facilitating me in all that is required for such a moment. My advancing spiritual alignment through the communion of His Holy Spirit with my spirit removed the fear. God guided my conversation, directed the words that I would say, and led me in the special prayer of thanksgiving for this miraculous event before I knew I needed it.

CHAPTER 5

THE DIVINE SYMBOLS

As the sacred vision was unfolding, I felt the sensation of a film being removed from my eyes, which became slightly blurred but instantly cleared up. My eyes were being specially prepared to see sacred things, to observe the revelation of a heavenly message. I sat still, unaware of the profound significance of all of this. I remained fully awake and experienced absolutely no other physical difference and certainly no fear at all. That is, at that moment.

The symbols were brightly colored shadows, the reflection of precious jewels—pure and clear. And the brilliance appeared as I have never seen anywhere on earth. They were of such that for several weeks following, the colors in our world seemed dull, muddy, dirty, dingy, and diluted.

The symbols were spread in three parts with two carefully determined spaces in length and placement that separate each set from the other. It was a gradual development—each set appearing by progression—and there were seven major symbols that I could immediately see.

First, two raindrops appeared. They were green—the reflection of the purest emerald. Imagine a raindrop and how it splashes on a dry surface, a sidewalk, or a pavement; that was how each of the two symbols was shaped. The only difference was that there was no water; these were shadows. Put another way, they were the reflection of emeralds in the shape of a drop of rain. They were situated together at the top, left corner of the left page, one immediately above the other.

There was a backdrop of other activity on the page, the presence of power or energy, resembling the shape of clouds.

Second, in the last verse that I had been reading when this began, in the center of the verse, another sacred symbol appeared. It was deep red—scarlet—and it was the reflection of a ruby or garnet gemstone. The color was pure. It was a round shadow, the size of my fingertip. This symbol lingered in the verse, pausing, allowing time as if to focus on me for a personal objective. I could see some subtle movement of the symbol, the slight movement of a steady hand. I became curious as I observed and was puzzled. This was beyond anything I could understand.

Third, as I watched, this sacred symbol moved up the page from the last verse to the right and over the center of the Bible to the next page. The divine action was deliberate and purposeful.

When the scarlet symbol, still in the form of a shadow as it moved across the center of the Bible, reached its special place (halfway between the first and the second placements but to the right), a third set of sacred symbols was initiated. Advancing much upon the first and second, this third set of symbols was a three-dimensional flame of fire, a burning light.

The scarlet symbol, as it became a flame of fire, was joined by another flame, green and sparkling like the purest emerald, and yet another flame, blue and gleaming like the purest sapphire. The colors together were exceedingly bright like a diamond the purity of which was unmatched in the earth as it formed the burning light.

Immediately, the three flames together formed a rainbow. The first color was green, and over that, the second color was red, and over that, the third color was blue. It was an emerging rainbow, the kind that looked as if it were perched upon or emerging from a cloud. At that time, I had never before seen an emerging rainbow like the appearance of this symbol in nature. It moved in an up-and-down manner to form a semicircular appearance, as rainbows do.

The flaming rainbow then flickered three times like a lamp or lighted candle and burned ferociously and vehemently like a furnace. I could hear the consuming fire, a buzzing sound that emanated from the furnace of burning light.

Emerging from the burning light, there was the last symbol, a tiny white light. It was as clear as crystal—or as the light reflecting from the purest diamond. It appeared at the end of the flaming rainbow. Then the other symbols disappeared, but the light lingered after all the other sacred symbols were gone, before it also disappeared.

The pages of my Bible were left untouched—not damaged in any way. And it is precious, particularly the pages where the symbols appeared, for they are most holy because this is where the presence of the Lord stood.

God Declares Himself God of Moses

I am reminded of the story of the burning bush, when the angel of the Lord appeared to Moses in a flame out of the middle of a bush. The Scriptures say, "And the angel of the LORD appeared unto him in a flame of fire out of the midst of a bush: and he looked, and, behold, the bush burned with fire, and the bush was not consumed" (Exodus 3:2). By the revealed similarity of this sacred vision, God is hereby declaring and affirming Himself the God of Moses.

The divine power around me was strong and the power of God so overwhelming that the light by my bedside suddenly flickered out, and I later discovered that my clock had also stopped.

CHAPTER 6

My Search for Answers

Because I did not understand how I would gain the interpretation, and was unsure of how I should delve further, I chose to set aside my thoughts of what had occurred. I certainly did not want to tell anyone. My first reaction was to wait upon God, hoping that eventually it would all become clear.

But soon thereafter, in my spirit, there became a sense of warning against ignoring this extreme intervention. And as the days progressed, I became more curious and my concerns grew. There was much I did not understand, and I developed uneasiness and a sense of urgency regarding how I would ever know what God was revealing.

One week had passed before I decided to tell anyone. I called the person with whom I had had the conversation. I recalled how we had discussed the level of corruption and violence around the world, how this grieves God, and how the rainbow was a symbol of God's promise never to destroy the world again with a flood but the next time it would be by fire. I described some of the details of the symbols. And as I summarized the conversation, I realized that this was indeed a divinely inspired conversation. I had been speaking prophetically without realizing it, and it became so stunning that God had not only heard but had directed the words. And through the symbols, God was affirming the words of the prophecy. Because the words are aligned with God's Word, God is confirming that they are truth.

Repeatedly, I recalled this astonishing divine intervention—after speaking of the rainbow, this symbol appeared upon the pages of my

Bible. And this confirmed the incontestable presence of God. And God was manifesting His part of the conversation.

Of all the numerous divine interventions I had experienced in the past, this was the most startling confirmation of the presence of God. And in wonderment, I pondered how the sacred symbols were perfectly aligned with my conversation. And the words were being confirmed by divine providence upon the pages of the Bible in spiritual language. It was stunning. There is great power available to us when we speak the words of God by faith through grace. For in the beginning, God spoke and all that exists was revealed and given life.

After grappling with all of this, I confided that I had become afraid, mainly because there was much I did not understand. I said, "God is in heaven, and I am on earth. How will I ever be able to understand what He is saying to me?"

I immediately ended the conversation and proceeded to pray in the posture of penitence, humility, and submission. With my face to the floor, I was putting myself at God's disposal. After my prayer, God gave me comfort and peace. I was confident that the answers I needed would eventually come. Yet it was puzzling as I considered why God would go to such great length to manifest Himself with this degree of openness, as He had done in ancient time.

And I reflected upon my life as it was in the previous weeks. Although it was the sacred season of Lent, I was not in prayer more than at any other time and had not been fasting. I had never fasted. I had simply resumed where I left off as a teenager in terms of the prayers I had been reading, in addition to studying the Bible daily. I was in the way of fulfilling my promise of developing a life of prayer and a relationship with God. Life at the time was uncomplicated, quiet, peaceful, and uncluttered from stress. I was contented. My college years were behind me, and I was beginning my career.

I called my mother. As I described to her some of the details, she told me that it meant that I was filled with the Holy Spirit. She said that in general, these kinds of occurrences contain warnings and I should speak with a priest immediately. She assumed that priests, being people of prayer, may have greater spiritual familiarity than others and may be able to help me in some way.

My mother instructed that God was calling me into service and that I needed to share His Word with others for the glory of God. She was convinced that my blossoming spiritual enlightenment was not given to me to be kept to myself but to be shared with others.

I wrestled with this, as I did not know how to share this information in a manner that made me comfortable. And I decided that initially I would share it with a few people who I trusted. Even so, in this brief conversation with my mother, we tried to find some answers, but to no avail.

Holy Week

It was now Holy Week, a busy time for the church in preparing for Easter, as I set out to find a priest. When I was in college, I had not been attending church. I had preferred to first take the time required to research the churches in the Washington, DC, metro area so that I could determine the best one for me. I had never found the time to do so while I was in college and working part time. Because of this, I was unsure of how to find the right priest to meet with.

I called my sister. She suggested I contact the priest of the First Congregational Church of Christ in Washington, DC. She had been worshipping at this church for some time. The priest kindly agreed. I also contacted a second church, as I tried to find opportunities to share this information. I made an appointment with the pastor of the Metropolitan AME Church in Washington, DC. I am grateful to both for meeting with me at such a busy time of the year.

Before each meeting, I felt the need to prepare to explain well, since this kind of information is unusual in modern times. I was overwhelmed by it. I did not understand it even while attempting to convey it to others. I was concerned regarding adequately communicating it, and I did not want to be misunderstood. I needed many answers.

Although they were unable to assist in my search for explanations, meeting with them was helpful. But I could see that they were puzzled. In the months following, I worshipped at the AME Church and continued daily Bible reading and prayer.

During the course of my spiritual growth, I learned that no one else is able to understand information of this nature that is meant for someone else, unless by the specific purpose, enablement, and power of the Holy Spirit who gave it.

Early in my search for answers, God gave me the knowledge that this sacred miracle had a definite connection with my salvation and the end times. I also knew that a rainbow is a symbol of God's promise and that the symbols were revealing the holy covenant between God and man. And I was confident that God was calling me into covenant by His grace. For the first time, I began to understand the deep significance of why Jesus died on the cross and by His death grace is made available to all people—to them who believe.

These were the first confirmations of spiritual knowledge that became clear to me as God began to give me enlightenment and bless me with deeper spiritual understanding. But I needed many more answers to all the questions I had regarding the symbols and why God was intervening. And I thought of God as being around us, but at the same time far away in heaven. I realized I had to wait upon God, and this would require time and patience.

CHAPTER 7

GOD WOULD PROVIDE THE INTERPRETATION

On a bright and windy day in late September 1996, I was jubilant and carefree as I strolled along my neighborhood in northern Virginia. Life was exciting and thoughts of having been covenanted caused me to ponder much, but they also brought me comfort. As I sauntered, I discovered that there was a library nearby—Aurora Hills Library. Since I had been unaware of it, I had used only the larger libraries on the college campuses in the Washington, DC, metro area. The moment I approached it, I thought it would be enjoyable to borrow some books for an entertaining evening of reading. But what transpired caused me to know with surety that my discovery was another blessing of divine providence and intervention.

As I dashed into the library, the first collection of books immediately ahead of me was the religious section. I reached for a Bible. It was the *Pilgrim Edition of the Holy Bible, Authorized King James Version* (Oxford University Press, New York, 1952). Because it had been published long ago and was worn from much use, instinctively I cherished it. I deemed it rich in knowledge and prized as its delicate pages had withstood the test of time. I seized it with care, and my heart pounded with excitement as I opened it.

Remarkably, I was told it had recently been donated to the library. In it was a hieroglyphic inscription written by the donor, I would imagine. The inscription appeared to be a kind of Arabic or Persian script by someone from a remote village of indigenous Arabic or

Persian heritage. I was unable to comprehend what was written and later sought assistance, but it was also difficult to decipher by language experts.

But now I proceeded to read the notes and commentary; I knew that this was an exceptional Bible. It was different in many ways from the one I had owned. I eagerly and randomly scanned the pages, and the Bible fell open at all the right places. The first words I saw were *rainbow, covenant,* and the meaning of the colors green, red, and blue, as well as the numbers and their meaning.

This was startling—though I thought of this as a special Bible, I had not initially grasped that this might be a source of interpretation. But instantaneously, when I saw these words in this brief initial review, I was able to make the connection because of this spiritual alignment. And because these words stood out, this was a sign that God had chosen it.

I was elated, and as my hands began to shake, I thought of this as a great miracle. It was a boost to my confidence that God would provide the interpretation and the answers to my questions as it gave me insight into the interpretation of some of the major symbols.

Additionally, this meant that the Lord was confirming the sacred vision. It was conveying that the source for my answers and interpretation was nowhere else but the Bible and that was where God was directing me.

I was convinced that God had guided me to this library and had directed this Bible to this library from a place far away. I took it home and read all night. The words were like mouth-watering food, for which I became insatiable. I sensed an awakening, an illumination, and an initial level of spiritual understanding as I read it.

This Bible became increasingly more precious as I pondered how it had been chosen by the hand of the Lord. And though it did not take me beyond my initial awakening in providing the answers I had been seeking, it was an instrument that God would use to show me how

He would guide and teach me and reveal spiritual knowledge. It was the answer to my prayer and would take me through the beginning of knowledge and truth as God imparts understanding. And because I knew it was of God, I cherished it greatly, and so I did not want to lose sight of it.

I borrowed it from the library repeatedly for a continuous period over the course of several months, and I read it every available moment in my quest for knowledge. I wanted to savor and digest all the information it contained. But after five months, the librarian told me I would not be allowed to keep it much longer. Although I knew that eventually I would have to give it up, that did not ease my disappointment.

I began my search—either to purchase or borrow. I contacted several bookstores, including those that specialize in rare books, but without success as it was out of print. There was not the availability of the Internet as we have today.

I was disappointed because of all the difficulty in locating a copy, but my disappointment only helped to strengthen my faith that God had provided it. And by this, I could see more evidently the work of God's hands.

As a next step, I visited the Library of Congress, but this Bible was rare, difficult to locate, and unavailable for loan. My exhaustive search confirmed that unless God had placed it in this small neighborhood community library, and had guided me there, there was no way that I could have found it in the first place. Furthermore, I would have no knowledge of it and would not have known I needed it. This caused me to pray even more earnestly for God to guide me to where I could find another copy.

The time came for me to return the Bible to the library for the last time. When I arrived at the reference desk, I thanked the librarian and told her how much I enjoyed it and wished I could have one of my own. The librarian suggested the Cokesbury Bookstore at the

Virginia Theological Seminary. I was grateful and endeavored to do so immediately.

It was February 1997 when I visited the Cokesbury Bookstore. It was exciting to see so many great books, several of which I wished I had had enough time to read. I searched diligently through all the shelves, but I could not find a copy of that special Bible. I explained to the salesperson the kind of Bible for which I had been searching, intending to settle for a similar one. He suggested a popular study Bible and offered to order a copy for me, without an obligation to purchase.

My earnest prayers and diligent search for God to guide me to the right Bible was because I had become aware that not all Bibles are accurate or appropriate for me. Some have become corrupted by their commentary and the way they present the Scriptures and interpretation. I wanted to know the truth and wanted God to guide me in understanding faithfully and precisely what He is saying. And my confidence in that truth is in knowing that the hand of God had chosen the right Bible. I prayed earnestly for God's protection from misinformation and false teachings.

Three weeks had passed. It was midmorning as I was briefly discussing the Scriptures with a colleague. I had not long finished speaking when I saw a sacred vision—the symbol was a printed page. There were the columns, and the verses were in deep red and black print, but the specific words on the page were not legible.

The design of the page was memorable, with elegant style and good use of bold and italics. Also on the page was a slight black ink smudge. This was a distinguishing factor that I can never forget.

Initially, I did not understand why this symbol was being given to me, though I was able to identify it with certainty as a page from the Holy Bible. And I recognized it as a page from the New Testament, because some of the verses were in red print. But it looked like no other book I had ever seen. Yet in fact, my prayers were being answered and God was informing. Nevertheless, at that moment, I did not link this to the Bible I had ordered.

A few hours later, I received a call from the Cokesbury Bookstore. It was the salesperson. "Your Bible is here!" he said.

To this, I replied excitedly, "Thank you so much. I'll be there this Saturday to see if it's the one I am searching for."

I visited the Cokesbury Bookstore the following Saturday, which was February 22, 1997, and was eager to see the Bible. But it was not the one. However, there was another salesperson standing nearby, a young Caucasian lady in her midtwenties, and she overheard my description.

She said, "I know what kind of Bible you're searching for. You're searching for a Bible with old-time notes."

I smiled, marveled at her insight, and said, "Yes! Yes! That's the kind of Bible I want."

She said, "I have just the right one for you. Here it is!"

The moment I saw it, my heart pounded with excitement. I said, "Yes, this is exactly the one!"

Truly, this Bible was quite different from the *Pilgrim Edition of the Holy Bible*; the one I wanted so much. It was a Bible for more advanced study; it was *The Matthew Henry Study Bible, King James Version* (A. Kenneth Abraham, general editor, World Bible Publishers, Inc., 1994). I was unfamiliar with this Bible, but even so, I was confident that this was the one for me. And indeed it was specially chosen.

Special Hands

The Lord blessed me through the help and support of the librarian and both salespersons. Through their hands, I was able to see the work of the divine hand. The hands of the first salesperson showed me the one that was not chosen, and the second showed me the one that was. With this distinction, I was able to recognize the divine hand of God, and this symbolism gives me divine verification.

The Lord chose this lady's hands to deliver specifically the Bible that He had chosen. This affirmed that it had been purposefully chosen and not left to chance but to God. Although I had been searching through my own strength of will and had received the support of the librarian and the sales gentleman, God intervened by providing her hands, at the right time and place, to deliver my Bible to me.

In the introduction to *The Matthew Henry Study Bible*, Ken Abraham tells us that Henry's notes have been around for nearly three hundred years. The print is large and the notes and commentary are generous. I purchased the Bible, along with a few other items, and could not wait to begin reading it.

When I arrived home, I immediately opened the Bible to look at the commentary and notes. The Bible fell open, and I was stunned to observe that the page where it fell open was exactly as I had seen in the sacred vision earlier that week. There was the ink smudge on the page just as I had seen it in the sacred vision, and the blood red ink, and the italic, bold font for the titles.

The Printed Page – Interpretation

First, by showing me the sacred vision of the printed page, God was showing me the actual page of the New Testament. This verifies the gospel. By revealing the vision, God was saying He had chosen the Bible He wanted me to have, and it was now ready.

Second, the smudged verse provided a second verification and confirmation. It immediately enabled me to make the special connection between the vision and the actual Bible. It was the distinguishing factor authenticating this specific Bible as the one chosen by divine appointment.

Third, the smudged verse was also consistent with my teenage prayer requests. It addressed the direction God has for my life. God was now describing the mission He had for me in spreading this message to facilitate the work of the kingdom of God on earth. It remains cherished and personal.

Fourth, this process of my discovery revealed that the interpretation would come from God Himself, committing His Word to my understanding by the enlightenment of His Holy Spirit. I learned that though this Bible was an instrument God would use, the interpretation must be revealed by the power of God. Nevertheless, I was confident that it would not misguide me or frustrate the work of the Holy Spirit but would be in harmony with God's guidance as I read each day.

Ultimately, God alone can give deeper spiritual understanding. And He who gives spiritual knowledge must also give the interpretation. I am aware that God has given me these Bibles (uncorrupted) as instruments of support in instruction as His Spirit communes with my spirit. But the impartation of knowledge, faith, and wisdom are the work of the Holy Spirit, and these are gifts of grace.

Fifth, the unavailability of the *Pilgrim Edition of the Holy Bible* had an essential message to teach. By its unavailability, God was revealing that He did not want me to stay with the same Bible but to move to the next level and to increase in knowledge and understanding. *The Matthew Henry Study Bible* was a symbol that meant that God would guide me to the next level of spiritual understanding.

Effectively, this is a spiritual process that God teaches by His guidance. Since these Bibles are instruments divinely chosen, our understanding is incomplete without the gentle guidance and direction of the Holy Spirit. Therefore, if we view them as such, as God's Word, we will remember that we rely upon God and not upon our own understanding.

Divine Process of Knowledge

As I advanced in knowledge, I discovered that this is a three-step process and these Bibles are symbols of God's guidance. In three stages is the way God imparts deeper spiritual understanding and wisdom.

First, God guided me to the King James Version of the Holy Bible, and this is a symbol of heightened awareness and awakening. Second, the *Pilgrim Edition of the Holy Bible* is symbolic of the beginning of knowledge. Third, *The Matthew Henry Study Bible* is the symbol of deepening awareness, the stage of maturity in deeper spiritual understanding and wisdom.

Waiting upon God

I realized I had to be totally available to God, without my own spiritual predetermination and preconceived notion, and I had to confidently wait upon God. I had to be free of determining where I think I should be going or what I thought I ought to do with regard to the sacred visions. Through prayer and patience, I depended upon God and trusted God to guide me. And the Lord taught me all that I do know, by the quickening power of the Holy Spirit.

If we seek God sincerely and with all our hearts, God will reveal Himself to us and will uphold us in strength and knowledge and will never leave us. And if we are diligently seeking Him, God will direct our path to Him. This I know for sure. "The Lord is good unto them that wait for him, to the soul that seeketh him. It is good that a man should both hope and quietly wait for the salvation of the LORD" (Lamentations 3:25–26).

CHAPTER 8

SEPARATION UNTO GOD

A Redirected Life

N ow that I had my new Bible, I was beginning to settle into a divine process while waiting to see how the interpretation would unfold. But I thought I might contact a few of my closest friends. We had been out of touch for several months, and they were unaware of how my life had changed. They and I had never discussed the Bible, and they were unaware of my spiritual experiences. I kept this information undisclosed, because I believed the details of a sacred vision like that of ancient biblical times might have been difficult for them to comprehend. I did not want to have them react negatively to hearing of the Holy Spirit and this astonishing information, which neither they nor I could fully understand.

This silence was good for me. It helped me to maintain an uncomplicated and stress-free life, and the opportunity for my faith to grow and flourish. But what I would discover in my effort to contact my friends was quite astounding.

Through another series of unexplained coincidences and divine providences, it became clear that everyone I knew—close friends and acquaintances—had left my life as they became unreachable for one reason or another. Popular electronic communication and social media did not exist. Several of my closest friends had left the Washington, DC, metro area and moved around the country. I discovered through happenstance that some had relocated abroad.

There was no forwarding information, and the contact information that I had for everyone was out of date in just a few months. Family was also far away. Additionally, friends with whom I spoke by phone on a regular basis, and whose numbers I never needed to write in my address book, unique to this particular circumstance, I suddenly and mysteriously forgot. God clears our thoughts in order to renew our minds and redirect our lives. The Bible says, "And be not conformed to this world: but be ye transformed by the renewing of your mind, that ye may prove what is that good, and acceptable, and perfect, will of God" (Romans 12:2).

At the same time, all the plans I had been making for advancing my career were suddenly canceled due to circumstances beyond my control. I was witnessing the work of God's hand so plainly, and to such an extent, and while I marveled, I scribbled a list of those with whom I had lost contact; the result was more than two lined pages of names.

The sudden manner in which this cluster of coincidences occurred grabbed me, and this scared me greatly. But when I accepted what God had done, I was able to continue more earnestly in prayer. The words of my childhood prayer was this, "Thou wilt shew me the path of life" (Psalm 16:11). God was redirecting me to the new pathway that leads to eternal life. I had to be aware and be willing. I prayed for God's guidance each day by reading generous portions of Psalm 119 including "Teach me, O LORD, the way of thy statutes; and I shall keep it unto the end. Give me understanding, and I shall keep thy law; yea, I shall observe it with my whole heart" (Psalm 119:33–34).

With these circumstances, it became palpable that God had been watching over me and had waited all these years until the time was right for Him to advance His purpose for my life. Now He was revealing Himself, seizing the moment, making sure that I understood that my obedience and redirection were required. By the power of the Holy Spirit, God guided me each day through this process of understanding, facilitating my discovery into His Word, but this was taking me beyond that.

A process of change would begin and my active participation, cooperation, and willingness would be required. I was discovering that I was now physically alone, but through this, I could see the presence of the Lord as a new friend and companion. There was now a new association. And the series of divine interventions regarding my friends, the renewing of my mind, and the change of my career are a trinity of symbols depicting a redirected life by the Holy Trinity of God.

God erases our thoughts to cleanse and change. God prepares us for a new beginning. Therefore, He erases what was there and writes His Word upon our hearts and gives us a renewed mind. One of the first actions God makes in order to reach us is to change the direction of our lives. God creates a new path that leads to Him.

Consecration

This mysterious occurrence is a symbol of consecration. God consecrates us by separating us. It protects us in many ways. His protection serves to ensure our obedience. It helps to strengthen our faith.

This separation caused me to be free of distractions, thus making it possible for me to have the time and ability to diligently inquire into the spiritual things that God was now revealing. God was creating the right circumstances for me to heed His Word, and by divine facilitation, He separated me to ensure my growth in wisdom and deeper spiritual understanding. And God provided the opportunity for a quiet life of peace, tranquility, and calmness, for this stillness would be the way that I would listen to God.

This separation is more spiritual than physical. God acts in physical ways in order to effectively reach us, but spiritual separation is what is important to God. Ultimately, this redirection is a spiritual symbol of separation from sin and has less to do with physical separation. It means sanctification, holiness, devotion, and being set apart for dedication to the service of God. One must be willing to consecrate oneself to be taught by God and to offer oneself for the service of God.

It is the initial stage of the blessing of grace for remission of sins and redemption. Christ consecrates us by His death. By this, we are able to approach and come near to the throne of grace. The Bible says,

> Having therefore, brethren, boldness to enter into the holiest by the blood of Jesus, By a new and living way, which he hath consecrated for us, through the veil, that is to say, his flesh; And having an high priest over the house of God; let us draw near with a true heart in full assurance of faith, having our hearts sprinkled from an evil conscience, and our bodies washed with pure water. (Hebrews 10:19–22)

God consecrates us to begin this process of purging, washing, and cleansing us from sin. There were many physical symbols in ancient times that are essentially representations of this spiritual work of the divine hand. And there were physical processes that the priests were commanded to follow diligently as symbols of spiritual purification, sanctification, and consecration. (Ezekiel 43:20–27).

How We Can Know That God Is Guiding Us

God separates us in order to lead us into the will of God. The psalmist, David, said of his life's journey, "The steps of a good man are ordered by the LORD and he delighteth in his way" (Psalm

37:23). We can know God is guiding us if we are aware of positive changes and redirections that have taken place. And we can know the will of God by diligence in prayer and study of His Word. "And ye shall seek me, and find me, when ye shall search for me with all your heart" (Jeremiah 29:13). If we are diligently seeking Him, we will be sure to find Him. He will reveal Himself to us when we are reconciled to Him, and we will know His will.

The Bible tells us much of the will of God, yet there are some who believe we cannot know the will of God for our lives. Naturally, we cannot know what people are thinking if we do not have a relationship with them and if we do not know them; likewise, it is with God.

The entire Bible is rich in knowledge regarding the will of God, and we can know of His intentions, among which is that He will come again. But if we invest the time in studying God's Word, He will guide us into understanding specifically what His will is for us.

The psalms are sweet and melodious, abounding in the knowledge of the will of God. Psalm 23 tells us much of the will of God. "The LORD is my shepherd; I shall not want. He maketh me to lie down in green pastures: he leadeth me beside the still waters. He restoreth my soul: he leadeth me in the paths of righteousness for his name's sake." (Psalms 23:1-3). This is physical in some ways, but more importantly, it is spiritual and truly a taste of God's will and intention for us.

God tells us what He wants from us and what we should want from Him. The Bible gives us His intentions, determination, motivations, and what delights and pleases Him. It gives us the intimate work of His Holy Spirit that dwells within us under grace.

The Bible tells us of the force of His anger, what He thinks of sin, and what grieves the heart of God. We learn of His infinite mercy, His wisdom, and His great power, and the purpose of it is His love. We know God's desire is for us to love Him, to worship Him, and to adore Him, to honor and glorify Him and to give Him thanks.

We know God wants our repentance and return and reconciliation. We know that God wants us to come to Him when we are weary of the world and of sin, and He will give us spiritual rest.

There is so much that we can know about God. He has revealed just enough of Himself so that we can please Him. He wants us to keep His commandments, and we know that He rewards obedience. We know that deep within His heart, His purpose is to redeem us.

One sure way to know the will of God is to learn what He has done for others and how He has dealt with specific situations. God's will for us is beautifully and wonderfully set out in these few words: "And thou shalt love the LORD thy God with all thine heart, and with all thy soul, and with all thy might" (Deuteronomy 6:5). This is our principle for living, and this is the simplest way to sum up the will of God for us.

If we do not know the will of God, how then can we be obedient? And how can we have harmony? Ephesians 5:17 puts it this way: "Wherefore be ye not unwise, but understanding what the will of the Lord is." God gives us the gift of an understanding heart, without which we cannot know the will of God. Jesus taught us to look to God, our heavenly Father, in prayer so that we may know His will. Thus, when we pray, we say, "Thy kingdom come, Thy will be done in earth, as it is in heaven" (Matthew 6:10).

Can we be of grace and yet not know the will of God? Knowing the will of God is an essential part of grace. Jesus prayed that God's will be done—His will was to do the will of God. Jesus said, "And this is the will of him who sent me, that everyone which seeth the Son and believeth on him, may have everlasting life: and I will raise him up at the last day" (John 6:40).

Unbelief and the lack of faith blind us spiritually to the will of God. Our will must be in harmony with God's. Our preconceived determination prevents us from the opportunity to know what God has personally established for us. "The meek will he guide in judgment: and the meek will he teach his way" (Psalm 25:9). When we know the will of God, our life will line up and be in harmony with God's Word. We will readily relinquish our will to the will of God, and there will be greater peace and contentment. But a spiritual struggle against God manifests in physical struggle that we sometimes encounter in life.

"I will instruct thee and teach thee in the way which thou shalt go: I will guide thee with mine eye" (Psalm 32:8). We will have a better sense of our life's purpose and an earnest in knowing truth because we have a desire to please God. God's Holy Spirit communes with our spirit to confirm His guidance and help our infirmities. God makes our steps secure so that we can grow in faith and confidence. God guides us continually and promises to be "our guide even unto death" (Psalm 48:14).

And when we are in the will of God, we are reconciled to Him with a longing and desire to please Him and to put Him first. And this is no burden; neither is it grievous to our spirit but is our joy and happiness.

"All Scripture is given by inspiration of God, and is profitable for doctrine, for reproof, for correction, for instruction in righteousness" (2 Timothy 3:16). This is how we know the will of God.

Being in the will of God is a holy covenant principle, for it is impossible to be in covenant with God and yet not know His will. This is why consecration—separation to be instructed by God in the will of God—is an indispensable part of a covenanted life.

CHAPTER 9

THE DIVINE PROCESS AND REWARDS OF SPIRITUAL KNOWLEDGE

Spiritual Milestone

I had now reached a spiritual milestone and looked back over all that transpired. I could see clearly how God had given me the parts and pieces that would come together at a later time. He was giving me incremental information, feeding me just enough—as much as I was able to absorb—and withholding knowledge appropriately to facilitate the correct timing of events and the sequence of my understanding. All of this was unfolding His perfect plan.

Spiritual alignment was being manifested to a greater extent. For instance, I would become aware of some spiritual knowledge today but would better understand it weeks or months later, when the occurrence of a related event made the knowledge more useful to me. On the other hand, I would gain knowledge through study of Scripture while a related event in harmony with that Scripture was occurring in daily life. Life clearly became a journey that paralleled the process of my study of God's Word. Natural was becoming in harmony with spiritual to break down the barriers to faith.

This confirmed that the spiritual knowledge I was gaining was truth, and it made sense. Flesh was continuing to line up with spirit as the Spirit of God communed with my Spirit. It made me feel secure that God was guiding me, and so I just let God guide me.

And in retrospect, I am convinced that if I had been determined to guide myself through this process, and if I had come to God's Word with preconceived notions of what He was seeking to say, I would never have been able to understand the direction that my life would take. I would not have been able to understand events as they were unfolding or be prepared for what was to come. But there was harmony because I did not know or understand much and had to be contented to wait, to depend upon God. I lived in quietness and peaceful contentment.

I understood that I could only learn by experience and by the providence of God, not faster or slower, but by the steps that are ordered by the Lord and at a pace determined by Him. It is a process of learning that involves renewal of the mind, and this can only be achieved by the patient and gentle direction of a divine hand. I learned that it is a course of personal change, spiritual growth, and the development of a divine relationship, not just the interpretation of symbols. And I discovered that it is a practice of wisdom and faith, a personal process that requires willingness and participation.

Although in the initial stages I looked to others for help in understanding the developments that were unfolding at this milestone, I became more confident that this is a process in which God alone could guide me. Yet I do know that God conveys spiritual messages through us for others and through others for us. But what I do mean is that God, who gives the dream, also gives the interpretation. Both the message and the interpretation are an inseparable process with God. So God does not commune with us and then leaves us on our own, expecting us to gain the interpretation without His guidance but by His care and attention. Only God is able to give wisdom and deeper spiritual understanding, and His intention is privy to Himself.

God Declares Himself God of Daniel

God gave Daniel the details of the king's dream and also the interpretation. And as God did for Daniel, likewise God would do for me. This was the message contained within this prayer of thanksgiving—God who gave me the sacred dream would, in like manner, also give me the interpretation. And though the divine providence would obviously and conveniently suggest that much, initially I did not understand. But I have since learned that God does the same for us consistently as He did for prophets of ancient times. This is one of the major reasons for this prayer, and God was mercifully leading me in thanksgiving before I knew how much I needed it. In fact, I would never have been aware of it, knew I needed it, or discerned any connection with it. And though this prayer blessed God, God also made it beneficial to me in many ways.

Not only is God mercifully directing me in prayer of thanksgiving, but it also served to confirm the prophetic contents of the dream. And it says, "I will give you interpretation and understanding."

By this consistent action, God is declaring and affirming Himself as the God of Daniel. And God is confirming His faithfulness. "Every good gift and every perfect gift is from above, and cometh down from the Father of lights, with whom is no variableness, neither shadow of turning" (James 1:17). "Jesus Christ the same yesterday, and to day, and for ever" (Hebrews 13:8).

Having this knowledge helped me to avoid doubt, error, misunderstanding, and struggle against the divine process and power of the Holy Spirit. It would have been exceedingly difficult and much harder to bear if I had not been prepared. Life would have been contrary to God's guidance, a constant and unbearable wrestle with the Spirit of God. Flesh would have been at war with spirit.

I realized that there was much being done on my behalf on a deeper spiritual level, of which I had little knowledge. But the Spirit of the Lord has caused me to walk in His way with peace.

Rewards of Spiritual Knowledge

An activity that continues to bring me special rewards of wisdom is the reading of the special prayers from Life-Study Fellowship—particularly the prayer for wisdom and deeper spiritual understanding, which I recite daily. After this prayer, I am rewarded by an incremental thrust of new knowledge. Thus, I know that God is pleased and takes pleasure in this prayer.

My mission to share the details of these sacred visions, as my mother had advised, was never far from my thoughts. But considering all that occurred, it was my desire to choose wisely those with whom I would share. Now that I am more aware of the constant presence of God, and always remembering that He is a silent party to every conversation, I am mindful of the need to put greater thought into what I say and do. Acutely aware that I have been entrusted with this divine knowledge, it is my responsibility to preserve its sacredness.

I was cautious. I was concerned that this information would be misunderstood, and I did not want to engage in conversation in which he/she was likely to utter something contemptible regarding the work of the Holy Spirit. I attempted to guard against this by speaking mainly to priests, though at this later stage, I was not expecting assistance with answers or explanations but just to share my experience. This level of caution and measured approach to dealing with this information was good for me and, as I later learned, was God's way of directing the divine objective.

After my meeting with the first priest, I was astounded by the reward of a sudden burst of new knowledge that significantly advanced my spiritual understanding and interpretation. And though the priests could not assist me, I benefited greatly from the rewards God gave me after meeting with each. This positive reinforcement was exciting. It confirmed that this pleased God.

Vocation of a Messenger

This tells me that God has a message for me to bring to the church and wants me to share my experience with the church for His glory. And for work, God effectively provides reward. This symbolism is communicating God's desire that I share this message.

The confirmation of the prophetic contents of the conversation by the divine symbols in substance is overwhelming in the knowledge that this reveals. But additionally, that it was immediate manifests a divine alignment that should leave no room for ambiguity in what God is seeking to affirm. This we will discuss throughout the course of these volumes.

The Priests

The Lord continued to bless me with the reward of wisdom and deeper spiritual understanding in more deliberate and highly noticeable increments as I studied the Bible. And as the Lord provided the opportunity, I would meet with a priest. I anticipated my heavenly reward thereafter.

But subsequently, these opportunities ended and there became no more occasion through my efforts or happenstance. This is surprising. But it offers significant knowledge within the context of spiritual interpretation, which we will discuss further in Chapter 29.

CHAPTER 10

VISIONS OF THE WORD OF GOD FACILITATE KNOWLEDGE

A nother way that God divinely inspired the interpretation is through visions of the written Word of God. And this appeared in printed and on occasion written form—written by the hand of an angel. But this was different from the vision of the printed page from the Bible that I discussed earlier.

The first time this occurred was immediately after God had chosen the second Bible, *Pilgrim Edition of the Holy Bible.* And there were several other occasions after God chose *The Matthew Henry Study Bible, King James Version.* This continued over several years as I advanced in knowledge.

I arrived home from work around 6:30 p.m. As I stood at the kitchen counter preparing dinner, suddenly I saw a sacred vision of God's Word, written in red. Although I knew this was the Holy Spirit, I was yet developing in faith and was startled so I looked to God for surety. I prayed that God would confirm Himself, showing me again the same vision so that I may know with surety. At this juncture, having experienced the many divine interventions, I rested my prayer peacefully with God and forgot it. But to my astonishment, the next evening at exactly the same time, as I was preparing my dinner, God blessed me with the same vision: the Word of God written in red. That was my answer, and I was secure that God was guiding me, even though I did not understand what this meant.

As time progressed, these sacred visions of written words occurred often, always the same image twice, one immediately following the other. As I studied the Bible daily, and my faith became strong, this subsided. Only before a pending significant advancement in knowledge or prophetic milestone that brought a major change would this occur. And these occurrences would take place in the evening, morning, or any time of day.

Ancient Languages of the Bible

On occasion, this kind of sacred vision would appear in English but more frequently would be in a foreign language: Hebrew, Greek, and Amharic. I was not familiar with any of these languages at the time of seeing these sacred visions. Neither English nor the foreign languages I could decipher clearly enough to be able to reproduce the information that was being given to me. But it was clear, beyond any shadow of doubt, that this was the written Word of God for my advancement in spiritual knowledge.

As this continued, I soon understood that these sacred visions were not meant for direct and instantaneous interpretation. Instead, they were meant to point me to the Bible. In other words, the interpretation means "the Word of God." They confirm the Word of God. This means divine instruction, and they are meant to direct me to the Word of God for some specific spiritual knowledge that would be revealed.

The gospel is complete in Jesus Christ. Therefore, now that we have the gospel, sacred visions of the written word are not meant for direct comprehension. This is for guidance in prayer and communion of the Holy Spirit. Visions of the written word do not supersede the Bible but are confirmations of the Bible. They are blessings of wisdom and understanding. They are evidence of the Holy Spirit and this is the way God was applying His Word to me.

They are therefore indecipherable; not intended to be legible, comprehensible, or directly understandable. They do not stand alone but support spiritual understanding by the power of the Holy Spirit. These visions mean that God is confirming His Word, the gospel of Jesus Christ.

After each occurrence, I experienced significant advancement in knowledge of the interpretation and illumination regarding the covenant, and these became milestones in my spiritual growth. All the while, life continued to parallel the Word of God; there was a certain increasing harmony between the study of the Word and what I was experiencing. For instance, suffering is a major part of the covenant. Therefore, while God was teaching me the role of suffering in the covenant, I suffered severely in daily life.

Generally, after receiving God's Word in a vision, the Scripture would parallel some activity occurring simultaneously and I would gain insights into the interpretation. By the power of the Holy Spirit, this knowledge is applied to my spirit as I read and study the Bible. This gave me enlightenment as I continued in the divine process. It strengthened me and helped me to bear my suffering. This is the way God teaches. I will discuss this covenant suffering more in a later volume.

With my increasing confidence, I received these blessings with peace and waited patiently to learn of their meaning from God, remaining available by prayer.

Word of God in Red or Black

I also learned distinctively that if the vision of the written word is in red, then I am being directed to the Bible—the New Testament, the gospel of Jesus Christ—for spiritual knowledge. But if the vision of the written word is in black, then this sacred image also points me to the Bible but is giving me knowledge of some important event that would occur that has direct spiritual interrelatedness that is important for my spiritual advancement. For instance, the written word in black refers to an important, life-changing event generally involving paperwork. Whether the words appear in red or black print, these visions are prophecies from God who alone knows the future. Although the words written are always indecipherable in the vision, God is pointing me to the Bible, showing what will take place and is giving me the mercy of preparation.

In early February 2000, I saw a sacred vision of a printed page, paragraphs of hieroglyphics in bold, black ink. The print was so distinctive that the look of it is forever etched in my mind. By this, God was preparing me for an event that would significantly affect me within the following weeks.

A friend who worked in the coffee shop on the first floor of the building where I also worked was having her first child and was now approaching her date of delivery. When I arrived at work on a Monday morning in early February, I was told that she had died the day before, during childbirth at a hospital in Washington, DC. This news was extremely devastating. It is not often that one hears of such an occurrence, and the fact that this had happened to someone I knew was particularly shocking.

It was a sad time. I attended her funeral the following Saturday. The moment I entered the church and someone gave me the program for her service, I was able to make the connection. As I looked at it, I shuddered. It was as if I were seeing the vision all over again. Consequently, I knew immediately that this was what God had been telling me one week earlier.

My friend was Ethiopian, beautiful, peaceful, soft-spoken, and of a quiet countenance. The program of her funeral service was written in Amharic, Ethiopia's official language. The Ethiopic script was exactly as I had seen it the week prior to her death in the sacred vision. God was showing me her pending death and was protecting me from the profound grief that I would soon experience. But I could only understand the meaning when I saw the program for her funeral. The good news is that her baby was born alive, a daughter the express image of her. The word of the Lord came to me as a pleasant reminder that He watches over all the details and is communicating His constant presence.

God Declares Himself God of the Bible

Through visions of the word of God, God is reaffirming Himself as the God of the Bible and is confirming the gospel of Jesus Christ. His indwelling Holy Spirit communes with our spirit, enabling this transfer of prophetic knowledge. This is the way God facilitates deeper spiritual understanding, enlightenment, and faith. In the words of Proverbs 4:11, "I have taught thee in the way of wisdom; I have led thee in right paths." I blessed the Lord.

Life Lines Up With Scripture

Life paralleled the Scripture as God guided me patiently through the same pathway, and through the same steps as those who have gone before. This harmony represents a walk with God. God causes us to follow the same footsteps as our predecessors to lead us similarly into faith, holiness and grace.

Consequently, by this parallel process of gaining knowledge from the Bible while a similar circumstance was occurring in daily life God has ordained and consecrated my life in a trinity of divine vocations. First, the footsteps of the saint to prepare me in sanctification for eternal life. Second, the footsteps of the priest to enable me to carry this message of preparation through the gospel of Jesus Christ. Third, the footsteps of the prophet to facilitate me in knowing what will befall us and to bring this message of warning. By this process of revealing similar favor, God is affirming Himself as the same Lord, Jesus Christ. This walk with God is an answer to my childhood prayer that God would let me walk close to Him all of my life.

CHAPTER 11

VISIONS OF THE WORD OF GOD IN ANCIENT TIMES

T here are numerous biblical prophets who received the blessing of visions of the written Word of God. While in my circumstances, the writing is illegible, it can be determined that in their circumstances this was different.

Inspired by God

We know that the Bible is inspired by God. The Bible also says, "Knowing this first, that no prophecy of the scripture is of any private interpretation. For the prophecy came not in old time by the will of man: but holy men of God spake as they were moved by the Holy Ghost" (2 Peter 1:20–21). It is of no private interpretation, meaning that it is not the product of individual and personal thoughts or imagination. And it is not developed by the wisdom, understanding, or skill of man but by the power and wisdom of God.

Through sacred visions, prophets of the Bible were given by the Holy Spirit the ability to see the writing of God and to hear His voice. It is evident that there had been a difference in the intensity and clarity of the writing and directness of the instruction in the visions given to them by God. This exceptional mercy was afforded them as part of the divine mission in developing the Bible for mankind. In order for them to perceive their instruction and gain deeper spiritual understanding and wisdom to do their work, God gave them spiritual abilities that are beyond that of physical senses and perception. And

God communed with them more openly and directly and in a manner that they could comprehend.

God spiritually advanced them in order for them to comprehend this spiritual knowledge and present it to us for instruction and knowledge. Now that we have the Bible, sacred visions of the written Word are not meant for direct comprehension. Instead, we look to the Bible, the Word of God, for advancement in spiritual knowledge.

The Bible, being no ordinary book but developed based upon divine inspiration, remains dependent upon the inspiration of God through the quickening of His Holy Spirit for its interpretation and comprehension.

We can be confident that the Bible is the inspired Word of God and is a faithful guide and true representation of God. God cannot lie; neither will God allow the world to be void of truth. It is the only book that allows us to know the gospel of Christ—God's goodwill to mankind under the liberty of grace.

It is the holy covenant, and this establishes that it is true, as no covenant can stand if it has error but is rendered null and void. "God is not a man, that he should lie; neither the son of man, that he should repent: hath he said, and shall he not do it? Or hath he spoken, and shall he not make it good?" (Numbers 23:19). God is faithful.

The Spirit of God communes with the spirit of man. And the power of God preserves the integrity of His Word. But if we come to the Bible depending upon our own knowledge, skill, worldly wisdom, or education without the quickening of the Holy Spirit, the result will surely be error, misinterpretation, and lack of understanding. Job said, "But there is a spirit in man: and the inspiration of the Almighty giveth them understanding" (Job 32:8).

You will notice below that visions that directly communicate the word of the Lord, as recorded in Scripture, occurred primarily in the Old Testament. They were legible, understandable, and comprehensible to those whom the information was given.

In the Old Testament, these words are often written: "The word of the Lord came unto … in a vision." But after the coming of Christ, the written Word of God points us to Christ, and the disciples preached the Word of Christ, the gospel. Now that we have Jesus Christ, God's Word is complete in Him. "The word became flesh and dwelt among us." And it says, "In the beginning was the Word, and the Word was with God, and the Word was God" (John 1:1). And this Word is Jesus Christ.

God Communicated His Word in Ancient Times

The Bible gives us extensively such occasions in which visions of the Word of God were given to beloved prophets. Some of those to whom this blessing was given include the following:

- **Abraham,** Genesis 15:1: "After these things the word of the LORD came unto Abram in a vision, saying, Fear not, Abram: I am thy shield, and thy exceeding great reward." The Lord was confirming His covenant with Abram and reassuring him of His promise to bless him by giving him a son.
- **Samuel,** 1 Samuel 15:10: "Then came the word of the LORD unto Samuel, saying, It repenteth me that I have set up Saul to be king: for he is turned back from following me, and hath not performed my commandments." The Lord sent Samuel to anoint Saul king over Israel, but because of Saul's sin, this was a warning that Samuel was delivering to him.
- **Nathan,** 2 Samuel 7:4–5: "And it came to pass that night, that the word of the LORD came unto Nathan, saying, Go and tell my servant David, Thus saith the LORD, Shalt thou build me an house for me to dwell in?" David wants to build a temple, but God is telling Nathan to tell him not to build it.
- **Gad, the Prophet,** 2 Samuel 24:11–12: "For when David was up in the morning, the word of the LORD came unto the

prophet Gad, David's seer, saying, Go and say unto David, Thus saith the LORD, I offer thee three things; choose thee one of them, that I may do it unto thee." David selects his punishment for conducting a census and numbering the people of Israel and Judah. God sent Gad to have him select one of three punishments: seven years of famine, to flee three months before his enemies while they pursue him, or three days of pestilence. David prefers to fall into the hand of the LORD, because God is merciful. He desired not to fall into the hand of man. So God sent pestilence upon Israel, and seventy thousand people died.

- **Solomon,** 1 King 6:11–13: "And the word of the LORD came to Solomon saying, Concerning this house which thou art building, if thou wilt walk in my statutes, and execute my judgments, and keep all my commandments to walk in them; then will I perform my word with thee, which I spake unto David thy father: and I will dwell among the children of Israel, and will not forsake my people Israel." God made the conditions perfect for Solomon to build the temple instead of his father, David, and he prepares to build the temple.

- **Jehu,** 1 Kings 16:1–2: The word of the Lord came to Jehu to convey a warning to Baasha, king of Israel, of pending punishment because of his sin. "Then the word of the LORD came to Jehu the son of Hanani against Baasha, saying, Forasmuch as I exalted thee out of the dust, and made thee prince over my people Israel; and thou hast walked in the way of Jeroboam, and hast made my people Israel to sin, to provoke me to anger with their sins."

- **Elijah the Tishbite,** 1 Kings 17, 18: The word of the Lord came to Elijah, whereby he was foretold concerning a long and grievous famine to punish Israel for its sin. God took care of Elijah in the famine by directing him to a brook where there was water for drinking and by sending ravens to feed him in the morning and in the evening. Three years later, the word came to him informing him that God was going to send rain again. "And the word of the LORD came unto him saying, get thee hence, and turn thee eastward, and hide thyself by the brook Cherith, that is before Jordan. And it shall be, that thou shalt drink of the brook; and I have commanded the ravens to feed thee there." (1 Kings 17:2–4). The word of the Lord came to Elijah on several occasions, including when he was fleeing into the wilderness from Jezebel, and the Lord sent angels to sustain him.

- **Isaiah,** 2 Kings 20:4–5: The word of the Lord came to Isaiah to deliver a message to Hezekiah who was sick and near to his death, that God had heard his prayer and was going to heal him. "And it came to pass, afore Isaiah was gone out into the middle court, that the word of the LORD came to him, saying, Turn again, and tell Hezekiah the captain of my people, Thus saith the LORD, the God of David thy father, I have heard thy prayer, I have seen thy tears: behold, I will heal thee: on the third day thou shalt go up unto the house of the LORD." The Lord not only healed him but added fifteen more years to his life. (Isaiah 38:4–5).

- **David,** 1 Chronicles 22:8: "But the word of the LORD came to me, saying, Thou hast shed blood abundantly, and hast made great wars: thou shalt not build an house unto my name, because thou has shed much blood upon the earth in my sight." David was commanded by God not to build the temple, but before his death, he gathered the materials for his son, Solomon, who would build it.

- **Shemaiah,** 2 Chronicles 11:2–3, 12:7: The word of the Lord came to Shemaiah with instructions for Rehoboam, the son of

Solomon, and for Israel in Judah, and Benjamin, as both sides were preparing for war. They were warned not to fight against their brethren but to return each man to his own house. When the Lord saw that they had humbled themselves His word came again to Shemaiah granting deliverance.

- **Jeremiah:** The book of Jeremiah: The word of the Lord came generously to Jeremiah the prophet as described all throughout the book of Jeremiah. He was a prophet most blessed by knowing the thoughts of God. First, the word of God came to deliver to him his assignment—the Lord had ordained him as a prophet. He was afraid to speak to the people and told the Lord that he could not speak because he was still a child. But the Lord said to him, "Say not, I am a child: for thou shalt go to all that I shall send thee, and whatsoever I command thee thou shalt speak. Be not afraid of their faces: for I am with thee to deliver thee, saith the LORD. " (Jeremiah 1:7–8). God is a sure protector of those whom He has called upon to deliver His messages. They are sure to meet with opposition. God is with him every step of the way to give him encouragement and protection and to deliver him from those who would oppose him. He is sent to Jerusalem to remind the people of the covenant God made with them, how God delivered them out of Egypt, and how He led them through the wilderness. Jeremiah is delivering warnings to Israel—because of their ingratitude they have forsaken God. He delivers warnings at the temple that they should change their behavior. He warns them in relation to the curses that are the consequences of breaking the holy covenant. God assured him of His protection by revealing to him the secret plots against him and God answered his complaints and delivered vengeance upon those who became his enemies.

- **Ezekiel,** the book of Ezekiel: The word of the Lord came also to Ezekiel, the prophet, generously as described throughout the book of Ezekiel. Ezekiel 1:3 tells us that the word of the Lord came expressly to him. He is a prophet most blessed by knowing the intention of God. God ordained him a watchman to warn the Israelites of the consequences of their sin. He is commanded not to fear those who would be opposed to his message but to go on with his work for the Lord. God provided him protection and gave him strength and courage to do the work that God had called him to do. He warns against false prophets and secret idols. He reminds Israel of the covenant God made with them and warns them against backsliding, adultery, and rebellion.

- **Hosea,** Hosea 1:1: The word of the Lord came to Hosea requesting him to take a wife who lived a corrupt life, symbolic of God's covenant with Israel. Israel broke the covenant and is a symbol of an adulterous wife. She was symbolic of Israel who had turned away from God and was serving other gods, yet God was willing to own them and show them mercy. Hosea predicted the destruction of the kingdom of Israel and the difficulties and trouble in captivity that was in store for Israel because of its rejection of God's love and mercy. They were giving up their relationship to God. Nevertheless, God wanted them to return to their duty in covenant with Him.

- **Joel,** Joel 1:1: The word of the Lord came to Joel. He predicted the destruction made by the plague of insects: palmerworm, locust, and cankerworm and the caterpillar that destroyed all the crops. He predicted God's judgment then and also pointed to the end of time. He was asking Israel to repent, with fasting, weeping, and mourning, then God would show mercy and the pastures would be green again. He predicted the pouring out of God's Spirit in the latter days.

- **Jonah,** Jonah 1:1–2: "Now the word of the Lord came unto Jonah the son of Amittai, saying, Arise, go to Nineveh, that great city, and cry against it; for their wickedness is come up before me." But Jonah took a ship to Tarshish instead, and as he was on the ship, the Lord sent a great storm. The mariners were afraid and prayed to their gods. But Jonah was fast asleep, so the shipmaster came to him and woke him up to pray to the Lord. They cast lots so that they could determine the person responsible for causing the storm, and they questioned Jonah. Jonah told them that he was a Hebrew who feared the God of heaven, maker of both sea and dry land. Hearing this, the men became more afraid and cast Jonah into the sea, because they believed it was for his sake that there was the great storm. The Lord prepared a great fish to swallow up Jonah, and he was in the belly of the fish for three days and nights. Then Jonah prayed to the Lord while he was in the belly of the fish, and the fish vomited Jonah onto dry land. Then the word of the Lord came to Jonah a second time requesting that he go to Nineveh to warn the people. This time, Jonah was obedient. He went to Nineveh and warned the people that within forty days the city would be overthrown. The people of Nineveh believed God and repented, and God changed His mind and did not allow Nineveh to be overthrown. But God's change of heart then displeased Jonah, and he complained to the Lord.
- **Micah,** Micah 1:1: "The word of the Lord that came to Micah the Morasthite in the days of Jotham, Ahaz, and Hezekiah, kings of Judah, which he saw concerning Samaria and Jerusalem." Here, Micah is warning the people regarding their sin and the approaching judgment of God upon them. Among his predictions was the destruction of Jerusalem.

- **Zephaniah,** Zephaniah 1:1–2: "The word of the LORD which came unto Zephaniah … I will utterly consume all things from off the land, saith the LORD." Zephaniah foretold of God's approaching judgment and the destruction of Judah and Jerusalem by the Chaldeans. He urged them to seek the Lord. He also reminded them of God's mercy and His promise to return them out of captivity and gave them hope.

- **Haggai,** Haggai 1:1: The word of the LORD came by Haggai, the prophet to Zerubbabel, governor of Judah, and to Joshua, the high priest. After Jerusalem was destroyed by Babylon, the Jews returned to Jerusalem and the word of the Lord came to Haggai requesting the rebuilding of the temple. But the people were concerned about their own daily lives and building their own homes. Haggai prophesied, and the Lord stirred up the spirit of Zerubbabel and Joshua and the people and encouraged them to return to their duty. They did the work and the temple was completed.

- **Zechariah,** Zechariah 1:1: The word of the Lord came to Zechariah in a warning to Israel of the Lord's displeasure. He warned the people that they should return to the Lord. The Jews were back in Jerusalem but were neglectful in their duty of rebuilding the temple. Zechariah prophesied to them, encouraging them to complete the rebuilding of the temple.

God communed with these prophets in visions of His word so that they understood the intention, the timing, and the providence of God. And God quickened them, enabled them with the capacity, the ability and faith to accomplish what was required.

These are but a few.

CHAPTER 12

ANCIENT VISIONS DEPICTING THE PERSON OF GOD

P rophets of old were blessed with other visions that include symbolism beginning in the Old Testament and continuing in the New Testament after the resurrection of Jesus Christ.

Some have seen visions of God, which means that what they must have seen are symbols of God, the Father, since no man hath seen God. These symbols point to Jesus Christ. In John 1:18, it is written, "No man hath seen God at any time, the only begotten Son, which is in the bosom of the Father He hath declared him."

Moses, a man beloved of God—a friend of God—beseeched God to show him His glory. God said, "I will make my goodness pass before thee, and I will proclaim the name of the LORD before thee; and will be gracious to whom I will be gracious, and will shew mercy on whom I will shew mercy. And he said, Thou canst not see my face: for there shall no man see me, and live" (Exodus 33:19–20). The Lord asked Moses to stand on a rock and God covered Moses with His hand while He passed by. And when God took away His hand, Moses saw the back of God but not His face. God also is described in 1 Timothy 6:16 as dwelling in unapproachable light, "whom no man hath seen, nor can see".

Visions of God

The following are brief examples of some of the visions of the appearance of God:

- **Abram,** Genesis 15

  The Lord appeared to Abram when He was making the covenant with Him (Genesis 12:7). He was visited by three angels that announced that he would bear a son (Genesis 18), and God talked with Abram when He tested his faithfulness (Genesis 22).

- **Jacob,** Genesis 28:12–13, 46:2

  Jacob dreamed of a ladder that reached from earth to heaven with angels ascending and descending. And the Lord stood above the ladder and identified Himself to Jacob in the dream and promised him the land of Canaan for an inheritance. God appeared to Jacob again in a vision to tell him he should go to Egypt.

- **Micaiah,** 1 Kings 22:19

  Micaiah in a sacred vision saw the Lord sitting on His throne and all the angels sitting beside Him on His right and left.

- **Isaiah,** Isaiah 6:1–3

  Isaiah "saw the Lord sitting upon a throne, high and lifted up, and his train filled the temple." And there were seraphim singing, "Holy Holy Holy is the LORD of hosts: the whole earth is full of his glory." Isaiah also heard God's voice as God was establishing him to be a prophet.

- **Ezekiel,** Ezekiel 1:4,28

  Ezekiel saw a sacred vision of the rainbow. He was generously blessed with knowing the secret treasures of knowledge. He gives details of the heavens being opened and he saw visions of God. He saw a whirlwind, a great cloud, a fire enfolding itself, and out of the fire was the likeness of four living creatures with the appearance of a man. And among the many other symbols he saw in this sacred vision, there was the likeness of the throne with the likeness of a man above it. And he saw the color of amber, and the appearance of the rainbow, and he describes this as the appearance of the likeness of the glory of the Lord.

Other Sacred Symbolism

- **Daniel,** Daniel 7, 8, 10

  Daniel was generously blessed with sacred visions of prophetic timing. He saw symbols portraying the sequence of historical events leading up to the second coming of Christ.

- **Peter,** Acts 10

  Peter in a trance saw heaven opened and a great sheet containing different kinds of four-footed beasts, creeping things, and birds. He heard a voice telling him to kill and eat. But he said he had never eaten anything common or unclean, and he heard a voice telling him that what God has cleansed, he should not refer to as unclean. This occurred three times, and then the vessel was received up again into heaven.

- **John,** Revelation 1:4–22

  This is another generous blessing of prophetic timing and complex symbolism. This is one of the most complex visions in the Bible where Jesus Christ Himself revealed to the prophet John the prophecy of the events that will come to pass throughout history, not necessarily in sequence but leading up to the second coming of Christ.

Those Who Heard the Voice of God

Here are two examples:

- **Proclamation of the Law, Exodus 19, 20**

  The people of Israel left Egypt and were in the wilderness of Sinai. "And Moses went up unto God, and the Lord called to him out of the mountain, saying, Thus shalt thou say to the house of Jacob, and tell the children of Israel; Ye have seen what I did unto the Egyptians, and how I bare you on eagles' wings, and brought you unto myself" (Exodus 19:3–4). And the Lord made promises to Israel, which Moses would convey, and he prepared them and sanctified them for the presence of the Lord. "And Moses brought forth the people out of the camp to meet with God; and they stood at the nether part of the mount. And Mount Sinai was altogether on a smoke, because the LORD descended upon it in fire: and the smoke thereof ascended as the smoke of a furnace, and the whole mount quaked greatly. And when the voice of the trumpet sounded long, and waxed louder and louder, Moses spake, and God answered him by a voice" (Exodus 19:17–19). And the Lord declared the law to Moses.

- **The Transfiguration, Matthew 17, Mark 9**
  On this occasion Peter, James, and John at the transfiguration of Jesus heard the voice of God. Jesus took Peter, James, and John up to the mountain and He was transfigured in their presence. His face shined as brightly as the sun, and His clothes became as light. And there appeared to them upon the mountain Moses and Elias in the spirit and they were talking with them. And while Peter was suggesting they build three tabernacles—one for Jesus, one for Moses, and one for Elias—a bright cloud overshadowed them and a voice out of the cloud said, "This is my beloved Son, in whom I am well pleased; hear ye him" (Matthew 17:5).

These examples should serve to strengthen our faith. For God has not entirely hidden Himself, nor does he withhold His will and intentions from us.

CHAPTER 13

THE GIFT OF PROPHECY AND THE EFFECT OF SACRED VISIONS

And it shall come to pass afterward, that I will pour out my
spirit upon all flesh; and your sons and your daughters shall
prophesy, your old men shall dream dreams, your young
men shall see visions: And also upon the servants and upon
the handmaids in those days will I pour out my spirit.

Joel 2:28–29

Our Lord has expressly told us that this will be a sign of the
last days and of His second coming. Why then should we
be surprised or startled that they do occur?

Sacred visions are divine revelations, glimpses into heaven
through symbols in which an aspect of prophecy is revealed by
the power and providence of the Holy Spirit. They convey deeper
spiritual truth. They open the secret treasure of heavenly knowledge.
They break down barriers between earth and heaven, natural and
supernatural, and time and eternity. They reaffirm spiritual truths of
the gospel of Jesus Christ.

Sacred visions were the way God brought us the Bible. Now
they are not an addition to the Bible but simply confirm it. And by
confirming the Bible, God sheds light upon it, opening to us deeper
hidden layers of knowledge that reveal Him more clearly as the day
of His return approaches. Visions are given to us in these last days

for confirming the people of God, for strengthening our conviction, and for preparation.

Because sacred visions are the source of wisdom and deeper spiritual understanding, they must convey a spiritual message and make biblical sense. Their interpretation must be revealed by the Holy Spirit through the pages of the Bible and prayer, not by our imagination through the pretense of scholarship or worldly wisdom. They must reaffirm the Word of God, advance the knowledge of God, and facilitate our relationship with God.

They reveal mystery and are therefore only possible by divine enablement. They serve many purposes, including facilitating the cleansing of sin and conformity to the image of Christ. Therefore, they support us in the way of redemption and serve to enlighten in ways that draw us closer to God. Their main purpose is to further our way in righteousness.

They are blessings of grace. "Grace and peace be multiplied unto you through the knowledge of God, and of Jesus our Lord, According as his divine power hath given unto us all things that pertain unto life and godliness, through the knowledge of him that hath called us to glory and virtue" (2 Peter 1:2–3).

God gives sacred visions because of divine love. Those who receive them are facilitated with a greater measure of empathy. Visions convey the gift of divine love. Because of love, God goes to great lengths to reach His people.

Often their main purpose is warning regarding pending judgment, the mercy of timing, and to call us to our duty. Sacred visions always convey God's intentions and instruction regarding something God wants us to do—a service He wants us to provide for the benefit of all.

God empowers us through visions with the knowledge and the will to obey what He requires. Jesus appeared to Saul on his way to Damascus in the form of a bright light from heaven. He wanted Saul to give a testimony to the people of what he had seen and that Christ had manifested Himself to him. The Lord wanted him to preach the gospel to the gentiles and enlighten them so that they could receive forgiveness of sins and sanctification by faith in Jesus Christ (Acts 26:12–18).

With instruction, God always gives understanding. God never gives a vision and then leaves us in a self-directed or misguided condition. God leads and guides, ensuring that His will is understood and accomplished. In the circumstances of Jonah, though, he was unwilling to do what God required. God ensured that he was able to carry out his task, though it was by the force of punishment, as he was swallowed up by the fish that God had prepared. God facilitates us in doing His will. It does not go unaccomplished because we fear what others might say or do, because we are unwilling, or because we believe that we are incapable.

By sacred visions, God conveys goodwill, assurance of protection, mercy, and safety. God protected Lot by sending an angel to hasten his escape before the imminent destruction of Sodom and Gomorrah (Genesis 18:15). God also appeared to Noah to let him know when the rain was going to begin and that it was time to come into the ark for safety. God revealed to Noah His presence, to see him into the ark to be safe from the flood seven days before the flood began. God gave them the mercy of timing.

God confirms His holy covenant and promised blessings by sacred visions.

Sacred visions facilitate the power of the gift of faith. They are given to support us when tested and provide assurances of God's presence. God communed with Abraham repeatedly to confirm the blessings He had promised, including the promised inheritance of the land of Canaan and the promise of a son, Isaac, with Sarah, his wife (Genesis 12:2; 15:1). God communed with Job when he was tested and under severe afflictions to give him strength, comfort, and hope.

When his testing had been accomplished, the Lord rewarded him double the material goods he had possessed in the beginning but had lost during his time of testing (Job 42:10). Sacred visions confirm the knowledge that God is constantly with us, which gives us faith to endure.

Since sacred visions forewarn of future events, they reaffirm God as Creator of the universe. They are a testament to His authority over creation. For God alone knows the future and is able to direct the course of nature. Thus, they are incontestable proof of God as Creator. They tell us that God is in control and has authority over all the ordinances of the earth.

A Beloved Condition

This gift of prophecy is a beloved condition. Daniel, greatly beloved by God, was given the secret details of King Nebuchadnezzar's dream and also the interpretation, whereas, no one else could assist the king with the interpretation, let alone the dream (Daniel 2:1–47). The king had a dream in which he saw an image of a person made of various metals, but he could not remember the details. But God blessed Daniel with the ability to tell the king the details of his dream and also the interpretation. He had the ability to know much more than others.

The same is true for all the prophets with whom God shared the secret treasure of knowledge regarding events that would come to pass, and whom God used to bring spiritual knowledge to the world.

Effect on the Physical Body

The blessing of a sacred vision is to be blessed beyond the measure of what is available by human capacity. Since divine wisdom is given to us only by the power of the Holy Spirit and is not a skill that we can acquire by our own efforts, we must be prepared by the quickening of the Spirit of God in communion with our spirit. God gives this empowerment through sacred visions. God engages us in ways that are beyond our natural condition and physical capabilities as a method of conveying these spiritual gifts.

The body must be prepared in order to receive the vision and the knowledge. Therefore, our physical systems, particularly the mind, heart, ears, and eyes, must be enabled in order to receive this level of divine openness. The eyes must be permitted by the power of God to see, and the ears to hear the supernatural. The body must be endowed with power to prevent fear and fainting and to maintain its physical capabilities in order to comprehend the mysterious experience. The body can be significantly affected by the proximity and expressed openness of the divine presence.

Such spiritual preparation is an individual gift. Therefore, a person who is present with someone during the revelation of a sacred vision is unable to see what is not meant for him or her, though he or she can be in some ways affected by the divine presence. And the person is unable to assist in spiritual interpretation.

In the case of Daniel, the Scriptures declare, "And I Daniel alone saw the vision: for the men that were with me saw not the vision; but a great quaking fell upon them, so that they fled to hide themselves" (Daniel 10:7). The men that were with Daniel felt the presence of God but were not equipped to withstand it. Their eyes were not divinely prepared for the vision that was meant only for Daniel, and their bodies were not prepared for the presence of God. Even so, Daniel himself had "fainted and was sick for certain days" on receiving revelations from the Lord (Daniel 8:27). He became dumb (Daniel 10:15). The effect was temporary.

Sacred visions are exceptionally beneficial to mental clarity and capacity. They impart enhanced analytical and problem-solving ability because the main purpose is to impart wisdom and understanding and other spiritual benefits. They provide superior coping proficiency including the capability to bear extreme suffering with fortitude, calm, and contentment. The Bible gives many examples of the fortitude of ancient prophets.

Our perspective on life becomes far-reaching with priorities that are structured upon an eternal rather than merely physical and temporal existence.

Misunderstandings in the World Regarding Visions

The word *vision* is much misunderstood because of the mystery, wonder, complexity, fear, and enormous curiosity that it entails. Because of their highly mysterious nature—and often the purpose is warning because of sin and pending judgment—visions can be a source of considerable fear and uneasiness. For this reason, the word *vision* often meets with opposition and rejection, and some would prefer to mock the message and the messenger. This has been the case from ancient times.

To add to the confusion, there are false prophets in our time who proclaim false visions. They speak and do evil, claiming the name of God, whereas they do so in the name of a false god and false Christ. This is the product of a corrupt imagination. Yet they are able to convince many. Today, it is becoming increasingly prevalent that we observe this kind of evil in the world—those who seek to deceive by pretending to speak on behalf of God when, in fact, they seek to further the cause of evil.

False prophets are (in the meaning of the word) bogus, incorrect, and wrong. What they speak is fabricated, deceitful, and insincere. They are contrary to the Word of God, and if we know the Word of God, we will be able to identify this evil and protect ourselves from it.

As I observe this spiritual mischief, and the response of many to this folly, I know that those who display such spiritual darkness are a detriment not only to themselves but to the souls of many. And I am acutely aware that God is present and watching the spectacle of arrogance and mockery.

Sacred visions, being gifts of grace, are not hallucination, figments of the imagination, delusion, or fantasy. Nor are they the result of psychosis or any kind of mental incapacity. Sacred visions do not cause anyone to do evil but further the cause of goodness and righteousness for the glory and honor of God.

As a matter of fact, it is dangerous to ascribe evil to the work of the Holy Spirit. This is highly irreverent and blasphemous. On the contrary, sacred visions lead us into greater peace, enhancing each aspect of a person's life. Consequently, the purpose of God through sacred visions is transformation, conformity, and restoration in holiness and grace.

Those who lack spiritual discernment are unable to differentiate. They know not what is truth or falsehood, or spiritual darkness from light. They believe what is false or they scoff at and ridicule information that ought to be held sacred. And they mock the things they do not understand.

Those who do not know the "voice" or the "alarm" of Christ (through the gospel) awake to the sound of the false alarm that is brought by the voice of the false prophet. They become disappointed. This is unfortunate and the cause of unnecessary fear, worry, and disillusionment. But most importantly, this is a great detriment to the soul.

There is much more to be said about false visions and false prophets in a later volume in this series. It will give insights into how we can protect ourselves and our souls from this evil.

CHAPTER 14

THE PROTECTION OF
THE HOLY SPIRIT

I n the early 2000s, my mother was having problems with a painful knee. But she loved to worship and looked forward to church every Sunday. She worshipped at an Anglican church in the parish of St. Peter, Barbados. With a slight limp, my mother made her way to church on the bus that was conveniently provided for churchgoers. Among the churchgoers was a woman who made fun of her limping, which caused her much discomfort and misery.

One Sunday evening, I called my mother to have a chat; I wanted to learn how she was feeling. With a heavy heart, she told me of the despair she was experiencing that stemmed from the snide remarks, mocking, and taunting of this woman. She was part of a group of four or five women that traveled together to church on the bus each Sunday. Her criticisms and ridicule caused my mother such suffering that she told me she was anticipating avoiding them by no longer going to church.

At that same time, there was I, with the burden in my heart regarding how I would ever be able to share the details of my experience with others as my mother had warned that I must do. And it was coincidental that I had called my mother to chat, in order to take my mind off the distress I was feeling but she was experiencing the same distress that I feared.

I believed I would be mocked and ridiculed as I tried to share this information with people other than priests. I was concerned regarding what they would say and think and how they would question my mental capacity. And with this burden, I called my mother. But instead of any comfort, she was telling me that she was being mocked at church because of the pain in her knee.

After hearing of my mother's misery, I did not disclose my own distress—that the burden I was anticipating stemmed from something so similar. But her circumstances disturbed me, and I became furious. This was now a bigger, spiritual issue. The woman was obstructing the worship my mother so loved to give to the Lord. And she was potentially impeding my mother's redemptive process and salvation. But I was also furious because it reinforced the matter of my own predicament. She was experiencing the same situation that I feared most.

I said boldly to my mother, "Are you going to let someone prevent you from going to church to worship the Lord? Is that really what you mean to say?" My mother said, in a soft and peaceful voice, as usual, "I no longer want to be among them!" It was a heavy burden to hear my mother say such words.

I ended the conversation pondering the malice and offensiveness of the woman. Although I was annoyed and bothered by what was being done to my mother, I thought there was nothing I could do since I was far away. And at the same time, I felt sorrow for the woman. She was engaging in the evil of obstruction while on her way to church, evidence of such spiritual darkness.

I could sense that from this coincidence that there was divine intervention and God was conveying a spiritual message to me.

Two weeks later, as I began a telephone conversation with my mother, she said anxiously, "Do you recall our conversation about the woman who was bothering me on my way to church?" But before I could reply, she said, "She had taken ill in church last Sunday. Less than five minutes into the beginning of worship, she fainted and never recovered. She died three days later. Services for her took place a few days ago. The other women, observing what occurred, took notice and were afraid, and now they help me as I get into the bus!"

My reaction was shock and fear as my heart pounded profusely—a thumping I could feel throughout my entire body.

Smitten by God

An angel of the Lord visited that church, and she was smitten by God. Her behavior created such provocation and anger in God's heart. It was as if to say He did not want her worship, because she was smitten in His church immediately as the worship service was beginning.

While she continued her mockery Sunday after Sunday, believing that all was well, she did not know that God was observing how she was preventing His worship and getting into the way of God's eternal purpose. God is zealous regarding His worship and all those who come to Him. He is determined to lose none.

What we do not realize, or hold in memory, is that God is observing each of us. He is present everywhere, at all times, and knows all things. And here again God has revealed Himself as a private listener to every conversation. He has manifested His presence on the bus and evidently in the church.

As God watched the behavior of this woman, likewise God watches each of us. But God, who is long-suffering, allowed her to continue as she did each Sunday morning. Then, suddenly, it pleased the Lord to intervene, making her a public example by smiting her in church, of all places. Neither the church nor my mother was aware of the deeply spiritual nature of what had transpired or how gravely serious it was.

The judgment of God is greater than physical incapacity. The fact that God intervened to bring about an end, and in His wisdom showed His power through the permanence of death, means that there are eternal consequences.

It is indeed dreadful when our behavior serves to create division, turmoil, and sadness to others, even in the sacred house of God. For this is the place where we should be in unity, love, and fellowship, and where primarily there ought to be peace.

God Provides Threefold Confirmation of Protection

First Confirmation of Protection: This divine providence and intervention represent a message that God is conveying regarding the burden in my heart and the covenant blessing of special protection. God protected my mother, but at the same time this incident represents God's protection of His message, worship, the holy covenant, and all that pertains to it.

It reveals peace and says that there ought to be no care or concern. Great lengths God would pursue in order to ensure that His work is done. God would allay my worry and fears. He would shut the mouths of those who would prevent my service or block the way of divine purpose. For no one is able to mock, denigrate, or prevent the work of God.

It provides warning. Such protection God has placed upon His message, that He is willing to fiercely defend and preserve it. He would ensure that it reaches the places it should go and bears the fruit that is intended. And God is willing to intervene, to ensure that none are lost who are His.

The power of the Holy Spirit is unstoppable, a shield that intervenes on our behalf and provides fortification when we are in physical and natural difficulty. But God's defense is particularly available when we are in spiritual difficulty and confronted by spiritual obstacles.

It is indeed horrible to mock the Holy Spirit. Elisha was filled with the Holy Spirit, for he was with Elijah just before he was taken up into heaven by a whirlwind. And before Elijah was taken up, He said to Elisha, "Ask what I shall do for thee, before I be taken away from thee. And Elisha said, I pray thee, let a double portion of thy spirit be upon me. And he said, Thou hast asked a hard thing: nevertheless, if thou see me when I am taken from thee, it shall be so unto thee; but if not, it shall not be so" (2 Kings 2:9–10). And Elisha watched as Elijah was taken up into heaven and was given a double portion of the Holy Spirit. And as Elisha went on his way, he was mocked by children who said, "Go up, thou bald head; go up, thou bald head" (2 Kings 2:23). Elisha looked at them and cursed them in the name of the Lord, and forty-two children were devoured by two bears. Those who mock God's people who have the indwelling Holy Spirit do not only mock them, for it is God they are mocking. And God takes this as a personal affront against Himself. Children must be aware that God is watching the things they do including when they bully.

Saul, who persecuted the church was on his way to Damascus when suddenly a light from heaven surrounded him. He fell to the ground and heard a voice saying, "Saul, Saul, why persecutest thou me? And he said, Who art thou, Lord? And the Lord said, I am Jesus whom thou persecutest: it is hard for thee to kick against the pricks" (Acts 9:4–5). At that moment, Saul was smitten with blindness and had to be led by his friends. He was three days without sight and did not eat or drink. Those who persecute God's people persecute Christ Himself. Saul's persecution of the church meant that he persecuted Christ. The consequences of such actions are severe, particularly when it relates to impeding the work of salvation and hindering the kingdom of God.

Today, I feel sorrow for the woman because of her awful spiritual demise. But I am aware of God's constant presence and hold in memory the words of my prayer that I may always be aware of how close God is to me.

This is testament to the spiritual environment of our time and the lateness of the hour in which we live. God is willing to manifest His presence through such direct and miraculous intervention. It represents the magnitude of spiritual activity that is occurring in the world, though many are unaware.

Second Confirmation of Protection: A major covenant principle is that God confirms His action and repeats His intention. It symbolizes the abundance of mercy.

In early July 2006, I received two job offers the same morning, between 10:00 and 11:00. Again, because of the coincidence, straightaway I knew that to be God's signature and His divine intervention. (Double is a covenant portion.)

I had been waiting for one month for the paperwork to be completed on the first position with a federal government contractor. But it was not ready until the morning I received the second offer. A representative from a recruitment agency was recruiting for a position with a well-established, prestigious American association, the world's largest membership organization of psychiatrists, including some of the world's most renowned. I had no knowledge of this association or the vacant position when I received the call. But by the providence of God, the agency moved quickly and effectively in finalizing the job offer.

Although I was eager to assume the first offer, after receiving the second, the choice between the two was not difficult, as there were many additional beneficial aspects to this position. Apart from the fact that it was a perfect match for me, there was a smooth and effortless series of interviews and recruitment process.

But the awareness that this was divine intervention raised my curiosity and caused me to wonder why I was being pointed in this direction. It appeared that I was being facilitated by God to work for this nonprofit organization. After accepting the position, my curiosity soon waned.

This association develops and establishes the standard criteria for diagnosis and classification of mental health disorders in every conceivable area of psychiatry. It establishes the psychiatric manual that defines what is and what is not a mental illness or disorder. This is the essential authority that is used throughout the United States of America and the world to define and diagnose mental illness.

And though I did not readily understand or identify the reason why God pointed me to this association, my first assignment should obviously have made me aware of what God was saying.

My first assignment was related to this manual as my boss assigned me the development of the revenue and expense projections in the early stages of predevelopment planning. When I assumed the position, they were just initiating the work on the revision of this manual. And through this first assignment, God was pointing me to the reason why I was there.

God was directing me to the definitions and classifications of mental illnesses and psychiatric diagnoses. It was as if to show me in the most comprehensive manner what is and what is not a mental illness or psychiatric disorder. And though I did not readily perceive what God was pointing out to me, this is a clear message—an ultimate message that speaks of total vindication and validation.

My work with this association is not in the area of psychiatry, and I do not speak in any manner on their behalf. But God having sent me to work among experts in the field of psychiatry, and furthermore where the very standards for diagnoses of mental illnesses and disorders are developed, is the ultimate support, justification, substantiation, and verification against any reproach. For they are witnesses to the exemplary nature of my work, intellectual capacity, and professionalism.

Years into my tenure, the two interventions of God became clear. First, God pointed out why I was there and then confirmed my validation. God was saying that after working with this association in the highly specialized and challenging areas of my profession, in finance and budgeting, and having interacted at all levels with such world-renowned experts in these comprehensive areas of mental health, it bears record against all who would mock or question my mental capacity or otherwise try to prevent my work.

And by addressing my concerns regarding those who would mock, God declares the level of seriousness He has placed upon His message and the work He has called me to do. God defends and protects it and would go to such extent against anything that would prevent it. By this special blessing of the opportunity to work at such a place and with experts whose authority is to develop the definitions of mental disorders, and by pointing me to the psychiatric manual, God would seem to say, "Let me show you. Here's what mental illnesses and psychiatric disorders are. This is not you. Fear not." By defining what this is, God distinguishes the difference and puts clarity, differentiation, and boundaries between what defines me and what defines mental illnesses and disorders. "For God hath not given us the spirit of fear; but of power, and of love, and of a sound mind" (2 Timothy 1:7).

God has presented me before the largest assembly of psychiatrists in the world to make a statement. God would again shut the mouths of those who would seek to mock. It is a message of warning to those who would denigrate and detract from the work that God would have me accomplish.

This is testament to the mercy of God, who is constantly available and involved in every aspect of life. On this second occasion, reaffirming the same message by different circumstances, God is manifesting the special protection of His work and covenant and allaying any concerns. It is a covenant principle. God's Word must go forth and must accomplish all that is intended.

Third Confirmation of Protection: God affirms yet on this third occasion. There is a trinity of divine protection in the covenant.

It was fall 2007, and I had been working on the computer until just after 1:00 a.m. when I became exhausted and sleepy. And as I lay on the bed and closed my eyes, not yet fully asleep, the Lord gave me a sacred vision. This time, the symbol was a woman's face. She was African American, dark skinned, had a round face, and her hair was short or pulled back, as I could tell from the split second this image flashed before my eyes. I was astonished because the image had such clarity. She was not someone I had known or had ever seen.

One week later, I was also working on the computer until approximately the same time in the morning. As I was about to go to sleep, I heard a loud collision on the street, but I did not look to see what was happening. The following morning, I had forgotten the incident and did not check. It had been snowing and I decided not to drive.

On Saturday, December 8, 2007, the snow had melted and I was absolutely shocked to discover that the loud collision was indeed my car being damaged. To add to my distress, the perpetrator left no note or contact information.

I reported the incident to the Springfield, Virginia, police. As I was awaiting their arrival to conduct an investigation, my heart pounded profusely as the Lord awakened me to the knowledge of where this was taking me. I remembered the sacred vision, the face of the woman He had shown me the week earlier. I was convinced that she was the one who had struck my car. This became much to assimilate. And as I accepted this reality, my heart throbbed mightily. I could feel the blood pulsating throughout my veins as I anticipated how this would unfold. Nevertheless, I had no idea if she might be someone living in the area or was a visitor who came and left shortly thereafter.

But I was convinced that this woman who did the damage would be revealed. I knew she would have to confess. The Lord had revealed her to me, even before the incident took place.

There were two patrol officers that arrived that Saturday afternoon, and after taking my statement, they told me to go inside; they would let me know if they discovered anything. But of course, I could not explain to the police what I already knew: that God had already shown me her identity. I was confident that within a short time they would locate her.

They proceeded to walk around the area. I was shocked when, in less than five minutes, they returned. There was a loud knock on my door. I knew they had found her. I jumped. Although I had been sitting by the door waiting for their return, this startled me. I struggled to put my shoes on. I was nervous with anticipation—eager to hear what they had to say. It was astounding to see the work of God's hand unmistakably before my eyes.

"We have found the person who struck your car," they said. "We would like you to come to meet her. She is a nice person." But in that moment, I was not persuaded that she could be a nice person and do as she had done.

My anticipation reached its peak, as I could not wait to confirm what she looked like and who she was. And indeed when I saw her, she was exactly the woman the Lord had shown me in the sacred vision the week earlier. I almost fainted. It was as if I had been in the trance all over again when I saw her face. She was my neighbor, who lived around the corner at #202. She was probably new to the area. I had never seen her in the vicinity.

She was African American, with a round face, her hair was pulled back behind her ears, and she was about just over five feet tall. She had confessed to the patrol officers that she and a friend had gone to the bar and were drinking alcohol. Her friend drove them home that night, but she was intoxicated. Having been so heavily impaired, when she tried to park the car, she struck my car.

There were several cars parked in the area, but the Lord caused traces of red paint to be left on my car, and this gave a clue to the patrol officers; the Lord led them to her door. They coordinated the exchange of her insurance and contact information. When the conversation was complete, as my heart pounded, all that I could say was, "God is so wonderful! God is so wonderful." But I could not explain to the police what that meant. They merely smiled when they saw how relieved and grateful I was. It was overwhelming!

The woman did not know that the Lord was watching while she and her friend drank alcohol until becoming intoxicated at the bar, and without any consideration for their own lives, or the lives of others, drove home under impairment, struck my car, and walked away.

The Bible tells us that the eyes of the Lord are in every place and nothing escapes Him.

The message from the Lord is that His protection is diligent, constant, and absolute. If God would keep watch even over my car, what wouldn't He? God not only protects us but all that concerns us as evidenced by the three distinct types of personal care and protection that are being demonstrated. This trinity of divine protection is the symbol of ultimate protection, extended care, and manifestation of His love and mercy.

God is great, yet He is willing to continually prove Himself, to show His loving attention and to be a shield to them that love Him. By invoking this trinity God provides proof of Himself. What this is saying is that with God as a shield and defender, I should have no worry but do what God has consecrated my life and has prepared me to do. By this trinity of defense and the surety of His watchful eye, the Lord has released me of that burden, and has set me free from the worry of mockers and critics. And by what God has done, He is demonstrating what He intends to do. "If God be for us, who can be against us?" (Romans 8:31).

What this also says is that though evil comes to us, it is not because God has turned his back, is unavailable, and does not see.

There are many reasons why, but we can be confident that whatever God allows is based upon a foundation of mercy and love. And there are spiritual underpinnings that we do not readily understand. Although we may be devastated in a physical and natural sense, we are much spiritually advanced if we use these occasions wisely.

The reasons are deeply rooted in the complexity of spiritual and eternal purposes of the holy covenant. Whatever God allows is for the purpose of bringing us back to Him with a passionate desire for mercy and redemption and to facilitate the opportunity for God to reach us and show us His love.

This incident did not end here. More noticeably, there were interrelated spiritual processes that were revealed by this manifested level of divine involvement. It revealed a spiritual milestone that relates to the overall message of the holy covenant and the processes that facilitate deeper spiritual knowledge. We will discuss this in greater detail throughout these volumes.

CHAPTER 15

DIVINE WISDOM AND DEEPER SPIRITUAL UNDERSTANDING

In the following chapters, we will examine the heavenly symbolism presented in the sacred visions. But let us first take a look at divine wisdom and deeper spiritual understanding, as this is the foundation of spiritual interpretation.

Divine wisdom and deeper spiritual understanding are not worldly skills, a measure of experience or mature sophistication, scholarship, or intelligence. They are not gained by years of education or any knowledge that we can learn or ideas we develop. They are spiritual gifts given by Jesus Christ under the new covenant of grace, by the communion and inspiration of the Holy Spirit. It is the knowledge of God and must therefore come from God.

This knowledge enables us to fear God. And what the Bible tells us is that "the fear of the LORD is the beginning of wisdom: and the knowledge of the holy is understanding" (Proverbs 9:10). If we fear God, it means that we honor and reverence His divinity and majesty and act in harmony with His will.

God reveals His divine intention by the blessing of divine wisdom and deeper spiritual understanding. It is a sign of grace and is the precursor to the multitude of other spiritual gifts. For the essence of grace is abundance, an opening of the treasure of God to the soul. It is a symbol of the abundance of grace.

Spiritual enlightenment, as the gospel becomes our light to show us the way to live, is evidence of this gift. We are unable to believe God without the power of the Spirit of Jesus Christ. Therefore, when we have the grace of Jesus Christ, we also have understanding. By the communion of the Holy Spirit, God imparts this ability through the study of His Word. It enables us to perceive and comprehend the Word of God and to live in harmony with the truth of the gospel of Jesus Christ. The Bible says, "Then opened he their understanding, that they might understand the scriptures" (Luke 24:45). We are unable to understand what God is saying without God speaking directly to our soul and spirit, giving us the spiritual awakening. And we are unable to understand the Bible, if we approach it (just as a book) without acknowledging God and desiring understanding. For this reason, there are many who do not believe it, or understand it. The true benefit of the Bible must come from its source.

Through the eternal Spirit of Christ, divine wisdom and deeper spiritual understanding give quickening and life to the soul. We are unable to follow Christ without this quickening and instead remain in spiritual darkness, in hostility, and in estrangement from God. Quickening is the process by which God gives life to the soul that is spiritually dead, a reviving effect by the Spirit of Christ that gives renewal and regeneration through wisdom and deeper spiritual understanding. It gives the soul freedom, as it is able to know the difference between life and death. Therefore, it does not desire to remain in the bondage of sin and condemnation, but the soul is able to hear, understand, and act according to the voice of Christ and heed the call to return to God for grace.

It gives life to the soul that has returned to God from the darkness of sin. It confers spiritual awakening that enables the soul to be conformed to a new nature, to the image of Christ. This life enables the renewal of our mind and transformation of our heart to the likeness of Christ. The soul becomes a new birth in Christ.

Wisdom and understanding are fundamental principles of a covenanted life. This facilitates the nourishment Christ gives to the soul under grace.

Therefore, it is the first sign of redemption as the quickening and life that come to us through wisdom enable the soul to recognize God, to know Him, to be at peace with Him, and to love Him.

In addition to the enablement of the Holy Spirit in the study of God's Word, God imparts wisdom and deeper spiritual understanding through dreams and visions. God communes with our spirit at a level that is greater and beyond words to give us the awareness of divine guidance and direction. And God imparts gifts that are beyond what are available to us on a physical level. Therefore, we are able to serve in a manner that is beyond the limitations of our natural and physical ability. "Daniel had understanding in all visions and dreams" (Daniel 1:17).

When the angel Gabriel came to Daniel in a sacred vision, the angel said, "I am now come forth to give thee skill and understanding" (Daniel 9:22). By giving him skill, God conferred to him grace. Daniel was blessed to understand the language of heaven and had glimpses into heaven and heavenly intent. God imparted to him such knowledge of prophecy spanning the history of the world. God granted him the ability to know much more than others, such that he was given the ability to describe to King Nebuchadnezzar details of his dream when even the king himself could not remember what he had dreamed. And Daniel also furnished him the interpretation when no one else could. The Holy Spirit bestowed upon Daniel such favor, for he possessed immense knowledge of the mysteries of the kingdom of God.

The foundation of faith is wisdom and deeper spiritual understanding. We are better able to believe the promises of God and have confidence and conviction to act in accordance with our belief when we have faith. God opens His secret treasure and removes boundaries of knowledge, and by so doing, removes also the boundaries to faith. This opening of boundaries of spiritual knowledge is a symbol of the return of favor. There is agreement and friendship as we are let into the secret treasure of God. Abraham, a man of great faith, was able to trust God and acted in harmony with the will of God according to the covenant. The Scriptures say, "Abraham believed God, and it was imputed unto him for righteousness: and he was called the Friend of God" (James 2:23). As a Friend of God, he was allowed access to the secret treasure of the knowledge of God. This is an essential principle of grace and is a symbol of reconciliation.

Wisdom and deeper spiritual understanding facilitate the gift of love. Our love of God increases as our knowledge of God develops and expands. We have a mindfulness of His loving kindness, mercy, and goodwill toward us, and we are aware of our responsibility to share the same with others. Consequently, greater also is our love for our fellow man.

When we understand more, we are able to love more and have an enhanced and acute level of empathy and compassion. Consequently, wisdom supports the essential bond of covenant love, fellowship, and communion.

These are covenant gifts to facilitate our duty in relationship with God, and in service to our fellowman, as this knowledge enables the soul to return to its duty. It gives mindfulness of God's constant presence and enables the soul in righteousness that keeps us in harmony with God. We are better able to accept God's authority with contentment and peace when we have wisdom.

And if we have harmony with God, we are able to serve Him and God helps us to do what pleases Him. Through the unity of spirit and promptings He places within us, we know what pleases God.

Therefore, it facilitates our obedience, and our obedience demonstrates that we love God, that we respect His autonomy and His will. God gives us these divine gifts to prepare us for service.

It gives us the ability to conduct our lives with consideration in accordance with the purpose of God. Therefore, we have discernment and good judgment and are able to better understand His instruction and submit to His guidance.

These are essential spiritual gifts that make us serviceable to God, not gained by our will but by divine appointment through the communion of the Holy Spirit. He who calls us also prepares us.

The gift of wisdom and deeper spiritual understanding is a precursor of work. In the book of Exodus, God gave the people wisdom and understanding to enable them for the work of building the tabernacle. The Scriptures tell us, "Them hath he filled with wisdom of heart, to work all manner of work, of the engraver, and of the cunning workman, and of the embroiderer, in blue, and in purple, in scarlet, and in fine linen, and of the weaver, even of them that do any work, and of those that devise cunning work" (Exodus 35:35). God granted them wisdom to understand how to perform their work well for the service of the sanctuary according to all that the Lord commanded (Exodus 36:1). With this knowledge, they were capable of exercising sound judgment and had insight to accomplish the building of the tabernacle to the glory of God.

The ability to act according to wisdom and divine knowledge is the foundation of good judgment. It provides insight, perception, discretion, and sound reasoning that are central to justice and fairness. It pleased God exceedingly when Solomon prayed for the gift of an understanding heart, for the ability carry out his duties well as judge of Israel, and discern between good and bad (1 Kings 3:8–10). And God blessed him extensively with wisdom and understanding, and riches beyond what he had asked. "And God gave Solomon wisdom and understanding exceeding much, and largeness of heart, even as the sand that is on the sea shore. And Solomon's wisdom excelled the wisdom of all the children of the east country, and all the wisdom of Egypt" (1 Kings 4:29–30).

God bestows upon us talent with the expectation that it should multiply. This is an essential principle of grace. Thus, the knowledge that God gives is not for the benefit of us only but to aid the progress of others. And there is always a spiritual mission for the work of the kingdom of God that comes with wisdom.

Accordingly, God gave Solomon wisdom to facilitate his work in judging the people of Israel. And having asked for an understanding heart, it presupposes that he also wants the gifts of righteousness and justice. The nature of his request assumes that he wants the knowledge of God and desires attributes of God to execute righteousness. It was to God such delight when Solomon asked for understanding that God bestowed blessings beyond measure in knowledge and material gifts, because he desired to do the will of God for the benefit of Israel.

God gives wisdom and understanding for His glory. The Bible says,

> But God hath chosen the foolish things of the world to confound the wise; and God hath chosen the weak things of the world to confound the things which are mighty; And base things of the world, and things which are despised, hath God chosen, yea, and things which are not, to bring to naught things that are: That no flesh should glory in his presence. (1 Corinthians 1:27–29)

God bestows spiritual gifts in a manner that enables His glory to shine forth instead of the glory of the messenger; God lets the world marvel at the glory of God instead of any worldly wisdom of the messenger. This way, there is no competition with God for His glory. For by the godly disposition of humility and submission of the messenger, the world is able to readily perceive that it is impossible for them, being weak and considered foolish, to have this wisdom by their own scholarship, but that it excels the glory of God in the world. They have no worldly glory or esteem and do not detract from the glory that is God's. So the Bible tells us, "That, according as it is written, He that glorieth, let him glory in the Lord" (1 Corinthians 1:31).

There is no greater detriment than to live without wisdom and deeper spiritual understanding. This leaves us vulnerable to evil— the evil that lives within us in the flesh and the evil that we face in the world. But more importantly, it is a detriment to the soul and therefore has eternal consequences. We live exposed to danger that is easily preventable with minimum care and attention.

Life is filled with errors, blunders, and spiritual stumblings when we do not have wisdom. We exist in vulnerability to life's circumstances, hostage to the state of affairs of the world, because we live without God. We ignore this truth—that we need God's care and protection—and we live in a manner that is open to the elements of danger, though we may be able to foresee. The Bible says,

> So shalt thou find favour and good understanding in the sight of God and man. Trust in the LORD with all thine heart; and lean not unto thine own understanding. In all thy ways acknowledge him, and he shall direct thy paths. (Proverbs 3:4–6)

The lack of wisdom impedes our ability to plan our lives and to make sound decisions. We can be easily fooled, falling prey to the deception of the world, including the deception of false prophets and false teachers. We are compelled to follow every whim that comes and goes. We more readily make our judgment based upon facades rather than substance. Our priorities are displaced and we are unable to determine the difference between what is important in life and what is not.

And above all, the lack of wisdom and deeper spiritual understanding renders us spiritually incapable. Just as in the flesh, a person may be mentally or physically incapable of taking care of himself or herself and managing the chores of daily living. Likewise, it is with our inability to care for what pertains to the soul. When we have no wisdom, we focus on the world and the flesh rather than the soul and spirit and we wander through life with a significantly diminished sense of purpose because we are detached from our soul. It has no life. It is spiritually dead. When the soul is dead, part of us has left us and so we are not whole but have a void that we are unable to fill.

Under grace, the gift of knowledge equips us for this mortal life but also for eternal life. It gives us strength and fortitude to cope with hardship and suffering with peace and contentment, because we are constantly reminded of the joys of eternity. When we have the knowledge of Christ, though we meet the challenges of bondage, burden, and affliction of the world, our soul is yet free.

"Wisdom is the principal thing; therefore get wisdom: and with all thy getting get understanding" (Proverbs 4:7).

CHAPTER 16

HEAVENLY SYMBOLS

S ymbols of the Bible constitute a heavenly language used by God to convey hidden spiritual truth. Symbols are used generously throughout the Bible, in both the Old Testament and New Testament. In the Old Testament, symbolism is used extensively in worship and often points to our Lord and Savior, Jesus Christ.

Necessary for Spiritual Understanding

A sound understanding of biblical symbolism is an essential part of deeper spiritual knowledge. Because they convey spiritual knowledge and prophecy, they are mysterious. They necessitate patience and diligence and encourage disciplined prayer and inquiry into the Word of God.

Since they speak of what pertains to heaven, we can only expect to know the message that they convey by the communion of the Spirit of God with our spirit. Their interpretation can never be gained through self-determination but by prayer.

God, who initiates the communion, must also give their meaning. And He does this by imparting the gifts of wisdom and deeper spiritual understanding. The revelation of the symbols is the initial stage of the gift of prophecy, and after that, God shares their meaning, which enables the opportunity for God to make Himself known to us—and for us to know more of Him.

God requires that we have a fervent desire to seek Him. The mystery of biblical symbolism encourages us to pursue heavenly knowledge, and this presupposes that we seek God. God has promised that those who diligently seek him will surely find Him. Biblical symbolism facilitates this diligence in our quest for knowledge of God.

As mentioned earlier, symbols are used in direct reference to the person and glory of God. They convey much of who God is and what He wants to say of Himself in a given situation. They are an expression of His presence. When God revealed Himself to Israel at Sinai, at the giving of the law, He came to them "in a thick cloud" (Exodus 19:9). "And the LORD went before them by day in a pillar of a cloud, to lead them; and by night in a pillar of fire, to give them light; to go by day and night" (Exodus 13:21). When God revealed Himself to Abram to confirm His covenant, God appeared as "a smoking furnace and burning lamp" (Genesis 15:17).

They show us that God is real, they reaffirm His existence, and they assure us of His involvement. The Scriptures say, "Behold the LORD our God hath shewed us his glory and his greatness, and we have heard his voice out of the midst of the fire: we have seen this day that God doth talk with man, and he liveth" (Deuteronomy 5:24).

Covenant Communion

The purpose of heavenly symbolism is to convey a covenant message for building a covenant relationship. Thus, God draws us closer by revealing Himself through symbols.

Symbols provide unity and commonality of communication. They put heavenly intent into perspective for us. Consequently, heaven and earth find commonality in symbols because they can be acknowledged and understood by man.

We are able to express them and relate to them in physical terms, yet they serve as an image of what is spiritual and God is able to commune with us in a manner that we are able to comprehend. They create a parallel of understanding between flesh and spirit, and between human and divine. They reveal mercy as God reaches us at our level, by symbolism, to reveal the mysteries of heaven.

God is Spirit. His way is superior and His thoughts are excellent. "For my thoughts are not your thoughts, neither are your ways my ways, saith the LORD. For as the heavens are higher than the earth, so are my ways higher than your ways, and my thoughts than your thoughts" (Isaiah 55:8–9). Symbols convert spiritual perspectives into a common denominator. The intention and purpose of God, and the finite thoughts and abilities of man can, through symbolism, effect meaningful spiritual communion. Thus, through symbols God confirmed the promised blessings of His covenant with Abraham (Genesis 12:1–8; 15:1–8).

Symbols break down barriers to prayer, love, mercy, and favor. They are the facility for spiritual exchange in a form that is greater, and absolute, and beyond what words can utter or have the ability to convey. They fulfill the purposes of the divine relationship because symbols allow us to commune with God on a deep, spiritual level during worship. Symbols add to the variety, vividness, richness, vibrancy, and depth of worship, particularly during the sacred season of Lent and Easter.

For example, under the grace of Jesus Christ, the symbol of the cross represents the reaffirmation of our belief that Christ died for us. By the sign of the cross, we are affirming that we belong to Christ according to the holy covenant. This represents that we are pledged to Christ forever and we come under His mercy, protection, and love. We declare our redemption and look forward to the resurrection on the last day—and to eternal life.

Convey Spiritual Gifts

Biblical symbols serve to build our faith because God is revealed by them.

They enable gifts of grace. The soul is transformed as we learn of God through them. And this transformation results from the multiple layers of spiritual gifts and benefits that are imparted by divine power and providence by the use of divine symbols. Certain of these we are aware, but there are numerous that we do not have the ability to comprehend in mortal life. When God communes with us, it is but finite what we can know. And it is infinite the good intentions of God that await us, of which we are unaware.

Consecrated Symbols

God delights in His symbols. God guards His Word and protects His symbols. In the Old Testament, we see how God provided exclusive details and instructions regarding their use. The knowledge that they are watched by God and protected gives confidence of His divine truth.

Thus, God used the same symbolism of the Bible to convey the message of the sacred vision. And by which we can be sure that He is speaking, and we can recognize Him as the true God. The manner in which God uses symbols is protected, and God is consistent in the knowledge that is revealed by them.

Thus, God defends them so that there is no opportunity for contradiction. For this would defeat His purpose. We know that with God there is no disorder or chaos. "For God is not the author of confusion, but of peace, as in all churches of the saints" (1 Corinthians 14:33). Instead, biblical symbolism is unifying. Knowledge of them comes from one source: the Spirit of Jesus Christ. They do not create misunderstanding, confusion of doctrine, or division among believers. They are harmonious with His Word and purpose of salvation.

Their interpretation must make sense in a manner that follows truth in covenant thought and holy reasoning. Because they serve to advance our knowledge of God, their effect on our life should foster our way in righteousness. The knowledge that is gained by them effectively renews our hearts to obedience, and love, and prepares our mind and spirit for service.

Thus, God has consecrated them so that no evil can infringe upon them. Their legitimacy is based upon the Bible, and they are set apart for holiness, having been blessed, hallowed, and dedicated to God. This is how we can be confident of truth. We must honestly represent and sincerely observe the same sacredness and holiness that are ascribed to them in the Bible.

CHAPTER 17

THE IMPACT OF SACRED
SYMBOLISM

I had never considered life from the perspective of spiritual symbolism until God gave me this divine miracle. In fact, symbolism was never a thought that would come to mind. But I am now more aware of the spiritual aspect of symbolism. After God directed me to the Bible and I discovered that all the symbols and their meaning could be found there, I developed an insatiable quest for deeper spiritual understanding, knowledge of symbols in the Bible, and the symbolism that is ever present in daily life.

Suddenness

Although God had prepared me through the many divine interventions and frequency of coincidences, this miracle was sudden. The suddenness of His presence has given me a new perspective on life, redirecting the way I perceive my own life and the world at large. As a result, I have a heightened awareness of how sudden the appearance of our Lord will be on the last day and an enhanced sense of the need for preparation.

This tells me that although we know that the coming of our Lord is approaching, and that we are living in the end times, the day and time of His appearance will be sudden and "as a thief in the night." The Bible tells us that our Lord will come "when we least expect and at a time when we think not." Jesus said, "But of that day and hour knoweth no man, no, not the angels of heaven, but my Father only" (Matthew 24:36).

This is how it was for me when I saw the sacred visions. Inclusive of those who are preparing, the coming of the Lord will be abrupt and unexpected.

God, the Creator

Another enormous benefit stems from having been witness to the fact that it is possible for something to come out of nothing that already exists. This may sound unreal for some, but what I have seen gives new meaning to the realm of possibility, as I witnessed the breaking of barriers between the natural and spiritual. "For with God nothing shall be impossible" (Luke 1:37). I watched, with my eyes wide open, the work of the divine hand as the symbols moved across the pages.

In Hebrews 11:3 it is written: "Through faith we understand that the worlds were framed by the word of God, so that things which are seen were not made of things which do appear." God created the world by the power of His Word.

The sacred vision reaffirms that this is true. And by this consistent action, God is affirming and declaring Himself God, the Lord and Creator. For by His Word all things exist—seen and unseen. The symbols came from God, the Holy Spirit, who I could not see. Only the supernatural symbols, by which the boundaries between natural and supernatural were broken, I could see.

Under grace, God's presence surrounds us and, though not readily accessible to our natural senses, is made available by the preparation and providence of God. This is extraordinarily compelling after experiencing the symbols suddenly appearing, originating from nothing. This has left an indelible mark. It has affirmed the essential element that constitutes faith—that it does "not stand in the wisdom of men, but in the power of God" (1 Corinthians 2:5).

Natural Symbolism

My understanding of the significance of natural symbolism stemmed from my advancement in spiritual alignment. We discussed earlier how the activities of daily life mirrored my study of the Word of God. And the awareness that this was occurring was by the profound and overwhelming number of coincidences—divine providences and intervention.

As the Holy Spirit communed with my spirit, I learned that there is correlation between the natural symbolism we have in our lives and the spiritual symbols that exist in the realm of the soul.

There is symbolism in every aspect of life, how we live, what we do and the things we say, how we perceive the world, and how we relate to God. They are indicators of our priorities, allegiances, commitments, values, beliefs, and ideologies that have implications of who we are. They affirm to God what is in the heart and reveal personal aspects of our character. They are signs, representations, images, characteristics, and marks of the condition of the soul. All the things we are, and all that are around us, declare us. They express verbal and nonverbal messages that declare our natural/temporal and eternal choices. They are rich with spiritual meaning, teach us lessons, and warn us of our consequences.

Symbolism can be our guide: The natural and physical aspects of symbolism run parallel to the spiritual and supernatural such that the natural and physical symbols in daily life become reminders of our spiritual condition.

We are created in the image of God and after His likeness. Physical/natural life therefore reflects the image of the state of our soul and spirit—the part of us that connects us to God, our source of life.

The symbols in our lives specifically, and in the world, are revealing a corresponding spiritual progression. And there is much for us to learn by them that could benefit us in leading a more meaningful life.

Our souls can flourish by them. They can serve to bring us closer to God. God enables us through symbols to check ourselves, to put limitations on sin, to return to God, and to assist us in the way of redemption.

In fact, symbolism can give us a sense of where we are in our redemptive process. Although there is no specific length of time or exacting sequence to life's path in the spiritual journey and redemptive process, symbolism reflects our spiritual state and serves to remind us of the association that our Creator has with each of us.

Symbols are intrinsic in all life events: Through the symbols around us, God facilitates us so we can return to our duty in the holy covenant. Whether a symbol is in the form of riches, marriage, the birth of a child, death, divorce, remarriage, crushing debt, struggle and suffering, poverty and lack, sickness and disease, strife, enemies, or any sin or any blessing, there is a corresponding spiritual message that is revealing the state of the soul.

All of life's symbols are inherent in the covenant. We are either under Christ and of grace, or under sin—under spiritual blessing or spiritual curse. Through prayer and discernment, an understanding of the symbols that permeate our lives can enable us to know where we stand. But the difference is never clear without Christ. These are questions we must ask ourselves. Do we have faith and confidence in eternal life? Are we straddling the fence with uncertainty of where we stand? Or maybe we have no knowledge at all of where we will be in eternity.

Complexity of symbolism: Symbolism is a complex subject that we will continue to discuss during these volumes. There is enormous difference in symbols' meaning in accordance with the difference in relationship that we have with Jesus Christ. For instance, under the grace of Jesus Christ, the symbols in our lives serve to bring us closer, to enable us in righteousness and holiness. They can be part of the perfecting process for the soul under grace. On the other hand, if we exist under conditions that are void of the perfecting blood of Jesus Christ, the soul remains under different conditions and we have different needs. The same symbols can serve different spiritual purposes and have different meaning, according to where we are in the redemptive process. Nevertheless, all are in need of the mercy of Christ.

To add to the complexity of symbolism, it can be of no benefit without a godly relationship. Their meaning rests upon an understanding of deeper spiritual knowledge, which is gained by the quickening of Christ. Knowledge of them is illuminating, and this is the spiritual element that will awaken us to the knowledge of God and our relationship to Him. But this knowledge is revealed by the quickening power of the Spirit of Christ through the Bible.

Therefore, we cannot know God without a godly relationship. And God will enable us to understand the symbolism that is personal to us, since this knowledge is given to us by the power of His Holy Spirit.

Through heavenly symbolism, God speaks to each of us. And the natural symbols in our lives speak to God. Our lives can speak to God by symbols of the bondage of sin, or it can reflect to Him the symbols of His grace.

God gives us divine discernment for the betterment and advancement of the soul. And though this engagement is beneficial to the natural self, it is enormously more for the benefit of the soul.

Without these benefits, we live in spiritual blindness from day to day, gaining nothing from what is being revealed. We miss the temporal benefits that are part of our preparation for eternity as we make our path through life.

Universal symbols: Apart from the symbolism that is peculiar to each of us, the world presents broader symbolism that also has peculiar spiritual correlation and meaning. We are all impacted by the symbols in the world. For instance, symbolism can serve the greater good.

Whether the symbol is a world authority, a public figure, worldwide events that impact upon us and those around us, or the wider society, these all play a role in God's eternal purpose. World events may convey the sign of the spiritual times and seasons. As we observe how the world is changing, we may learn from the symbolism, be resolved to reorder our priorities, and redirect our lives.

As we perceive the symbols that declare the state of the world, this can awaken us to its correlating spiritual condition. This in turn can move us to make a difference or discover our life's purpose.

The impact of the symbolism in the world can bring out the good or evil in us. But with symbolism, regardless of whether it is good or bad, there is always a spiritual revelation of mercy, as through it all, God calls us to return. The good in the world ought to remind us of the goodness of God, and the evil ought to summon us to turn away from sin. And by both, we are called to return to our duty.

All of life's symbolism serves the purpose of facilitating the work of Christ as He prepares us for eternity. Thus, the Scriptures tell us, "And we know that all things work together for good to them that love God, to them who are the called according to his purpose" (Romans 8:28).

PART 2

THE SYMBOLS
AND THEIR
INTERPRETATION

CHAPTER 18

THE SHIELD OF GOD

The interpretation of the sacred vision is set out in six volumes. But let us begin by breaking down each symbol and laying the foundation for the first layer of interpretation. Subsequent volumes will detail the greater meaning of each symbol and reveal the cohesive message.

Late at night on March 6, 1996, as I had just completed bible reading, God gave me a sacred vision of an image—a head of gold wearing a king's golden helmet, shiny armor to shield the head and face. The coincidence that followed, by the providence of God, confirmed the image in Daniel's prayer, as God guided me to its verification and led me in prayer of thanksgiving.

There are multiple blessings in this prayer. It confirmed that the image is of God as its description is established in the Bible. The fact that the image and also its verification are revealed by divine intervention and divinely inspired prayer provides incontestable proof of the presence of God. It blessed me with the interpretation, and at the same time, it enabled me to give thanks and glory to God.

The Sixth Day of March

The number six represents work. It points to God's work of creation and redemption. We know that "in six days the LORD made heaven and earth, the sea, and all that in them is, and rested the seventh day: wherefore the LORD blessed the Sabbath day, and hallowed it" (Exodus 20:11). God's work of creating the universe and the recreation of the soul to cleanse it from sin are of parallel spiritual interconnectedness. We know that "if any man be in Christ he is a new creature: old things are passed away; behold, all things are become new" (2 Corinthians 5:17). God will recreate the soul and the world to cleanse sin. Thus, this symbol points to God's work of redemption and the resurrection when Christ will reveal the new heaven and earth. The Scriptures say, "And he that sat upon the throne said, Behold, I make all things new" (Revelation 21:5). (Later we will discuss the symbol of the number seven.)

Six speaks of the work of grace, the divine process of cleansing, renewal and replenishment that God would enable upon the soul. This work includes the way God would impart deeper spiritual understanding and wisdom, as these are gifts of grace.

Spiritual gifts make us serviceable to God. As with all sacred visions, they contain instructions regarding God's mission, and there is always something specific God wants us to do. And God revealed Himself in a manner that enables me and gives me understanding and confidence in what I am called to do. Having experienced this process, I must share the knowledge of it with others for the glory of God. This symbol is depicting the work of sharing the message of the kingdom, so that many would be awakened as I was.

And Christ is able to do the same for others, so that many who would come to Him in these last days could be so facilitated and led by Him through the redemptive process, and be delivered by the power of His Holy Spirit. God is mercifully manifesting Himself in order to prepare His people.

Gold

Gold is symbolic of trial and testing and points to the afflictions I would undergo. Fine gold is a spiritual symbol that refers to what results from the trial and testing of faith and is associated with work. Gold is refined by being pressed, melted, and molded in the furnace to bring out its purity. The beauty of gold when refined is a symbol of grace. This refers to God's work of redemption and the process that I would undergo to separate me from my sins and bring out the refinements of grace of Jesus Christ. By fire, gold is purified, and this refers to the purity of the soul when it has been refined by suffering and affliction. The soul is made pure by the work of Jesus Christ under grace. It is the symbol of God's work of preparation, and it means preparedness.

Gold represents reward. It is the product of God's work. This symbol speaks of heavenly rest and reward that comes after labor. Job in the agony of his trials said, "But he knoweth the way that I take: when he hath tried me, I shall come forth as gold" (Job 23:10). Also, 1 Corinthians 3:12–15 states,

> Now if any man build upon this foundation, gold, silver, precious stones, wood, hay, stubble; Every man's work shall be made manifest: for the day shall declare it, because it shall be revealed by fire; and the fire shall try every man's work of what sort it is. If any man's work abide which he hath built thereupon, he shall receive a reward. If any man's work shall be burned, he shall suffer loss: but he himself shall be saved; yet so as by fire.

We build upon the foundation of Christ, we follow His example, we conform to His image and likeness, and the grace of Christ Himself is our reward.

The symbol gold also has a broader meaning as it points us to the period of the tribulation just before the return of our Lord. This refers to the preparation and refinement through trials of the redeemed who will be delivered by God from the fire of affliction through tribulation. "Many shall be purified, and made white, and tried; but the wicked shall do wickedly: and none of the wicked shall understand; but the wise shall understand" (Daniel 12:10).

The Head of Gold

The head of gold is the symbol of the greatness of God, the head of all creation. The head of gold is the symbol of God as King. God is "King of Kings and Lord of Lords." The gold is a symbol of His deity and relates to the throne and kingdom of God. This is the symbol of Christ. "His head is as the most fine gold" (Song of Solomon 5:11).

Gold represents the presence of God. In 1 Chronicles 28, in the temple that Solomon built, we learn that the altar of incense was made of refined gold, the instruments, candlesticks, lamp, the tables of showbread, and also were the cherubims that spread their wings over the ark of the covenant of the Lord. The ark of the covenant representing the presence of God was overlaid with gold (Hebrews 9:4).

The Shield, the Amour of God

The armor of gold is the symbol of the armor of God and represents God as shield. The shield also means faith and points to the Word of God, the gospel of Christ. "Above all, taking the shield of faith, wherewith ye shall be able to quench all the fiery darts of the wicked" (Ephesians 6:16). We are told in Ephesians 6:6, "Put on the whole armour of God, that ye may be able to stand against the wiles of the devil." The deceitfulness and deception of the Devil is indicative of the tribulation of our current time. But the period of the tribulation is also a time when faith is refined.

God is our defender, support, and protector. And the shield confirms God as being present and available, our help in the time of afflictions. God provides special protection under spiritual affliction.

It is a blessing of grace. The shield points to God's favor, as God is our safety and salvation, our hiding place. "Thou art my hiding place and my shield: I hope in thy word" (Psalm 119:114). This is confirmed in Psalm 18:35 and 2 Samuel 22:36: "Thou hast also given me the shield of thy salvation." And Psalm 28:7 says, "The Lord is my strength and my shield, my heart trusted in him, and I am helped: therefore my heart greatly rejoiceth; and with my song will I praise him."

How God Approaches: When God calls us to any service, He will Himself enable us to carry out our mission. And when God approaches us to initiate and confirm the holy covenant, He approaches us with a greeting, with peace and assurance of His protection. He confirms mercy. He assures us of His goodwill toward us and quiets our fears. God's approach to us is the same whether in ancient time or today—for God never changes.

God's Greeting: The shield invokes and represents the covenant God made with Abraham. The sacred vision is a confirmation of this covenant, and it points to righteousness and grace. When God approached Abraham to confirm His covenant, the word of the Lord came to Abraham in a vision: "Fear not, Abram: I am thy shield, and thy exceeding great reward" (Genesis 15:1). This is the way God greeted Abraham, and it is remarkable that this first symbol, the head of gold/the shield, denotes a divine greeting, the way God approaches to confirm His covenant.

God Declares Himself God of Abraham, Isaac, and Jacob

All those who are of faith and grace are the seed (the spiritual descendants) of Abraham and are blessed with Abraham. God imputes to us through Jesus Christ the same favor and blessings given to Abraham. It follows logically that God would renew the greeting of that covenant and confirm it. The expressed harmony of the symbolism and the greeting affirms that God is confirming His Word and covenant.

Daniel speaks of what will come to pass in the latter days—that God will confirm His covenant with many. In these last days, God is hereby confirming His covenant made with Abraham. The covenant made with Abraham points to the new covenant in Jesus Christ.

God's approach is by repeating/confirming the greeting given to Abraham, our forefather: "Fear not, I am thy shield and thy exceeding great reward." By repeating the greeting, it represents that God is hereby repeating/confirming the holy covenant. This astounding miracle is confirming the truth of the gospel of Christ.

God is declaring His presence by the symbol of the shield. And God is affirming Himself as the God of Abraham, Isaac, and Jacob.

Divine Link between this First Vision and the Second

In the two interconnected parts, first God revealed the greeting and then the message. In the first God approaches by taking away the fear of His presence. It follows logically that on March 15, I was not afraid in the midst of the manifested display of divine presence. There was already spiritual preparation, though I was unaware. God had prepared me well.

Thus, on March 15, God continued the conversation and proceeded to reveal by symbols what He would say. And God linked both sacred parts by Daniel's prayer of thanksgiving. (And immediately as I concluded this prayer, God revealed the symbols.)

Coincidences

The most astounding coincidence took place at this moment. In general, the coincidences confirm an important covenant principle, which is that all the blessings of the covenant are given in double measure—even the revelations of God.

Under the grace of the covenant, the divine providences, coincidences are symbols depicting a double portion. But what is remarkable is that there were multiple coincidences in the course of this specific message.

The abundance of them speak to the fact that these revelations are confirmed as truth and are everlasting, firm, secure, and readily given in abundance. (Abundance is a symbol of grace.)

Life Becomes a Parable

Coincidences that are works of grace reveal spiritual alignment. With spiritual alignment, flesh lines up with spirit. What occurs in the flesh is a reflection of what is occurring in the spirit. And this is the divine process of transformation, renewal, and conformity.

The soul is realigned, turned away from sin, to the adoption under grace. Thus, coincidences—two incidences occurring in unexplained sequence—are representing the simultaneous awakening, quickening, and transformation of the soul (the spiritual body) and this benefit is reflected in the natural body.

This awakening and awareness is the beginning of spiritual knowledge. In order for God to initiate His covenant with us, we must be aware and we must be a willing party to the agreement. Thus, as God works upon the soul, it is made known to us in the natural body as the Spirit of God communes with our spirit.

In this impartation of spiritual knowledge the Holy Spirit dwells within us. This awareness that is given means that we are able to respond to God. The soul is awakened from spiritual death.

And God made my life become a parable, through coincidences/ double events (natural in alignment with spiritual). A parable is an earthly story with spiritual and heavenly meaning. It is a parallel process. Thus, what I was experiencing is the parable of life, in that it became an earthly story with a heavenly meaning. God taught me the spiritual meaning by means of what was occurring in daily life. This is the way God imparts deeper spiritual knowledge. It is a process that we must be aware of and personally engaged in order to benefit and be established in the guidance of God.

Flesh is an image of the spirit, and therefore the activities of life become an image of the spirit. Therefore, when we are of grace, Christ enables this harmony. Life lined up with Scripture, and the activities of daily life paralleled spiritual knowledge that God was revealing.

This is the way I learned the interpretation of these symbols by the careful guidance of God. As the coincidences gave me awareness, they provided a link to the Bible, and the activities in daily life became in harmony with the way of grace. God works within our limitations in the flesh to bring us knowledge of the spirit. The two must come into alignment in order for us to understand what God is revealing.

The life of Abraham is presented by parable in order to reveal the deeper spiritual meaning of the holy covenant. God is also hereby affirming that by way of parable He imparts spiritual knowledge.

This harmonious alignment denotes covenant agreement. Therefore, life becomes in harmony with the Word of God. And harmony with His Word, the Bible, is a symbol of harmony and agreement with God.

"We walk no longer after the flesh but after the Spirit". And the words that we speak are of the Spirit. It follows logically, therefore, that if one has this spiritual alignment, by the gift of grace of Jesus Christ, we are able to speak prophetically without realizing that the words that we speak are of the Spirit. Our thoughts are redirected to think "spirit" instead of "flesh."

This is the way deeper spiritual knowledge is facilitated. With this knowledge comes the gift of prophecy. Prophecy is of the spirit and not of the flesh. And one is unable to prophecy under the power of grace without the Spirit of God dwelling within.

Parable Declares God Our Lord Jesus Christ

A life guided by parable is evidence of the presence of Christ. Jesus taught heavenly knowledge to multitudes and to His disciples by many parables when He was here on earth. The Bible says, "All these things spake Jesus unto the multitude in parables; and without a parable spake he not unto them" (Matthew 13:34).

Christ is revealing Himself in our time by the manifestation of parable as Christ is the only one who taught by parable. All knowledge of heaven is of Him. He is the heavenly teacher—by parable is the way heavenly symbolism is taught by God. Therefore, the presence of parable declares our God, our Lord, Jesus Christ, the One who gives us wisdom and deeper spiritual understanding.

CHAPTER 19

GOD, THE DELIVERER

The second part of the sacred vision occurred on March 15, 1996. The date March 15 is an exceptional day in many ways. I assumed it was of special significance because it was within the holy season of Lent. But it was astonishing when I discovered how truly blessed a day it is. It is a day that God holds in memory.

Early in this divine process of interpretation, I just opened the Bible, and there it was. I was stunned! Until that day, I had not known this was a consecrated day described in the Bible.

Fifteen is a symbol of divine protection, safety, and deliverance. In the great flood, God covered the mountains by fifteen cubits and ensured that Noah's ark was kept safe floating above the highest peaks (Genesis 7:20).

Confirming Purim

The Feast of Purim: March 15 is hallowed because it is the day God showed great mercy and protected the Jews against the plot by Haman to destroy them (in the book of Esther). March 15 is the Feast of Purim. At that time, I had never heard of the Feast of Purim.

Purim comes from the Hebrew word meaning "lots." "In the first month, that is, the month Nisan, in the twelfth year of King Ahasuerus, they cast Pur, that is, the lot, before Haman from day to day, and from month to month, to the twelfth month, that is, the month Adar" (Esther 3:7). It refers to the time when the lot was cast to decide the intended day of the annihilation of the Jewish people.

God delivered the Jews and gave them rest from enemies and persecution. March 15 is the day of feasting in celebration of their deliverance. Esther 9:18 states that "the Jews that were at Shushan assembled together on the thirteenth day thereof; and on the fourteenth thereof; and on the fifteenth day of the same they rested, and made it a day of feasting and gladness."

The month of Adar is the month of March. It was established that the Jews should observe the fourteenth and fifteenth days of the month of Adar annually. And God has commanded that this feast be celebrated by "every generation, every family, every province, and every city; and that these days of Purim should not fail from among the Jews, or the memorial of them perish from their seed" (Esther 9:28). This feast was celebrated not only by Jews but by "all such as joined themselves unto them, so as it should not fail that they would keep these two days according to their writing, and according to their appointed time every year" (Esther 9:27–28).

Confirming the Covenant

The book of Esther details the marriage of Esther to King Ahasuerus. The king was being remarried after his divorce from his wife, Vashti. Esther prepared a great banquet of wine in celebration of their covenant. This was the occasion and instrument for deliverance of the Jews. The king loved her so much that he was willing to grant her whatever was her wish, even to half of his kingdom. Her request was the safety of her people. Their enemy Haman who was plotting against them, was hanged.

This symbol, the fifteenth day of March, points me to the confirmation of the holy covenant. The marriage of Esther and the remarriage of the king is symbolic of the remarriage of Christ to the redeemed. It is a symbol of reconciliation and grace. The banquet of wine that Esther prepared points to the blood of Christ and to the banquet of heaven. This is symbolic of the reuniting of the elect with Jesus Christ, the Bridegroom whose blood was shed for us. God is affirming that the covenant of grace in Jesus Christ is the instrument of our deliverance.

God Declares Himself God of Israel

God chose this date for this miraculous intervention, declaring and identifying Himself, through this symbolism, as the Lord, God of Israel, just as God has repeatedly described Himself in the Bible.

He is the God of spiritual Israel, the congregation of the redeemed of Jesus Christ, those that are sealed by the Holy Spirit, by His blood, from all corners of the earth.

God Declares Himself God, the Deliverer

And by the symbol of March 15, God declares Himself as the deliverer. By the symbol of Purim, God is confirming Himself as the true God. For it is God Almighty who delivered Israel and decreed this holy day to be held in remembrance forever.

This is one of the many incontestable revelations of Jesus Christ, and it is infallible proof of His identity in the sacred vision. Jesus is the messenger, author, creator, and seal of the holy covenant.

This symbol represents deliverance from tribulation. It signifies that God will deliver His people, the congregation of the redeemed of Jesus Christ. In a broader sense, the Feast of Purim is a symbol of the faithfulness of Christ. He will protect His covenanted people in troubled times.

Therefore, protection and deliverance are promised to God's elect, the spiritual Israel, from every nation. It points to certain and timely deliverance and represents that the time is near for the coming of the kingdom of heaven. It follows logically that this is the day God has chosen to reveal this divine message.

It was remarkable to discover that this divinely appointed day remains a sacred symbol just as God commanded thousands of years ago. God protected it in ancient times and affirms that it is protected forever.

God's Word never changes, and the interpretation remains constant. But it also represents that God is present in the world and observing all that is occurring. Thus, this story of Purim has significance for us even today. It bears striking similarity to events of our time, with much violence and threats regarding the annihilation of natural Israel. But the Feast of Purim is God's way of signaling that deliverance will come to those who believe in Jesus Christ and have the seal of protection by His blood, the Israel of the Spirit.

March 16

It was approaching the end of the day on March 15, 1996, so let us also look briefly at the sixteenth day of March. Sixteen, four times four, and eight times two are numbers that signify covenant, completion, and eternity. "Number 4, perhaps from the four points of the compass, has to do with completeness" (English, and Bishop Bower, 1952: 1,708).[v]

It represents that the time of deliverance is approaching. Since it represents completeness and covenant, it points to finality of preparation. In the book of Revelation, the symbolism given to John speaks of "four angels standing on the four corners of the earth, holding the four winds of the earth, that the wind should not blow on the earth, nor on the sea, nor on any tree ... till we have sealed the servants of God in their foreheads" (Revelation 7:1–3).

For those that are sealed, God testifies that they are His. Four times four is symbolic of covenant principle. From the perspective of this sequence of events, sixteen represents preparation for the sealing of God's people in that God does the final work of grace.

Ten Days Later

The period of waiting between the two parts of the sacred vision—the greeting and the message—was ten days. Ten represents waiting, a spiritual period of trial and testing. It is not literal but a specific period that is known only to God. It represents the duration of preparation in the divine process of latter-day redemption while the elect of God await deliverance.

Ten days is representative of the tribulation. The Bible says, "Fear none of these things which thou shalt suffer: behold, the devil shall cast some of you into prison, that ye may be tried; and ye shall have tribulation ten days: be thou faithful unto death, and I will give thee a crown of life" (Revelation 2:10).

CHAPTER 20

PREPARATION FOR DIVINE PRESENCE

Physical and Spiritual Preparation

In addition to the special preparation God gave me through the period of divine providences, and alignment leading up to this day, there was also special preparation at the moment of the sacred vision.

We discussed the physical effect upon the body, but there is also a greater spiritual effect that takes place within the soul as the Spirit of God communes with our spirit and seals us to Christ. God must prepare us physically and spiritually for heavenly access.

Preparation for God's Presence

The presence of God requires calm, peace, and quietness from the noise of life that drown out the "voice" of God. "Be still and know that I am God" (Psalm 46:10). It necessitates freedom from unnecessary worldly care and the self-imposed busyness of the modern world. It demands a life without clutter, from what keeps us in spiritual blindness, and obstructs the divine presence. It requires setting aside a special time each day to spend in the Word of God, developing knowledge and fellowship.

But preparation for God's presence requires divine power. The Holy Spirit must enable us with the ability to withstand God's glory.

Our responsibility is simply to be available, and Christ will ensure that there are all the right conditions, both physical and spiritual.

Although it is God who prepares us, God will not force us. Force is not consistent with principles of the holy covenant. Therefore, God will not reach us if we are not available. Jesus said, "Behold, I stand at the door, and knock: if any man hear my voice, and open the door, I will come in to him, and will sup with him, and he with me" (Revelation 3:20). If we are available, we will be able to readily open that door to Christ when He calls for us. But if we are too busy with the world, then we are unable to hear God's call. Consequently, we must set our priorities that we know what is important in life and what is not. And this was my prayer, which the Lord has answered. For it is the Holy Spirit that determined the way for me, redirecting my life at a time when I would benefit most.

Preparation for Heavenly Access

Just as we are unable to see God's glory in the world without the quickening of Christ, we are unable to have access to heavenly treasure of spiritual knowledge but with the power of the Holy Spirit. The world declares the immense natural treasure of the work of God's hands, yet many are blinded to the existence of God. This is the way we all are before Christ gives us the blessing of quickening, awareness, and access under grace.

Through Christ's death, there is access to heaven and we have bold access to God's throne. And through Him, there is freedom of access to the hidden knowledge and treasures that God has promised in the covenant. Access to heaven presupposes that we have revelation of the glory of God in the earth. Thus, it necessitates God's preparation in order to have the ability to look around us and see His glory and know that God is real.

God must open our eyes to give us quickening and light, putting away the loss of sight and the darkness of sin forever. Sin creates darkness in the soul, takes light away from our eyes, and blinds us to God.

God Opens Our Eyes

Our eyes are created to behold the natural and physical world, but in order for us to see into the spiritual world, it requires the gift of spiritual sight.

As the sacred vision was unfolding, I felt the sensation of a film being removed from my eyes. This is symbolic of the opening of my eyes to spiritual light, sight, and knowledge.

The Bible refers to this as the "removal of scales" from the eye. It represents the removal of spiritual blindness, enlightenment, and the impartation of spiritual gifts. Opening the eyes is one of the ways God prepares us for His presence. This is how God gives access to the treasure of heavenly revelation that prepares us for service.

Instruction for Service: God gives us instruction and prepares us for the service of spreading the gospel. Saul was stricken with blindness by an angel. The Lord Jesus appeared to Ananias and sent him to lay his hands upon Saul in order for him to receive his sight. Immediately, Ananias laid his hand upon him "And immediately there fell from his eyes as it had been scales: and he received his sight forthwith, and arose, and was baptized" (Acts 9:18). Straight away, he preached Christ in the synagogues, that He is the Son of God. The Lord removed not only physical scales but spiritual ones as well, giving him understanding and filling him with the Holy Spirit to prepare him to preach the gospel. The removal of the film, as it felt to me, really is the removal of scales and similarly represents preparation for service.

God Declares Himself God of Job

This is the divine way that God gave Job his instruction. "In a dream, in a vision of the night, when deep sleep falleth upon men, in slumberings upon the bed; Then he opens the ears of men and sealeth their instruction" (Job 33:15–16). By the opening of our eyes, the ears and the heart are also opened. This consistent action declares God the God of Job.

By opening our eyes, God causes us to love instruction, and with instruction comes wisdom and deeper spiritual understanding. And God prepares us in righteousness: by first opening our eyes and giving us understanding. This enlightenment is the way we are made serviceable to God. Psalm 25:9 tells us, "The meek will he guide in judgment: and the meek will he teach his way." But a disobedient heart despises instruction, because it has no light.

This symbol represents access to the treasures of heaven, to God's throne and kingdom, to be serviceable to God and to do the work of heaven in the earth. This access is an eternal work completed while we are yet in the world.

God Declares Himself God of Ezekiel

Ezekiel said "that the heavens were opened, and (he) saw visions of God" (Ezekiel 1:1). This means that God prepared his eyes and there were no barriers to heavenly access. The heavenly realm was opened when his eyes were opened by the power and preparation of the Holy Spirit. The ability to see heavenly revelation represents that heaven is opened.

The sacred vision is establishing through the display of heavenly symbols that God opened the hidden treasures of heaven. By this consistent action, God is affirming Himself as the God of Ezekiel.

God Opens the Covenant of Grace

By the opening of the eyes, God opens access to the covenant. He teaches grace by showing what it is. He demonstrates that His favor toward us is not dependent on any work on our part: no obedience or righteousness of our own and no desire for Him that is of ourselves. He lets us see that we must depend on the completed work of Christ. We must depend upon His righteousness and obedience.

God imparts wisdom and deeper spiritual understanding by opening the eyes. And this is the initiation of spiritual gifts. Paul's prayer for the saints is this:

> That the God of our Lord Jesus Christ, the Father of glory, may give unto you the spirit of wisdom and revelation in the knowledge of him: The eyes of your understanding being enlightened; that ye may know what is the hope of his calling, and what the riches of the glory of his inheritance in the saints. (Ephesians 1:17–18)

The eyes of spiritual understanding are the eyes of the heart and of the mind, which God opens for quickening, so that we may be amenable to conformity and transformation to the likeness of Christ.

Covenant Gifts of Enlightenment

God gives us light, for God is light. By opening our eyes, God opens Himself to us. We can look to Him. The book of Matthew describes the eye as "the light of the body" (Matthew 6:22). When our eyes are opened, we have Jesus Christ, for Christ is "the light of the world." Christ can give us that light by opening the eyes of the soul. Thus, the removal of the scales is a symbol of the light God gives to the body to enable us to follow Him, but it is the gift of spiritual light and enlightenment to the soul.

Separates us from sin: God separates us from our sins and from darkness by giving us the light of the gospel. Christ opened my eyes to remove doubts, to make my direction sure and clear, to protect me from misinformation, and to give me the will, the conviction, and the confidence to follow the truths of the gospel with unquestionable surety. This light gives us quickening and the ability to understand the gospel. It gives us the willingness to please God. "The statutes of the LORD are right, rejoicing the heart: the commandment of the LORD is pure, enlightening the eyes" (Psalm 19:8). The gift of the light of the gospel of Christ (the commandment of Christ) opens the eyes and turns us from spiritual blindness to spiritual sight.

Daniel said that in these latter days, many will be purified, made white, and tried, but the wicked shall do wickedly, and none of the wicked will understand. But the wise will understand. Wickedness hardens the heart and blinds our eyes. It creates blindness in the soul so that it cannot see. Therefore it has no understanding.

Guidance: By opening our eyes and giving us light, God guides us and shows the way of righteousness. By guiding Israel out of Egypt and into the wilderness, God's intention was to give them a "heart to perceive, eyes to see and ears to hear." By opening the eyes, God also gives us the gift of an obedient heart and the disposition to receive and be amenable to our direction in righteousness, as well as to willingly accept God's guidance.

When our eyes are opened, we walk in meekness but with confidence in God and are able to relinquish our will to the will of God. With the opening of the eyes, an obedient life and an understanding heart are all functions one of the other.

The opening of the eyes is the divine direction. God shows us a new path through life, walks with us, and guides us through redemption.

Overshadowing of the Holy Spirit

The symbols appeared in the form of brilliantly colored shadows, the reflection of precious gemstones. Since a shadow is a silhouette of a real and existing object or being, the shadows confirm the overshadowing of the Holy Spirit, directing this divine action, as I observed the unfolding of the miracle.

The overshadowing also confirms the presence of the heavenly messenger/angel of God, and this confirms the presence of Christ who is our mediator and advocate. Hebrews 12:24 speaks of Jesus as "the mediator of the new covenant and … the blood of sprinkling."

Overshadowing represents the baptism of the Holy Spirit. It is a symbol of divine cleansing through the immersion of the Holy Spirit, and this is the baptism made possible by the precious blood of Jesus Christ.

To be under the shadow of God means to be under the will and power of God. This too is a symbol of divine guidance and speaks of the divine relationship, made possible through Christ.

We become in harmony with God as we walk with Him in His shadow. This represents covenant agreement. We are made in the image and likeness of God, and our physical state is an image and likeness of our spiritual state. Therefore, to be under the shadow of God means that life becomes reflective of a harmonious relationship with God. "Two cannot walk together unless they are in agreement." The natural and physical are shadows of greater spiritual gifts. The shadows are reflective of conformity and transformation, a life lined up with Christ.

Overshadowing is a symbol of divine safety, both natural and spiritual. "He that dwelleth in the secret place of the most High shall abide under the shadow of the Almighty" (Psalm 91:1). God gives assurance of divine protection and deliverance in time of affliction. These are the words of David: "Be merciful unto me, O God, be merciful unto me: for my soul trusteth in thee: yea, in the shadow of

125

thy wings will I make my refuge, until these calamities be overpast" (Psalm 57:1).

God overshadows us as we grow in faith. Jesus likens the kingdom of God to a grain of mustard seed, "which, when it is sown in the earth, is less than all the seeds that be in the earth: But when it is sown, it groweth up, and becometh greater than all herbs, and shooteth out great branches; so that the fowls of the air may lodge under the shadow of it (Mark 4:31–32). With a small amount of faith, as much as the grain of mustard seed, God will enable us by His power to accomplish all that is required of us, and to do great things.

The shadows also mean spiritual healing through the divine power and presence of Christ. Acts 5:15 tells us that "they brought forth the sick into the streets and laid them on beds and couches, that at the least the shadow of Peter passing by might overshadow some of them" (Acts 5:15). The presence of the shadow of the Holy Spirit of Christ brings healing to the body and also the soul.

God Declares Himself the God of Mary

The angel Gabriel appeared to Mary and told her she would be overshadowed by the Holy Spirit and would conceive of a Son and His name would be called Jesus. By this consistent action of overshadowing, God is in our time affirming Himself as the God of Mary and the God and Father of our Lord and Savior, Jesus Christ.

CHAPTER 21

Divine Placement, Spaces, and Movement of Symbols

The purposeful placement, the spaces, and the movement of the symbols are critical factors that are essential to the interpretation. These features convey their own wisdom. Every word of God is the ultimate precious gem, nothing is to be ignored, and certainly no aspect is to be without meticulous and in-depth inquiry by prayer and meditation.

There were three distinct placements by progression, across both pages of my open Bible. The symbols were decidedly placed, not random or accidental, as God does nothing casually, indiscriminately, or unintentionally but in systematic arrangement and logical sequence.

Thus, the first set of symbols appeared at the top left corner, and there was a wide space from the top to the last verse on the page where the second symbol was positioned. This second symbol was guided by the celestial hand upward, then over the center of the Bible to rest on the opposite page to the right, and finally stood midway between the first and second positions.

Placement

The interpretation is threefold. The three placements are symbolizing the plan and purpose of God. We will discuss this in detail throughout these volumes.

Encompassing the entire process is a special order in the timeline of God's plan and includes milestones of the tribulation of our time.

Spaces

The spaces that resulted from the placements formed an organized layout. It indicates a particular portion of space or location chosen and designated for something.

There were two spaces between the three sets of symbols. The interpretation is twofold.

Time: First, the spaces symbolize duration, specific periods of time, and stages of a divine process. It points to activities set within a time constraint. God's work upon the soul is a process, and this is symbolic of the process of God's work of redemption and grace. The process of redemption and divine grace is not hurried. It takes time and will be fully perfected on the day of the coming of our Lord. Change in us takes time, and God is willing to work within our abilities and constraints. God can transform us instantaneously, but our acknowledgement, awareness, enlightenment, understanding, obedience, and repentance are a lifetime process. And we must continue to guard our righteousness and faithfulness. The Scriptures tell us, "be thou faithful unto death and I will give thee a crown of life" (Revelation 2:10).

The spaces also specifically refer to the period of time and the stages of tribulation, a period of testing, trial, and affliction. And in a much broader sense, the spaces also represent the process leading up to the timing of prophetic covenant events.

Distance: Second, the spaces are symbolic of expanse, distance, and measurement, and they represent a place, area, or lot. This is symbolic of heaven, the land of our spiritual inheritance, the land of promise, the ultimate blessing of the holy covenant.

One day, I decided to draw with a pencil a sketch of the placements. After joining the position of the symbols, this revealed a mysterious and unexpected shape—a shape that is now most familiar but by which I had been puzzled for over seven years.

The shape was that of the lot, the land where my home was located in Virginia, four years after the sacred vision. Astoundingly, by divine intervention, it was Lot 15. God directed me to this number and location by coincidence/divine providence, without my predetermination. It was totally unexpected.

As we discussed, the number fifteen is symbolizing a place of deliverance and points to heaven, the land of our deliverance. God does not speak of the covenant without also speaking of the land of inheritance. This is the primary promise of the covenant and a divine principle that, when we have returned to God, there is a home prepared for us. The promised inheritance is integral to the covenant because it represents a heavenly home, our spiritual inheritance.

God gave all that He had created to Adam, to be under his ownership and dominion in the covenant in the beginning. And God planted a garden for Adam, appointing him a special place where God dwells. God promised Abraham an inheritance when He made covenant with Him. The inheritance promised to Abraham is also promised to his spiritual generations. For "those who are of faith are also blessed with Abraham."

The land is a symbol of grace, a place at home with God, appointed and reserved for God's people. Jesus said, "In my Father's house are many mansions: if it were not so, I would have told you. I go to prepare a place for you" (John 14:2).

Another principal observation that is revealed by this layout is determined by its link to the great flood. The waters prevailed, and all the hills and mountains were covered fifteen cubits high. In accordance with the providence and the will of God, "The waters were dried up from off the earth; and Noah removed the covering of the ark, and looked, and behold, the face of the ground was dry" (Genesis 8:13).

The dry land that was revealed, and which Noah so eagerly longed for, was a signal that God's mercy had been restored. It is a symbol of deliverance. Likewise, the mysterious shape that emerged when I sketched and joined the symbols is symbolic of dry land revealed, and it is also a symbol of mercy restored.

It also is symbolic of the resurrection in that the earth appeared again from under the deluge. This is symbolic of restoration and the return of mercy after the cleansing of sin. Heaven is a place of restoration of grace for God's people, salvation, settlement, reconciliation, joy, and rest.

Movement

The first and second placements were by sudden appearances, but when the second symbol moved to the next purposefully determined placement, the third set of symbols was developed by gradual formation.

Movement symbolizes the progress of time, developments, advancements, and changes. It denotes moving forward toward a purpose or conclusion, an intended and planned action toward accomplishing an end. There were purposeful changes in the positions, and the placements were predetermined by the Holy Spirit. The locations had been decisively organized to achieve the heavenly purpose and reveal the intention of God.

The upward direction symbolizes rising higher, or rising from beneath, and represents rising from the dead.

Movement represents life and resurrection to a new life. It is the Holy Spirit that moves and gives life to the soul and makes it a new creation. It is the Spirit that moved in the beginning and was the first action of creation. The Scriptures say, "And the Spirit of God moved upon the face of the waters. And God said, Let there be light: and there was light" (Genesis 1:2–3).

To overcome: The movement of the symbol over (to the right) represents to overcome or to have victory over death. It also speaks of overcoming the suffering of trial and tribulation. Jesus said, "These things I have spoken unto you, that in me ye might have peace. In the world ye shall have tribulation: but be of good cheer; I have overcome the world" (John 16:33). The Bible says, "For whatsoever is born of God overcometh the world: and this is the victory that overcometh the world, even our faith" (1 John 5:4). "To him that overcometh will I grant to sit with me in my throne, even as I also overcame, and am set down with my Father in his throne" (Revelation 3:21). Jesus, after He had conquered death on our behalf, is seated at the right hand of His Majesty in heaven.

CHAPTER 22

THE NUMBER THREE—
SYMBOL OF DIVINE NATURE

Three Parts of the Holy Covenant

T he number three is the most sacred. The three sets of symbols represent the three parts of the holy covenant: the beginning, middle, and end. This testifies of the presence of God in the holy covenant.

Holy Trinity

This sacred number symbolizes the Holy Trinity and affirms the three Persons of the Godhead: the Father, the Son, and the Holy Spirit. Consequently, it signifies divine nature. God is identifying Himself and declaring that He is the Godhead. The majesty of the Lord is addressed in the words "Holy, holy, holy" (Isaiah 6:3).

The three sets of symbols each represent the Trinity of Persons in Jesus Christ. Christ is from eternity past, present, and eternity future. "I am Alpha and Omega, the beginning and the ending, saith the Lord, which is, and which was, and which is to come, the Almighty" (Revelation 1:8). They signify His eternal nature and pertain therefore to eternal life of believers through Jesus Christ.

By revealing symbols of Himself and His Holy Spirit in the sacred vision, Christ is therefore manifesting His presence, and these point to the second coming of Jesus Christ.

The Bible speaks of "the third heaven," the place where God dwells (2 Corinthians 12:2). Heaven is described by symbolism as having twelve gates. "On the east three gates; on the north three gates; on the south three dates; and on the west three gates" (Revelation 21:13).

Peter spoke of building three tabernacles (Matthew 17:4). Saul was blind for three days when he was smitten by the angel on the road to Damascus (Acts 9:9).

The Divine Purpose

Three is a symbol of the divine purpose of the Trinity of God. Here we see examples of God's process revealed in Jonas and Christ. The Bible says, "For as Jonas was three days and three nights in the whale's belly; so shall the Son of man be three days and three nights in the heart of the earth" (Matthew 12:40).

There is a three-step process of grace, and likewise is deeper spiritual understanding. "First the blade, then the ear, after that the full corn in the ear" (Mark 4:28). This is the process in which believers in Jesus Christ become the fruit of righteousness and grace. There are three levels by which the soul is cleansed from sin.

The three parts of the sacred vision correlate with the divine method and progression that identify how God imparts the gifts of wisdom and deeper spiritual understanding.

The three Bibles are symbols of three levels of spiritual knowledge. God chose each at different stages of my growth. The Bibles represent God's personal care and divine attention that are available to each of us. The knowledge of God is from God only.

The fact that God chose them affirms that wisdom and enlightenment, and deeper spiritual understanding, are gifts of the Holy Spirit under grace and must come from God only. They are reserved gifts and represent that God Himself would guide me into truth and lead me into deeper spiritual knowledge. The three levels represent that the process of grace is a patient process by the communion of the Holy Spirit. Mankind is chosen for grace by the work of Jesus Christ.

The Bibles are symbols that gave me glimpses into how God would guide and impart the gift of faith. And I learned to depend upon God for the knowledge that guided the interpretation as God used them as instruments. I could not understand by reading the Bible but by the patient enlightenment of the Holy Spirit. And as I read the Bible, God followed along with me and I with Him.

The three Bibles represent a trinity of heavenly guidance. There are levels of wisdom—as wisdom is the knowledge of God: the Father, the Son, and the Holy Spirit. They are symbolic of the work of the Holy Trinity in the process of grace.

They are three levels of regeneration through wisdom. As I read, God was able to flourish my heart, mind, and soul and enable transformation and conformity. Therefore, the three bibles represent that God would guide me by His Holy Spirit through three levels of spiritual knowledge, as God would impart levels of wisdom by awakening the soul. And as I prayed and read God's Word, the Holy Spirit revealed the interpretation, and my understanding blossomed as the opening of divine rosebuds day by day.

Therefore, from the three sets of sacred symbols come this multivolume interpretation and levels of spiritual knowledge for the service of the kingdom of God. Thus, there are three miraculously chosen by divine hands as God reveals Himself and mysteries of His kingdom. God sows the seed and prepares for the gathering of the "fruits" of the harvest of the kingdom. "The sower soweth the word" (Mark 4:14). These three Bibles are representing how God sows the seed, waters and nurtures it, so that it may grow into "pleasant fruit" of grace. Then God takes that fruit and scatters the seed so that it may multiply and bring forth more fruit for the kingdom.

God loves to multiply. It is a principle of the covenant. When God said, "Be fruitful, and multiply, and replenish the earth," His first intention and purpose is the multiplication of the seeds of grace.

Thus, God describes the stages of the fruitful seed. It takes root as it gets its life from God, becomes fruitful, and multiplies.

1) The first level is "first the blade" symbolized by *The Holy Bible, Authorized King James Version Personal Gift Edition* (Tyndale House Publishers, Inc., 1976, 1979).

2) The second level is "then the ear" symbolized by the *Pilgrim Edition of the Holy Bible, Authorized King James Version with Notes Prepared with Utmost Simplicity for Readers of Every Age* (Oxford University Press, New York, 1952).

By divine power and providence, God guided this Bible from a remote corner of the world to my community here in the United States of America, conveniently placing it in the library nearby. It represents the purposeful work of God in revealing divine truths, ensuring that His work and purpose are accomplished. The Bible had been brought to this country by someone from a remote area of the world as indicated by the inscription written in Arab or Persian script. Because it could not be understood, it is likely an indigenous local dialect from a remote village of an Arab or Persian nature. The fact that God guided this Bible from across the world represents that God will likewise guide His Word to remote places in the corners of the world and use it for His glory, just as God used this Bible to effect His purpose for me.

3) The third level is "the full corn in the ear" symbolized by *The Matthew Henry Study Bible, King James Version* (A Kenneth Abraham, general editor, World Bible Publishers, Inc., 1994).

The ink smudge that defines this Bible as the one specifically chosen by God reveals a divine purpose. It is given this special spiritual mark in the sacred vision and then confirmed by the natural mark, the actual smudge, which appears in the physical copy. There is an explicit purpose for this.

That purpose is defined in the parable of the sower. This parable speaks of the sower who is Christ as He scatters the seeds of grace, which is the Word of God, the gospel of Jesus Christ, throughout the earth so that it may bear the fruits of the harvest of the kingdom of God. Thus, God is declaring His purpose—to multiply the seed of grace.

God's work of salvation in this time of tribulation is to gather the elect, even from the remote corners of the earth. Jesus taught the multitude by the seaside this parable. He said,

> Hearken; Behold, there went out a sower to sow: And it came to pass, as he sowed, some fell by the way side, and the fowls of the air came and devoured it up. And some fell on stony ground, where it had not much earth; and immediately it sprang up, because it had no depth of earth: But when the sun was up, it was scorched; and because it had not root, it withered away. And some fell among thorns, and the thorns grew up, and choked it, and it yielded no fruit. And other fell on good ground, and did yield fruit that sprang up and increased; and brought forth, some thirty, and some sixty, and some an hundred. (Mark 4:3–8)

Jesus explains the parable.

> And these are they by the way side, where the word is sown; but when they have heard, Satan cometh immediately, and taketh away the word that was sown in their hearts. And these are they likewise which are sown on stony ground; who, when they have heard the word, immediately receive it with gladness; And have no root in themselves, and so endure but for a time: afterward,

when affliction or persecution ariseth for the word's sake,
immediately they are offended. And these are they which
are sown among thorns; such as hear the word, And the
cares of this world, and the deceitfulness of riches, and
the lusts of other things entering in, choke the word, and
it becometh unfruitful. And these are they which are sown
on good ground; such as hear the word, and receive it, and
bring forth fruit, some thirtyfold, some sixty, and some an
hundred. (Mark 4:15–20).

The unfruitful seed fell in three places: by the wayside, on stony
ground, and among thorns. But God's Word must accomplish that
for which it is intended. This parable is detailed here because it is of
such importance. And Christ points us to this prophecy that is being
fulfilled in this time of tribulation.

The Work of Tribulation

The book of Revelation reveals enormous symbolism in this
number as it points to aspects of the tribulation. This is revelation of
judgment. "The third part of the sea became blood ... the third part
of the creatures which were in the sea, and had life, died; and the
third part of the ships were destroyed ... the third angel sounded, and
there fell a great star from heaven ... and a third part of the waters
became wormwood" (Revelation 8:8–11).

Three points to the opening of the third seal in the book of
Revelation, a time of hardship and famine indicative of our present
time. Tribulation is a time of turmoil and limited judgments. "And
when he had opened the third seal, I heard the third beast say, come
and see. And I beheld, and lo a black horse; and he that sat on him
had a pair of balances in his hand. And I heard a voice in the midst
of the four beasts say, A measure of wheat for a penny, and three
measures of barley for a penny; and see thou hurt not the oil and the

wine" (Revelation 6:5–6). This speaks of a time of famine for many even as there is great excess, the display of overindulgence, and waste of resources in the world.

The book of the Revelation speaks also of the sounding of the fourth angel.

> And the third part of the sun was smitten, and the third part of the moon, and the third part of the stars so as the third part of them was darkened, and the day shone not for a third part of it, and the night likewise … an angel flying through the midst of heaven saying with a loud voice, Woe, woe, woe, to the inhabiters of the earth by reason of the other voices of the trumpet of the three angels, which are yet to sound! (Revelation 8:12, 13) This is a precursor to judgment.

The Trinity in the Resurrection

The number three also points to the resurrection. Jesus rose from death on the third day. For, He said to the Jews concerning His body, "Destroy this temple, and in three days I will raise it up" (John 2:19). As Jesus rose from the dead so likewise will the dead in Christ rise unto eternal life on the last day.

CHAPTER 23

THE NUMBER TWO—SYMBOL
OF HUMAN NATURE

The sacred vision asserts that the number two has godly symbolism. Consequently, it emerged in three instances, and this correlates with divine purpose. There were two parts (the greeting and the message). The first symbols were two raindrops, and there were two spaces between the three sets of symbols.

The numbers three and two are the principal symbols in the holy covenant. Whereas the number three is the symbol of divine nature, two is the symbol of human nature. Both are critical as they encompass the foundation and framework of the covenant and form common threads that permeate covenant doctrine. There are several layers of spiritual knowledge that they reveal. This chapter uncovers and introduces precepts that bring this to light and will be advanced throughout the course of this multivolume series.

God's Signature and Code of Creation

Mankind is identified in the covenant by the number two. And the natural universe is also identified in the covenant by the number two. This is the covenant possession that God has placed under the dominion of mankind in the beginning.

The number two is the spiritual code of creation, a symbol of the signature of God upon His handiwork. It therefore testifies of God as Creator and originator of all life. And all life is formed upon the foundation of the holy covenant. This is one of the primary and most central numbers in the covenant and the universe.

The Divine, having created all that exists, has written His signature. In writing His signature, God writes His name, and this is evidence that God created mankind and the universe for Himself. He writes His name as a sign of belonging, ownership, authority, and autonomy.

And it is a sign that the act of covenant is also the very act of creation. Our design affirms this incontestable truth: that God has written the covenant upon mankind. He has written it so that we may never forget it and that it may be forever before us.

And God has written the covenant into nature also. Therefore, animal, bird, reptile, fish, and all things that live bear the signature of God and the traits of the covenant, having been created under the aegis of the covenant.

Thus, the holy covenant is everywhere in the earth. Consequently, the signature of God is everywhere. This number is incontestable proof of God's presence. It cannot be denied that God exists when we see ourselves and observe the world around us.

Mankind and the universe bear the everlasting mark of Christ by whom the covenant is made possible, for it is forever sealed by His precious blood. It is undeniable that mankind was created by Christ, for covenant.

Two Bodies

Mankind was created by God with two bodies. Two is a sign of covenant and it relates to those things pertaining to the flesh. Mankind was created under the original intention of grace and has a natural body and a spiritual body. We are created of flesh and of spirit. The Scriptures reveal, "There is a natural body, and there is a spiritual body" (1 Corinthians 15:44).

Two Births

While the natural body lives, if we do not have the indwelling Holy Spirit, our spiritual body is dead because of sin. It is relegated to a spiritually corrupted condition called spiritual death. Thus we have natural life but yet are spiritually dead. And this spiritual condition is also manifested in the natural body by its thoughts, words, and deeds. In order for the spiritual body to live again, it must undergo regeneration and a new birth. It must be born again, given a new life by Christ who is our Creator. This life comes by the Holy Spirit that dwells in us. Wherefore Jesus said to Nicodemus, "Except a man be born again, he cannot see the kingdom of God" (John 3:3). The scope of this topic will be illuminated throughout these volumes.

Two—The Design of Mankind

God has embedded in us the holy covenant.

Internal Design: The design of our natural body bears the mark of the covenant. The design of our internal organs shows that we are created with this code of creation deep within. Our internal organs and bones are noticeable evidence of this for everyone to see, in numbers of two or multiples of two. To name a few, for example, we have two tonsils, lungs, and kidneys, and male and female endocrine systems constitute pairs of organs. We have organs with dual main functions and bones and muscles that work together in pairs. Thus, with the code of this symbol indelibly within us, God has created us with the purpose and intention of grace (in that we have two bodies) according to the edict of the holy covenant. Our innermost parts declare that we depend upon God for life and all that we need to exist.

Accordingly, the Bible says, "The spirit of man is the candle of the LORD, searching all the inward parts of the belly" (Proverbs

20:27). God refers to the inward parts when He evokes the covenant. "But this shall be the covenant that I will make with the house of Israel; After those days, saith the Lord, I will put my law in their inward parts, and write it in their hearts; and will be their God, and they shall be my people" (Jeremiah 31:33). The inward parts are where God points us to knowledge of the covenant. In the words of David, "Behold, thou desireth truth in the inward parts: and in the hidden part thou shalt make me to know wisdom" (Psalm 51:6).

External Design: When God looks upon mankind, He never forgets His covenant. God has put His name and signature upon mankind. Our external design bears witness that we are created by God, for God, with the covenant on the mind of God. And mankind is created with the unchanging and indelible mark of the everlasting covenant that affirms that mankind was created as eternal beings. The covenant is written upon us so that we too may never forget God or the covenant He has made with us in creation. Mankind has duties and responsibilities in the covenant.

Without delving too deeply into human anatomy—and as you know, mankind is created with two eyes, eye brows, ears, nostrils, cheeks, jawbones, lips, shoulders, arms, hands, breasts, hips, thighs, legs, knees, ankles, feet, etc.—these are incontestable evidence of covenant design.

And in addition to these fundamental characteristics, each person is irreplaceable and one of a kind. Each person is different in many fundamental ways, ranging from our peculiar bodily design including facial features to the sound of our voice, our speech, our walk, our DNA and fingerprints, etc. And we have our own tastes, likes and dislikes, skills, abilities, talents, and interests. These are marks that say we are each the individual craftsmanship of God. And this verifies that the covenant is individual and personal. This bears out incontestable proof of our undeniable association with our Creator, Jesus Christ.

Singular Systems and Organs: Mankind has systems and organs that constitute three parts. We have the pancreas, liver, and gall bladder that work together, and intestines that are made up of three parts and must work together.

Mankind is created in the image and likeness of God. Though this is spiritual it can also be identified in our physical body. As we discussed, God is three Persons but one God. All the systems and subsystems of the body must work together as one. This is a covenant principle, and our organs and systems are symbolic of our association to one God, one Creator.

There are organs of which we each have only one, and these also bear the mark of the holy covenant. We have one nose, but this is divided into two nostrils. The air we breathe is the breath of one God, from a single source of life: Jesus Christ. "And the LORD God formed man of the dust of the ground, and breathed into his nostrils the breath of life; and man became a living soul" (Genesis 2:7). And from the first man, Adam, is the whole world overspread with his descendants.

We have one brain, but it is divided into two parts—left lobe and right lobe—with their own characteristics and responsibilities. Our mind, once renewed in accordance with the covenant, is toward one God with a desire to serve Him only with single mindedness. The Bible says, "A double minded man is unstable in all his ways" (James 1:8). Double mindedness is evidence of sin, fickleness, and deceit, a mind at enmity with God and alienation (serving another god). These are proof of a broken covenant. The Scriptures, in the book of James, say, "Draw nigh to God, and he will draw nigh to you. Cleanse your hands, ye sinners; and purify your hearts, ye double minded" (James 4:8).

The head consists of several pairs of organs. It is a symbol of one God and Creator, the Head of the universe. Under grace, mankind is consecrated to one God. We are created to bow our heads in worship to one God, one Ruler, and one Judge on the last day: Jesus Christ.

The neck also has pairs of nerves, arteries, muscles, and glands. In accordance with the covenant, the "spiritual neck" is a symbol of grace. The Lord watches the neck and adorns it with "ornaments of grace." It demonstrates what is in the heart. This follows logically that we only have one. The neck is a symbol of a life in harmony with God and freedom through Jesus Christ. But the Bible often speaks of a neck that has no grace—it is a symbol of sin: hardened, stiff, and with the spiritual yoke of bondage.

The heart is divided into four major parts: two atriums and two ventricles. One heart is evidence that there is one God. For God has given us a heart to love one God, to be "single hearted" toward God. It is the place where God puts understanding, wisdom, and love. "No man can serve two masters: for either he will hate the one, and love the other; or else he will hold to the one, and despise the other. Ye cannot serve God and mammon" (Matthew 6:24). Singleness of heart is the desire to serve God only, a symbol of unity, harmony, and agreement in covenant. The four parts of the heart symbolize complete and perfect devotion and love.

The liver is a single organ in the abdomen but has two main lobes. This complex system regulates what we take into the body and detoxifies the blood. The liver is a spiritual symbol of deep passion, love, anger, and mourning. We read of such passion in the book of Lamentations. "My eyes do fail with tears, my bowels are troubled, my liver is poured upon the earth, for the destruction of the daughter of my people; because the children and the sucklings swoon in the streets of the city" (Lamentations 2:11). The liver represents the soul where the deep sorrow of repentance, and longing is toward God, the single foundation, the ultimate source of goodness and grace, and of the knowledge and wisdom we absorb and digest. The soul under grace looks to God as our passion, zeal, delight, and love.

Two and Three: Five—The Symbol

Teeth: Our teeth tell us much of the covenant. Mankind, with two rows, top and bottom, has thirty-two for adults and twenty primary teeth for children. Thirty-two equals five multiples of two (two times two times two times two times two equals thirty-two), and twenty consists of two multiples of five of (five times two times two equals twenty). And two of each tooth is identical in design, adhering to the covenant principle of a double portion.

Fingers and Hands: Our two hands and ten fingers also bear this peculiar mark of the covenant (two times five), with one finger on each hand identical to one on the other hand. God created mankind with hands to uphold His commandments.

Toes and Feet: Our two feet and ten toes also bear this indelible mark (two times five) with two of each toe being identical in design. Mankind is created with feet to walk upright, with God, in the way of righteousness.

Our hands and feet represent that God has designed us to live a covenanted and obedient life. Consequently, God has given us Ten Commandments on two tables of stone, corresponding with two hands and two feet with ten fingers and ten toes.

This speaks to us of God's command that we do His will by acting in accordance with our responsibility in the covenant. Our hands and feet facilitate our work and our will. God has affixed the covenant to our hands and feet and has designed them for the service of God and to live in accordance with the will of God. Our hands are made to uphold His law and our feet to walk in uprightness. They are instruments of our deeds, of good and evil, right and wrong. They declare what is in the heart and carry out the secrets of the heart.

Our hands and feet are created with an ethereal design. Our hands and fingers are comparable in shape to the wings of angels that are elongated to reach up to heaven in prayer. And our feet with toes

145

sloping from big to small would seem to facilitate a gradient ascent up to heaven.

God has designed us to long for heaven, our ultimate inheritance and place of eternal service to our Creator. Our hands and feet represent symbols of heavenly service and mankind has been created to do the work of the kingdom of God.

Mankind is created to be in harmony with God, and therefore our hands represent His ethereal nature. They are correlated with commandments of Christ, which is love. Mankind and God in harmony is a symbol of grace. Our hands and feet ought to remind us each day that we are created in covenant to live in harmony with God and to walk with Him in agreement through the path of life. The way we walk, the path that we take, and our deeds speak to God. This number establishes that mankind was created for grace and to spend this temporal life in preparation for grace and eternity.

Redemption and Grace: Five represents the way of redemption and grace. The numbers two (human nature) and three (divine nature) represent man and God jointly in harmony and grace— hands working together and feet walking together. Although God and mankind are opposites, they agree in covenant because of the justification of Christ.

Two represents the law, and three represents grace. This affirms that all flesh is first under the law, but then by repentance, mankind is shown the way to Christ for cleansing of sin and the gifts of faith and grace.

Consequently, there are five stages of grace. The two spaces and three sequences of symbols of the sacred vision are representing this divine process. Two signifies those things natural, and three represents things spiritual. We are first born of flesh, and then we are reborn of the spirit. The two together are symbols of redemption and ultimately grace.

Two Is the Code of Creation in Nature

The design of the animals, birds, fish, reptiles, and all creatures bears the code of creation and all are created with the design of the holy covenant. They too are included in the covenant because they were created for mankind and were put under the dominion of Adam, and his descendants, as covenant possessions. "And God said, Let us make man in our image, and after our likeness: and let them have dominion over the fish of the sea, and over the fowl of the air, and over the cattle, and over all the earth, and over every creeping thing that creepeth upon the earth" (Genesis 1:26).

They bear the sign of the covenant because they are under the ownership of mankind. All life is from a single source under the ordinances of the covenant. Thus, God writes the sign of the covenant, His signature, upon creation.

Two Genders—Male and Female

God created male and female and blessed all creatures under ordinances of the holy covenant with the ability to reproduce and multiply. The Bible says, "So God created man in his own image, and in the image of God created he him; male and female created he them. And God blessed them, and God said unto them, Be fruitful, and multiply, and replenish the earth and subdue it" (Genesis 1:27–28). This is one of the most critical areas of the holy covenant. This command to be fruitful and multiply is essential to the covenant, because it fulfills the blessings of abundance. And abundance is an essential component of grace.

God established that all creatures be male and female, because therein is the fulfillment of the essential replenishment that God has commanded. Since the covenant is everlasting, it is generational, and therefore replenishment fulfills this fundamental characteristic of the covenant. Male and female define the core principles of the covenant. It was God's intention that grace would be replenished in the earth through the seed established in male and female. And this indispensable principle cannot exist without both.

Thus, God created every creature with the ability to reproduce according to its own kind (its own likeness) just as God created mankind in His image and likeness. (And children do carry the traits of their parents and heritage.) There is no creature that evolved from what it was not in the beginning of creation. The ability for life to reproduce according to its own seed remains forever in keeping with the everlasting nature of the covenant as God established in the beginning. Thus, the design of all creatures, of two genders, and the ability to reproduce bears the mark of the covenant.

And God also designed the animals bearing the code of creation, with two or varying multiples of two as the code of covenant design. Animals have four legs, and birds have two wings and two feet. But the centipede has varying and numerous pairs of legs, as well as spiders, scorpions, octopuses, squids, and other creatures. And whether it is two eyes, two ears, or simply the ability to multiply, their design is evidence of the covenant, and they manifest the glory of God.

God created the universe and put it all under the dominion of mankind, and consequently all of nature bears the mark of the covenant.

Two—The Code of Creation in the Earth

The earth also carries this code of creation with the symbol of two and its multiples. There are two lights: sun and moon. And the earth has several doubles that are developed from opposing conditions, such as day and night. The Bibles says, "And God made two great lights; the greater light to rule the day, and the lesser light to rule the night: he made the stars also" (Genesis 1:16). We have darkness and light, morning and evening, hot and cold, wet and dry. There are sea and sky and the heavens above and the earth beneath. And these all declare the glory and majesty of God. "For as the heavens are higher than the earth, so are my ways higher than your ways, and my thoughts than your thoughts" (Isaiah 55:9).

And the earth is also twice doubled in the seasons and elements. God created four seasons: winter, spring, summer, and autumn. These seasons are also everlasting in accordance with the enduring, replenishing, and generational nature of the covenant. God has declared that while the earth remains, the seasons will never cease.

There are four elements: water, wind, fire and earth. The Bible speaks of "four winds from the four quarters of heaven" (Jeremiah 49:36), "the four winds, from the uttermost part of the earth to the uttermost part of heaven" (Mark 13:27), and "four angels standing on the four corners of the earth, holding the four winds of the earth" (Revelation 7:1).

Created According to Principles of Divine Justice

Opposing and contrasting but complementary doubles constitute an essential covenant principle. Thus, we have male and female, the opposite sexes in mankind and other creatures, and we have the above opposing and contrasting conditions that are characteristic of nature. Summer is hot, winter is cold, spring is the beginning of life when blossoms are in bloom, and autumn is the end of life when the summer fruit has been harvested and the leaves die and fall to the ground.

Scales of Divine Justice: These opposing and contrasting characteristics in creation constitute symbols of the divine justice and are reminders to us of the justice of God. Thus, in the covenant, there are good and evil, blessing and curses, and with God, there are defined conditions of right and wrong, righteousness and unrighteousness.

The scales of divine justice stipulate and affirm that there are two eternal conditions; they are opposing and contrasting but complementary. These contrasting conditions are heaven and hell. The two must be congruent or matching and must agree in proportion, in order to have balance—balance that is essential to justice. Thus, heaven and hell are opposite eternal conditions by proportion. And this is the foundation of fairness, evenhandedness, and divine justice.

Consequently, we have two places where the soul continues in two opposing forms and states of being called heaven and hell. Heaven is where the soul has eternal life and restoration of goodness given by Christ as a gift of grace. But hell is where the soul is separated from God, its source of life, and continues in a corrupted form called the second death.

We have, on the one hand, life through Jesus Christ, and on the other hand, we have eternal separation from God, which is death. The soul cannot live and have goodness and viability without the only source of life and goodness: Jesus Christ.

Natural justice originated in creation and follows the principles of spiritual and eternal justice. And in accordance with divine law, there are debt and payment—sin is a debt that must be paid. The scales of divine justice stipulate that, in accordance with our actions, there are two systems: rewards and consequences. In these two opposing systems, justice is satisfied when there is harmony in proportion reached between both.

In natural concepts of justice there must be opposing arguments (for and against) in order for there to be equality, fairness, and justice. There is no justice unless there is a measure of harmony between both.

I can recall when I was a child my grandmother had antique weighing scales and balances. There were two equal bars like shoulders on each side. From the bars, there were three chains that resembled arms that hang on each side. And from each arm hung equal pans called the balances. In the balances, a set of standard weights was used to achieve the desired proportions.

For example, in biblical times, these scales were used to weigh money in the balances. So in one balance, the standard weights would be added, and in the other, the weight of the money by proportion until both sides agreed and were congruent. In order to achieve a just and equal proportion, the bars, the chains, and the balances on both sides had to be exactly horizontal to reach equilibrium. This evenness/balance is a symbol of fairness, equity, and justice. Since biblical times, these scales and balances were used as symbols of justice and continue to be a universal symbol of justice.

These scales and balances are of the likeness of our upper skeletal frame. God instilled this scale and symmetry within us in creation. Consequently, we have left and right, and we have everything by two or multiples of two that are symbols of balance, equilibrium, and agreement. The holy covenant is God's system of law and justice, and this spiritual symbol has been engrained within us by the way we are created.

Two Eternal Choices: These contrasting yet complementary doubles in our bodies signify that mankind is created under divine justice. They are symbols of our two eternal choices. As we weigh our spiritual choices, there is heaven on the one hand and hell on the other, as well as blessings and curses. Mankind has contrasting choices: to do good or evil or to be of sin or grace. There are two directions that our feet will take in the spiritual path through life. And the path that we take declares to God our eternal choice. Thus, in the parable of life, our natural state speaks to God of our spiritual state, and our choice.

Rewards and Recompense: The Bible speaks of rewards, and recompense and consequences. Jesus said, "And, Behold, I come quickly; and my reward is with me, to give every man according as his work shall be" (Revelation 22:12). The work of our hands, our deeds, will be rewarded according to divine justice, whether they are works of faith and righteousness through Christ or works of sin and evil.

Sin establishes that there is debt that is left unpaid. Therefore, when God weighs according to divine justice, the balances remain unequal. As the Bible declares, "Thou art weighed in the balances, are art found wanting." One side has come short of its measure and proportion but must balance. And this is a terrible thing.

These rewards and recompenses are double on either side in accordance with covenant principles and divine justice. The Bible says, "For her sins have reached unto heaven, and God hath remembered her iniquities. Reward her even as she rewarded you, and double unto her double according to her works: in the cup which she hath filled fill to her double" (Revelation 18:5–6). Justice is reached when there is equal measure and harmony on both sides. And these are the principles that are evident in creation and the covenant.

Created under Principles of Agreement

Consequently, mankind is designed with symmetry, scale, balance and equilibrium, consistency, and evenness and uniformity. We have left and right as well as parts of the body that belong to the front or the back. Our organs are by proportion, and God has instilled within us stability and harmony in the body. Harmony, accord, and synchronization and coordination are symbols of agreement. This is the essence of what it means to be in agreement with God. It signifies that mankind is created in design that correlates with covenant harmony. Consequently, when God created us with the design of the holy covenant, God also instilled within us the fundamental nature of covenant agreement, reflecting the ordinances, rules, and laws of agreement.

Accordingly, God did not violate His own covenant when He created mankind, but He created based upon the ordinances of the covenant. And God created the universe with this common symbol that defines the harmony, uniformity, and stability between mankind and nature, and with God.

God could have created mankind with any design according to His infinite imagination, and in any form. But instead, He created mankind according to a covenant system of grace with rules of agreement and with symbols of unity, fairness, evenhandedness, and righteousness. And this balance, equilibrium, and consistency are also engrained in the elements of nature.

God is divine and mankind is sin, and there is great contrast, yet through Jesus Christ both are brought together in harmony according to the divine system of justice. In the covenant, only the blood of Christ is worthy to bring balance in the scales of divine justice. For there is the debt of sin on one hand, and the payment (wages) which is death, required on the other. But it is impossible for mankind to pay. In divine justice, sin cannot pay for sin—righteousness must pay for sin.

Not an Accident

God has created us with all that we need for life and godliness, according to the covenant that is written all over us and is deep within us. Our design can never be altered, and this is evidence of the everlasting nature of the covenant. It affirms that the original intention of God toward mankind is only goodness and mercy. But the covenant of grace is rejected, and the mercy of God is mocked, when we live as though God does not exist and did not create us.

What defines the way in which mankind is created is far removed from accident, explosion, survival of the fittest, natural selection, or any other product of human imagination.

The world's theories are based upon hypotheses that speculate. They propose the necessitation of chaos and confusion, probability, uncertainty and vagueness, ambiguity of method, and lack of defined purpose. And these are assumptions of guesswork, doubt of individualistic viability of species, and lack of clarity in matters pertaining to the origination, formation, and generational continuation of life.

Instead, the way we are created reveals the power, will, and purpose of God and His covenant relationship with man. For all life could not result in such symmetry and ordered complexity without the work of God. The covenant revealed as the foundation of all life affirms this.

God's method of creation is clear, logical, and harmonious. It is based upon orderliness, uniformity, organization, and evidence. "For God is not the author of confusion, but of peace" (1 Corinthians 14:33). Confusion is a symbol of sin, not grace. But the covenant is grace, wisdom, understanding, peace, and harmony, which are revealed as the original intention of creation.

God Is Declared Our Creator

God created with the covenant on His mind, and creation is the product of an infinite imagination.

By revealing this number in the sacred vision as part of the holy covenant, God is affirming and declaring Himself as Creator of the universe and Creator of mankind.

CHAPTER 24

TWO RAINDROPS— SYMBOL OF WATER

The two raindrops were the first set of symbols that appeared. They were shadows on the page, and their color was green, resembling the reflection of the purest emerald. They were close to each other, one a little higher than the other in the top left corner of my Bible where this pair of symbols dropped onto the page.

Double Coincidences

God of the Bible: As we discussed, the sacred vision was divided into two parts, and each part was revealed by coincidence. God repeats Himself throughout the Bible, and by this consistent action, God is confirming who He is—He is the God of the Bible, the gospel of Jesus Christ. These two distinct coincidences/divine interventions reveal knowledge of prophetic timing.

When an incident happens twice, it means that God has confirmed it and will soon bring it to pass. The Bible reveals, "And for that the dream was doubled unto Pharaoh twice; it is because the thing is established by God, and God will shortly bring it to pass" (Genesis 41:32). God gave Pharaoh the same dream twice in one night.

In the current circumstances, the same sacred vision with two parts and each part also doubled means that it was doubled twice. This establishes that the prophecy is established by God, and God will shortly bring it to pass.

God Reveals and Affirms Himself as the God of Joseph

God revealed to Joseph what it means to have the same dream twice. By this consistent action, God is revealing Himself as the God of Joseph. God is consistent and unambiguous.

Pharaoh, King of Egypt, called all the magicians of Egypt, but there was none who could interpret his dream. Then Pharaoh sent his servants to call Joseph, who they hastily brought out of the dungeon to Pharaoh. And Joseph did not hesitate to point out that the interpretation was not his but God's. And after Pharaoh described the dream to Joseph, he was able, with the help of God, to reveal the interpretation. "And Joseph said unto Pharaoh, The dream of Pharaoh is one: God hath shewed Pharaoh what he is about to do" (Genesis 41:25). The interpretation of the dream was that there would be seven years of plenty and seven years of a great famine in the land of Egypt. The King was able to prepare by gathering enough food during the years of plenty. Our current circumstances also speak to us of our need for preparation.

A Covenant Portion

Double is the portion of the covenanted. It symbolizes the abundance of grace and represents all things freely given under conditions of grace and righteousness.

God gave Joseph a double portion of the land of his inheritance. "Thus saith the Lord God; This shall be the border, whereby ye shall inherit the land according to the twelve tribes of Israel; Joseph shall have two portions" (Ezekiel 47:13).

After his afflictions, the Lord prospered Job greatly. "The Lord turned the captivity of Job … also the Lord gave Job twice as much as he had before" (Job 42:10).

Speaking from personal experience, when God is ready to double, He does not double from where we have suffered losses. God takes us back to the value of the blessings we had in the beginning when our trial and testing under grace began, and then God doubles that. In other words, God restores so that we forget we suffered losses. He restores what we had before the losses, and then God doubles that. This is testament to the justice of God.

Double Blessings and Afflictions: The two raindrops are a symbol of double blessings and double afflictions. Double is the way God deals with the covenanted in all things. Isaiah 61:7 explains, "For your shame ye shall have double; and for confusion they shall rejoice in their portion; therefore in their land they shall possess the double: everlasting joy shall be unto them." The afflictions are double; likewise, also there is double restoration.

Firstfruits unto God: Two means firstfruits unto God and Christ and are those who are of the covenant of grace. God calls us His firstborn and represents the first fruits of the Holy Spirit, the product of God's work. We are by our new birth firstfruits unto God. "Of his own will begat he us with the word of truth, that we should be a kind of firstfruits of his creatures" (James 1:18; 1).

And the firstborn is entitled to a double portion. "But he shall acknowledge the son of the hated for the firstborn, by giving him a double portion of all that he hath: for he is the beginning of his strength, the right of the firstborn is his" (Deuteronomy 21:17). This is our entitlement under grace. Therefore, a double portion is a symbol of abundance (a second portion on top of what is already enough). And abundance is a major principle of grace.

Future Blessings: Rain denotes future blessings, as rain fertilizes the soil and makes everything grow, and causes it to bring forth fruit in abundance according to its season—the fruit that we become is the result of God's work, and this is the fruit of grace.

In Leviticus 26:4, God speaks of rain. "Then I will give you rain in due season, and the land shall yield her increase, and the trees of the field shall yield her fruit."

The future blessings that are represented are the blessings of grace and refer to a period of work and spiritual preparation by the patient guidance of God. Wisdom and understanding fertilize the soul and cause it to flourish in the gifts of grace.

Faith, Cleansing and Purification

Rain is a symbol of faith, hope, and patience, as we must wait for rain from God to provide the food we need. "Be patient therefore, brethren, unto the coming of the Lord. Behold, the husbandman waiteth for the precious fruit of the earth, and hath long patience for it, until he receive the early and latter rain" (James 5:7). We must have patience in our afflictions and patience in waiting upon God. These are attributes of grace.

Rain also points to a time of testing and afflictions mixed with mercy. The Lord rained manna from heaven when the children of Israel were in the wilderness. The Lord said to Moses, "Behold, I will rain bread from heaven for you; and the people shall go out and gather a certain rate every day, that I may prove them, whether they will walk in my law, or no" (Exodus 16:4). It denotes God's patient impartation of the gift of faith.

The raindrops are symbolic of the water of sprinkling, which means spiritual cleansing and purification. "And thus shalt thou do unto them, to cleanse them: Sprinkle water of purifying upon them, and let them shave all their flesh, and let them wash their clothes, and so make themselves clean" (Numbers 8:7). Water washes away impurities, and so, it means cleansing and purification of the soul from sin. "And now why tarriest thou? arise, and be baptized, and wash away thy sins, calling on the name of the Lord" (Acts 22:16).

Two Covenant Conditions

The two raindrops are also symbolizing the two sides of the holy covenant. There is natural and spiritual, flesh and spirit, and sin and grace. And there are two processes within the covenant. The Spirit of God communes with our spirit under grace, and therefore we are able to "walk according to the Spirit." But under sin, we "walk" according to the flesh, and sin.

This is confirmed in the book of Job, which states, "And that he would show thee the secrets of wisdom, that they are double to that which is!" (Job 11:6). The secrets of wisdom are taught by God by parable. Thus, there are two sides, the natural and physical side of this knowledge and the spiritual side. They are reflective of each other.

Salvation, Safety, and Mercy

Salvation is represented in this symbol. After confirming His covenant with Noah, God commanded, "And of every living thing of all flesh, two of every sort shall thou bring into the ark, to keep them alive with thee; they shall be male and female. Of fowls after their kind, and of cattle after their kind, of every creeping thing of the earth after his kind, two of every sort shall come unto thee, to keep them alive" (Genesis 6:19–20). They were set apart for mercy. This is the special protection of them that are the redeemed of Jesus Christ.

Water also is symbolic of salvation and is spoken of in the book of Isaiah, which says, "Therefore with joy shall ye draw water out of the wells of salvation" (Isaiah 12:3).

Testimony

And Moses turned, and went down from the mount, and the two tables of the testimony were in his hand: the tables were written on both their sides; on the one side and on the other were they written. And the tables were the work of God, and the writing was the writing of God, graven upon the tables. (Exodus 32:15–16)

Two is a symbol of testimony, witnessing, and prophecy. It is written, "And I will give power unto my two witnesses, and they shall prophesy a thousand two hundred and threescore days" (Revelation 11:3). It signifies the work of witnessing of the holy covenant— giving testimony to the world of what God will do, so that the benefit of it might be to all people. It brings prophecy and warning that signals a need for preparation. It is the sign of the witness of the gospel of Jesus Christ, the new covenant.

God, the Holy Spirit

Water confirms the presence of the Holy Spirit. By the symbol of water, God affirms Himself as the Creator, the Person of the Godhead who was first in creation. This is a declaration of Christ.

The sudden appearance of this symbol is depicting the sudden appearance of our Lord, and Savior, for cleaning of sin and recreation of the soul. Because it reveals cleansing, this symbol is revealing preparation.

The voice of the Lord is represented as the "sound of many waters" in the book of the Revelation (Revelation 1:15). And Genesis 1:2–3 says, "And the Spirit of God moved upon the face of the waters. And God said, Let there be light: and there was light." This symbol denotes wisdom, understanding, and enlightenment. God takes away our sins and enables us with the gifts of grace.

Baptism

Water refers to holy baptism. We baptize babies by the sprinkling of water upon their foreheads. The raindrops symbolize the water of sprinkling, and this is the water of baptism that represents the work of Christ. With baptism, there is also resurrection.

New Birth: Water being the instrument of our baptism is a symbol of our new birth. Jesus said, "Except a man be born of water and of the Spirit, he cannot enter into the kingdom of God" (John 3:5). This is symbolic of our death to sin and our rebirth in righteousness through Jesus Christ.

Consecration

Water is a symbol of holiness, separation unto God, consecration and sanctification. God separates us from evil and from our sin. "As far as the east is from the west, so far hath he removed our transgressions from us" (Psalm 103:12).

Water denotes cleansing and therefore represents separation from sin. The Bible speaks of the water of separation used symbolically in the Old Testament as part of the purification process. "And a man that is clean shall gather up the ashes of the heifer, and lay them up without the camp in a clean place, and it shall be kept for the congregation of the children of Israel for a water of separation: it is a purification for sin" (Numbers 19:9).

Healing

Water also symbolizes the healing of Christ for the body and soul. The book of Ezekiel speaks of the river of healing. The river produced the tree with the leaves that were used for medicine. Ezekiel 47:9 says "that everything that liveth, which moveth, whithersoever the rivers shall come, shall live: and there shall be a very great multitude of fish, because these waters shall come thither: for they shall be healed, and everything shall live whither the river cometh."

In Jerusalem by the sheep market was a pool called Bethesda where a great multitude of the helpless, and the blind waited for the water to be moved by an angel that came at a certain time to stir the water. Whosoever then came first into the water after the angel had touched it was completely healed (John 5:2–4).

Regeneration

Water is symbolic of regeneration and renewal of the soul and spirit to a new life in Christ. We are saved "not by works of righteousness which we have done, but according to his mercy he saved us, by the washing of regeneration, and renewing of the Holy Ghost" (Titus 3:5).

Eternal Life

Eternal life is the special meaning of the sacred vision and is particularly revealed by this symbol. If we drink the water of Christ, we shall never thirst. Two raindrops symbolize the abundant water of Christ, a symbol of everlasting and abundant life. Jesus said, "But whosoever drinketh of the water that I shall give him shall never thirst; but the water that I shall give him shall be in him a well of water springing up into everlasting life" (John 4:14).

In the book of the revelation of St. John, we read, "And he shewed me a pure river of the water of life, clear as crystal, proceeding out of the throne of God and of the Lamb" (Revelation 22:1).

Green

The raindrops were green, the reflection of a deep-green emerald. "And he that sat was to look upon like a jasper and a sardine stone: and there was a rainbow round about the throne, in the sight like unto an emerald" (Revelation 4:3). The color green is widely used in the Bible and is a symbol of life. "For he shall be as a tree planted by the waters, and that spreadeth out her roots by the river, and shall not see when heat cometh, but her leaf shall be green; and shall not be careful in the year of drought, neither shall cease from yielding fruit" (Jeremiah 17:8).

Green is the color of eternity, a symbol of everlasting life and righteousness. It is a symbol of the eternal nature of God. It also means renewal, refreshment, regeneration, and replenishment with the graces of God.

A new beginning, a new life in Jesus Christ, is revealed by this symbol and it denotes spiritual rest from enemies, from troubles, and from trial. It symbolizes rest after labor, restoration, healing, and contentment. As a result, it also is deliverance that comes with grace. "He maketh me to lie down in green pastures" (Psalm 23:2).

Tribulation

The rain, water, and the emerald green suggest a body of water like a flood or the ocean. The ocean is constantly restless with waves that rise and fall, and with continuous flow. The Bible says, "And I saw a new heaven and a new earth: for the first heaven and the first earth were passed away; and there was no more sea" (Revelation 21:1). It is the symbol of the afflicted soul that is without rest. It is a symbol of tribulation. And God has set boundaries upon the ocean, they are lined by the sand that is upon the seashore. And God sets boundaries upon our suffering and our tribulation. When God permitted Satan to try Job's faith and patience through the afflictions that came upon him, the Lord said to Satan, "Behold, all that he hath is in thy power; only upon himself put not forth thine hand" (Job 1:12). This symbol points to the period of tribulation. And God has determined that it has a beginning and an ending.

The sea is a symbol of the Law (Old Covenant) and of sin. The Law and sin are made obsolete by Christ when we are under His grace. When the soul is existing under conditions of the law it has no rest just as the sea does not rest but has waves that ebb and flow. This represents afflictions that are not meant to harm but to try us and point us to Christ just as the Law points us to Christ. And God sets limitations upon them just as God has put limitation upon the existence of the sea. It shall not continue forever but is made obsolete just as the Law and sin are made obsolete by Christ.

Clouds

As we know, clouds come with the rain. Clouds represent the majesty of the presence of God and are a symbol of God's glory. When God revealed Himself to Israel at Sinai, at the giving of the law, He came to them "in a thick cloud" (Exodus 19:9). The cloud also stood above the tabernacle in the wilderness journey of Israel and led them toward the Promised Land (Exodus 40:34).

Clouds indicate the overshadowing of the Holy Spirit. A bright cloud overshadowed Jesus during His transfiguration upon the mountain in the presence of Peter, James, and John. And they heard the voice of God, the Father, saying, "This is my beloved Son, in whom I am well pleased; hear ye him" (Matthew 17:5).

This symbol reveals God's faithfulness. God went before Israel by day in "a pillar of a cloud" to show them the way, and He stayed with them each day (Exodus 13:21–22). The Lord spoke with Moses as he "entered into the tabernacle, the cloudy pillar descended, and stood at the door of the tabernacle" (Exodus 33:9).

The clouds symbolize guidance and direction. They confirm the presence of God's Holy Spirit and they denote communion. This is the way God imparts knowledge of Himself. And by His Spirit, God leads us, takes away fear and gives confidence, faith, and assurance of His care.

They cover the light of the sun and are therefore symbols of afflictions and darkness. But the clouds and the rain are symbols of afflictions tempered with mercy. Consider Psalm 147:8, which states, "Who covereth the heavens with clouds, who prepared rain for the earth, who maketh grass to grow upon the mountains." They symbolize God's mercy as they are accompanied by rain.

The day of our Lord is described as a cloudy day as we read in the book of Zephaniah. "The great day of the LORD is near, it is near, and hasteth greatly, even the voice of the day of the LORD: the mighty man shall cry there bitterly. That day is a day of wrath, a day of trouble and distress, a day of wasteness and desolation, a day of darkness and gloominess, a day of clouds and thick darkness" (Zephaniah 1:14–15). It is a day when God cleanses all sin and blots it out forever. It is the day of redemption.

Clouds also symbolize the blotting out of transgressions. Our Lord says, "I have blotted out, as a thick cloud, thy transgressions, and, as a cloud, thy sins: return unto me; for I have redeemed thee" (Isaiah 44:22).

CHAPTER 25

SCARLET DROPLET—
SYMBOL OF BLOOD

T he second part of the sacred vision was a scarlet symbol, the reflection of a ruby or deep red garnet, a saturated red in its purest form. This also was a shadow, a droplet, with a round shape and the size of my fingertip. It appeared directly in the middle of the verse that I was last reading when this miracle began; it was the final verse on the page in Daniel's prayer of thanksgiving. The scarlet droplet focused on me personally, as it lingered, and my eyes remained affixed upon that verse. There was a pause, and then I could see the delicate movement of the symbol as it was guided by the divine hand but stayed within that spot in the middle of the verse as it achieved its sacred mission.

Christ Is Affirmed Our Savior

This scarlet droplet is the symbol of the blood of Jesus Christ. It affirms His presence in the sacred vision and in the holy covenant. It declares Christ as our Savior. It represents a drop of blood and signifies His shed blood on the cross, which is reaffirming payment for our sins.

Second Presence of Christ

This symbol is the second part of the sacred vision. Consequently, it is depicting the second presence of Christ. It declares that He will come again and that His coming is near. The blood of Christ cleanses sin, and this is representing God's desire to cleanse the world of sin and herald everlasting peace.

Deliverer

Christ is affirmed as God, our Deliverer. It speaks of the coming of our Deliverer who will bring everlasting righteousness, and only through Him, we might have eternal life.

The Seal of the Holy Covenant

This symbol represents the seal of the holy covenant and affirms the presence of Christ as the Messenger of the covenant. The new covenant of grace is sealed with His sacred blood for the remission of our sins. The seal of the blood is confirmation of eternal life. For eternal life is in the blood of Jesus Christ that was shed in payment for our sins.

Mediator

The seal also represents Christ as the Mediator of the new covenant. He is our advocate. This symbol appeared in the middle of the three sets of symbols and in the middle of the verse that I was last reading. It is Christ who reconciles us to God. This middle symbol of His blood represents Christ as He who represents us and reconciles us to God the Father. He is in the middle. He goes between the two parties, mankind and God to bring us together into the agreement by interceding for us.

Ratification

The book of Hebrews says, "This is the blood of the testament which God hath enjoined unto you" (Hebrews 9:20). The blood ratifies the covenant. Jesus said, "For this is my blood of the new testament, which is shed for many for the remission of sins" (Matthew 26:28). It is the precious blood of Christ that makes us acceptable to receive all the promised blessings, privileges, and benefits of the new covenant.

In Old Testament times, covenants were ratified and made secure with blood. Blood was sprinkled upon the altar in offering sacrifice to God (Leviticus 8:19). "And Moses took the blood, and sprinkled it on the people, and said, Behold the blood of the covenant which the LORD hath made with you" (Exodus 24:8). The drop of blood is a symbol of the blood of sprinkling which is a symbol of the blood of Christ.

Cleansing and Purification

Blood and scarlet were used in cleaning and purification (Leviticus 14:49, 51). Also, "a red heifer without spot, wherein is no blemish" was used in sacrifice as a symbol of purification and points to Jesus Christ (Numbers 19:2). Old Testament symbols are shadows that point to Christ, the only perfect sacrifice. "For the law having a shadow of good things to come, and not the very image of the things, can never with those sacrifices which they offered year by year continually make the comers thereunto perfect" (Hebrews 10:1). But Christ is the perfect and everlasting sacrifice.

It is confirmation of redemption and grace to them who believe in His finished work. The blood of Christ purifies our souls and makes us acceptable to God, the Father.

Atonement

This is deliverance and liberty through Jesus Christ. His blood is the instrument of our pardon; that is, we are freed from the uneasiness that arises from a sense of guilt for our sins and we are free to draw near to God. The Scriptures tell us

> This is the covenant that I will make with them after those days, saith the Lord, I will put my laws into their hearts, and in their minds will I write them; And their sins and iniquities will I remember no more. Now where remission of these is, there is no more offering for sin. Having therefore, brethren, boldness to enter into the holiest by the blood of Jesus, by a new and living way, which he hath consecrated for us, through the veil, that is to say, his flesh. (Hebrews 10:16–20)

And this is the symbol of atonement, as the blood of Christ, the only perfect payment for sin, makes atonement for the soul. "For the life of the flesh is in the blood: and I have given it to you upon the altar to make an atonement for your souls: for it is the blood that maketh an atonement for the soul" (Leviticus 17:11).

When Jesus was crucified, He was stripped of His clothing and Roman soldiers put a scarlet robe on Him (Matthew 27:28). In Isaiah 1:18, our Lord tells us, "Though your sins be as scarlet, they shall be as white as snow; though they be red like crimson, they shall be as wool."

Sanctification and Reconciliation

The blood is also a symbol of sanctification and reconciliation. "And Moses took the blood, and put it upon the horns of the altar round about with his finger, and purified the altar, and poured the blood at the bottom of the altar, and sanctified it, to make reconciliation upon it" (Leviticus 8:15). The blood was also sprinkled upon the priest and his garments for sanctification. The blood of Christ is the appeasement to God, the Father, that makes reconciliation possible because of our sin.

Salvation

Scarlet is the symbol of salvation, as it declares deliverance and it declares Christ as the God of our salvation.

The blood is a symbol of safety, mercy, and special protection. Rahab and her household were saved by the symbol of a line of scarlet thread in her window (Joshua 2:18, 21). At the Passover Feast, the Lord commanded Israel to take the blood of the sacrifice and

> strike it on the two side posts and on the upper door post of the houses, wherein they shall eat it … And the blood shall be to you for a token upon the houses where ye are: and when I see the blood, I will pass over you, and the plague shall not be upon you to destroy you, when I smite the land of Egypt. (Exodus 12:7, 13)

Redemption

The symbol of the blood means redemption through Christ. "In whom we have redemption through his blood, the forgiveness of sins, according to the riches of his grace (Ephesians 1:7).

Justification

Scarlet/red also means justice and justification. God's justice is perfect and requires the blood of Christ to make us perfect. It is only by His blood that we are justified. The Scriptures say, "Therefore as by the offence of one judgment came upon all men to condemnation; even so by the righteousness of one the free gift came upon all men unto justification of life. For as by one man's disobedience many were made sinners, so by the obedience of one shall many be made righteous" (Romans 5:18–19).

Declares the Gospel

This symbol points also to the fulfillment of the gospel of Christ. "And the scripture, foreseeing that God would justify the heathen through faith, preached before the gospel unto Abraham, saying, In thee shall all nations be blessed" Galatians 3:8).

The Divine Mission and Purpose

Initially, this symbol of Christ's blood and its divine action I least understood, but its positioning, the pause, the delicate movement, and the personal focus caused an elevated level of curiosity.

It was overwhelming enough to know that this sacred vision is covenant confirmation, that I was being called into covenant. But I did not completely understand a great deal concerning this specific symbol. Consequently, it took more than three months before I was able to fully comprehend that God would show me such great favor and immeasurable mercy.

Seal of the Holy Covenant is the Blood

Nevertheless, it is the symbol most sacred, and this divine action was the sealing of the covenant, as Christ applied His precious blood and confirmed His holy covenant. And the interpretation of this action can be summed up in the words God said to Noah when He confirmed His covenant. "But with thee will I establish my covenant" (Genesis 6:18).

My heart pounded the moment my spiritual eyes were opened to this truth. There are no words to fully express the unspeakable joy that I felt when God gave me enlightenment, that the blood of Christ has cleansed my sins, for there is no other surety of heaven but the precious blood of Jesus Christ.

Covenant Confirmation—Sealed by Christ

The delicate movement of this sacred symbol represents the moment that God applied the seal, the blood of Christ, by the power of the Holy Spirit. Its position in the center of the verse where my eyes were affixed represents the placement of the seal in the center of my forehead. And I watched as I was being sealed, although at that moment unaware of the enormous significance of all of this.

Of all the symbols, this symbol was closest to me (at the bottom of the page), and its lingering, personal focus confirms the intimate nature of the covenant as God draws us to Himself. The sealing of the covenant is the action of Christ, as He alone must administer His blood. The pause denotes divine attention, as God focused at that moment on that action. God Almighty pauses to care for each of us.

After the pause for my sealing, the symbol continued across the page, becoming part of the third set of symbols that formed the rainbow (the symbol of the covenant). This represents the divine connection, the process of inclusion by the sealing and confirmation into covenant.

Convergence of Time and Eternity

And so, upon this divine action of Christ, there is a convergence of time and eternity. For this is the moment that God ordained this divine appointment and revealed this heavenly secret. The covenant confirmed in heaven, before the earth was created, is sealed until the day of redemption. What had been accomplished in eternity past, and in the spirit, is now manifested in time, in the flesh and continues until the day of redemption. It is an everlasting appointment that cannot be altered.

Within God's heart, the decision was made to reveal this heavenly secret. It signifies the pinnacle of a divine process, a sacred milestone, for it reveals what was once hidden deep within the Lamb's Book of

Life. It is the book that only Christ is worthy to open. Now the secret treasure of heaven is open for all who would come to Christ.

Sealing of the 144,000

This is establishing the sealing of the 144,000 and the fulfillment of Bible prophecy that is described in the book of Revelation.

At the opening of the sixth seal, the servants of God are sealed in their foreheads. The angel from the east said to the four angels at the four corners of the earth,

> And after these things I saw four angels standing on the four corners of the earth, holding the four winds of the earth, that the wind should not blow on the earth, nor on the sea, nor on any tree. And I saw another angel ascending from the east, having the seal of the living God: and he cried with a loud voice to the four angels, to whom it was given to hurt the earth and the sea, Saying, Hurt not the earth, neither the sea, nor the trees, till we have sealed the servants of our God in their foreheads. (Revelation 7:1-3)

When the seal is being administered, there is a pause consistent with the pause in the sacred vision. There is silence in heaven as God attentively seals His people. It denotes God's individual care in recreating the soul.

The seal is an invisible and spiritual mark that cannot be seen with the naked eye but which is the mark of Christ. This mark seals and confirms the new covenant and makes it everlasting and secure. We are sealed with Christ's blood as belonging to Him, set apart for safety, mercy, and peace in these troubled times, and this is the earnest security of everlasting life.

When God seals us, we are brought into agreement with God and are one with Christ. Our lives are conformed to His image.

When I spoke earlier of how my life became in alignment with Scripture through the divine coincidences and intervention, this is denoting transformation and conformity. It means being in agreement with Christ as one with Christ in covenant. With the debt of our sins having been paid by the cleansing of the soul from sin, we are confirmed in faith, grace, and righteousness, and "sealed unto the day of redemption" by the power of the Holy Spirit (Ephesians 4:30).

The sealing of the covenant means betrothed to Christ, awaiting the day of heaven's banquet. Yet it also means that we are already married to Christ in that the covenant is made secure from before the foundation of the earth. The seal makes the relationship secure, and nothing can pluck us out of His hand.

God seals His Word upon our hearts. He confirms His love for us, and we are given the understanding and the quickening that cause us to love His law under grace (the gospel). God gives us the precious gift of love so that we are able to love Him sincerely in return, and with the passion and delight of divine love. The Song of Solomon puts it this way: "Set me a seal upon thine heart, as a seal upon thine arm: for love is strong as death" (Song of Solomon 8:6). (Evidence of the sealing of the one hundred and forty-four thousand will be discussed in further detail in an upcoming volume.)

Resurrection

After the sealing, this scarlet droplet moved up from the last verse and then over the center of the Bible to the right. This symbol of the blood represents the death of Jesus Christ. But since the blood displayed movement, it also indicates life. The rising of this symbol signifies that Christ is risen from the dead and sits at the right hand of God, the Father. It also affirms that "the dead in Christ shall rise." Therefore, it speaks of pending redemption and the resurrection.

CHAPTER 26

THE RAINBOW

T he third set of symbols included the rainbow, the token of the covenant. This was the object of my conversation after discussing the level of violence and corruption in our world. I was repeating the prophecies that I had read in the Bible weeks earlier. This chapter will examine the interpretation of that conversation.

The rainbow is mentioned in sacred visions on three separate occasions in the Bible.

God Is Declared the God of Noah

First, in Genesis, when God made the covenant with Noah and all of nature. "And God said, This is the token of the covenant which I make between me and you and every living creature that is with you, for perpetual generations: I do set my bow in the cloud, and it shall be for a token of a covenant between me and the earth" (Genesis 9:12–13). By this consistent action, God is, in the sacred vision, affirming Himself as God the God of Noah.

God Is Declared the God of Ezekiel

Second, in the book of Ezekiel, Ezekiel saw the glory of God in a vision. He saw the likeness of God's throne "as the appearance of a sapphire stone … (and) the appearance of fire, and it had brightness round about. As the appearance of the bow that is in the cloud in the day of rain" (Ezekiel 1:26–28). By the replication of these consistent symbols that were given also to Ezekiel, God is affirming that He is the God of Ezekiel. And God is confirming heaven, as these are symbols of heaven that were given to Ezekiel and are hereby repeated in the sacred vision in our time.

God Is Declared the God of the Beloved Apostle John

Third, in the book of the Revelation of John, when he was in the spirit, he saw the throne of God, "And He that sat was to look upon like a jasper and a sardine stone; and there was a rainbow round about the throne, in sight like unto an emerald" (Revelation 4:3).

The rainbow is one of the most precious heavenly symbols. For God has not only established it within the foundation of the universe, it is also established in His throne and kingdom. It is a symbol pointing us to Christ, and by pointing us to Christ, we are pointed to the holy covenant.

The revelation of this symbol means that God is revealing heaven and is affirming the vision of John in the book of Revelation.

God Confirms His Word and Covenant

- The vision is a confirmation of the Bible, the Word of God. The words that God put upon my lips and God's symbols in harmony represent confirmation of God's Word. My words are natural and God's words are spiritual by the use of symbols, but they convey the same message. And God confirmed the natural language by immediately revealing the spiritual and heavenly language.
- It is confirmation of prophecy. God's way of confirming His prophecy is by setting His seal to it, by placing His symbols directly upon it, and by confirming that it is true.

The immediate divine action also testifies (without hesitation) that these words are true.

- God always warns before He acts in judgment. God spoke through Noah to the people of his time to warn them against the violence and corruption. He spoke through Ezekiel to warn Israel. In Ezekiel 12:25, it is written, "For I am the LORD: I will speak, and the word that I shall speak shall come to pass; it shall be no more prolonged: for in your days, O rebellious house, will I say the word, and will perform it, saith the Lord GOD." God confirms His Words to strengthen the faith of His servants, to give them the confidence to speak His words, and to do the work He has called them to do. Consistently, God is hereby warning before He acts.

- This is confirmation of the tribulation and the deliverances that will come to many in these times. In Daniel's vision (Daniel 9:27), it is written, "He shall confirm the covenant with many for one week." Daniel 12:1 says, "There shall be a time of trouble, such as never was since there was a nation even to that same time: and at that time thy people shall be delivered, every one that shall be found written in the book." "One week" is the prophetic period of time that symbolizes a milestone in the period of tribulation, the actual duration of which is known only to God—when this will occur, its beginning and ending.

Symbols Divinely Placed on the Bible

The fact that the symbols were divinely placed on the pages of my Bible point to several important facts:

a. This is another way God is confirming His Word as if to put a stamp upon it. It is proof that the Bible is written by the inspiration of the Holy Spirit. We can be assured that the Bible is the sacred Word of God.

b. This also points to the Bible as the only source of interpretation by the power of the Holy Spirit.

c. The fact that all the symbols are located in the Bible confirms the symbols as truth—that they are all God's symbols, and that they are ancient yet relevant to us today and are everlasting. Their continued relevance as in ancient times confirms God's Word as true, perfect, infallible, and unchanging. The same principles hold true today as in biblical times, and God is setting His seal to it. Hence, we can be certain that the interpretation of this divine revelation is truth. God is pointing us to what He has done in the past to give us knowledge of His intention for the future.

The Immediacy: The purposefulness of the placement speaks of a divine determination. The immediacy by which this occurred is strikingly significant, as this too is a sign of confirmation, but the sense of urgency tells us that the time of our Lord's revelation of Himself is near. The promptness, efficiency, and suddenness are indicative of an event that will not be prolonged or delayed.

This also is indicated by the sense of urgency that I felt in the days following. God will enable us to know that the time is near, yet we cannot expect to know the day or the hour. Therefore, it will be sudden to all, even those who are looking for Him and expecting Him.

The Prophetic Conversation

Because the symbols align with my conversation, they confirm it. The time of Noah, and the covenant God made with him, has become our frame of reference. The following are excerpts from that prophetic conversation that show how this compares our time to the time of Noah and that it was guided by the power of the Holy Spirit:

"We have so much violence in the world today." The earth was filled with corruption and violence and God made the covenant with Noah, for "Noah found grace in the eyes of the LORD." The covenant was confirmed with Noah, yet the divine revelation that Noah received was universal in that it was warning for the benefit of all, and the consequences pertained to all flesh—the rainbow was a "token of the Covenant God made with all flesh."

My conversation focused upon our world filled with violence sequentially advancing from country to country while discussing the violence all around the world. In our time, the focus again within the heart and mind of God is that the earth is filled with violence and corruption.

The rainbow, the symbol associated with the cleansing of sin, points the world to the consequences that result from great violence and corruption. The whole world was impacted by the consequences, and similarly it is now as it was then. Likewise are the promises of the covenant available to all who would call upon the name of Jesus.

"Just as it was in the time of Noah." This prophecy states,

> But as the days of Noah were, so shall also the coming of the Son of man be. For as in the days that were before the flood they were eating and drinking, marrying and giving in marriage, until the day that Noe entered into the ark, And knew not until the flood came, and took them all away; so shall also the coming of the Son of man be. (Matthew 24:37–39)

Although the earth was filled with violence, for many life continued as usual. They were unaware of the serious nature of the time and the tremendous consequences that would follow. Likewise, it is also today. Many are consumed by the busyness of life, by frivolity and play, by immense wealth, or by poverty and worldly care, and as such, are apt to miss the warnings that are indicative of this present time. Some are being penny-wise by focusing on the short term and the temporary —how they will live from day to day, and are neglecting preparation for eternity.

"The heart of God is grieving over us." The Bible tells us, "And it repented the LORD that he had made man on the earth, and it grieved him at his heart" (Genesis 6:6). God confirmed His covenant because it was a time of great turmoil, when corruption, and violence was at its peak, and because sin abounded in the earth. Likewise, this confirmation calls our attention to the state of the world today.

There was grief in His heart. He conveyed His anger. This is the magnitude of the impact of violence and corruption in the world upon the heart of God. It is so great that it causes God to look upon His creation with regret. That which was the object of His pleasure, in the beginning when He declared that it was "good," is now the object of great sorrow, grief, and anger in God's heart.

"Likewise God's wrath will follow this level of violence." Because this confirmation is so directly linked in similarity of circumstances to the confirmation with Noah, it represents the way that God feels and similarly it is revealing His intention. The rainbow is the symbol associated with the cleaning of sin and destruction. It was after the destruction that the rainbow, the token of the covenant, was revealed. And when God made the covenant with Noah, the destruction was already declared. This means that it was sure. The Scriptures say

> And God saw that the wickedness of man was great in
> the earth and that every imagination of the thoughts of
> his heart was only evil continually … And the LORD said,
> I will destroy man whom I have created from the face of
> the earth; both man, and beast, and the creeping thing,
> and the fowls of the air; for it repenteth me that I have

made them ... And the earth also was corrupt before God, and the earth was filled with violence. And God looked upon the earth, and, behold, it was corrupt; for all flesh had corrupted his way upon the earth. And God said unto Noah, the end of all flesh is come before me; for the earth is filled with violence through them; and behold, I will destroy them with the earth. (Genesis 6:5, 6, 11–13)

God waited for Noah until he had completed the work of building the ark, and then God brought the great flood upon the earth. The ark is the symbol of Christ, in whom alone there is salvation. In our time, our ark is the gospel of Christ. God waits as it is preached to all the world and has accomplished all that it should and its work is done. "And this gospel of the kingdom shall be preached in all the world for a witness unto all nations; and then shall the end come" (Matthew 24:14). It is time for an invigorated evangelism.

"But God sent the rainbow because He promised never again to destroy the earth with a flood, the next time it will be by fire." God said to Noah,

And I will establish my covenant with you; neither shall all flesh be cut off any more by the waters of a flood; neither shall there any more be a flood to destroy the earth ... And it shall come to pass, when I bring a cloud over the earth, that the bow shall be seen in the cloud: And I will remember my covenant, which is between me and you and every living creature of all flesh; and the waters shall no more become a flood to destroy all flesh. (Genesis 9:11, 14–15)

And after the flood, Noah worshipped God and offered sacrifice, and this pleased God. "And the LORD smelled a sweet savour; and the LORD said in his heart, I will not again curse the ground any more for man's sake; for the imagination of man's heart is evil from his youth;

neither will I again smite any more every thing living, as I have done. While the earth remaineth, seedtime and harvest, and cold and heat, and summer and winter, and day and night shall not cease" (Genesis 8:21–22). This was the heart of God, after the cleansing of the earth from sin, and the return of worship, sacrifice, and righteousness.

But the world has returned to this original condition that grieved the heart of God and has progressed much in corruption and violence over what was prevalent in the time of Noah. And God's justice means that He will again cleanse the earth of sin. Yet God will not contradict His promise "never again to destroy the earth with a flood." Consequently, the next cleansing of the earth will not be by a flood (the deluge of water); it will be by the deluge of fire. The Scriptures say, "But the day of the Lord will come as a thief in the night; in the which the heavens shall pass away with a great noise, and the elements shall melt with fervent heat, the earth also and the works that are therein shall be burned up" (2 Peter 3:10).

The symbol of the rainbow is affirming the many similarities with Noah's time and is confirming this prophecy in the book of Peter. Hence, the sacred vision is depicting a flaming rainbow. This flaming rainbow is confirmation of the prophetic words: "The next time it will be by fire." And God is confirming this truth by immediately revealing this heavenly symbol.

Sacred Vision, Unique and Biblically Sound

In addition to the above similarities with Noah's time, this sacred symbol reveals additional unique but sound biblical characteristics. They confirm these prophecies and declare these truths in a unique way, and they provide many biblical messages for us within the context of our time.

- ○ **First Water, Then by Fire:** The order of the revelation of the symbols affirms this truth. Consequently, the symbols of the vision are depicting water and the flood, as symbolized by the raindrops, but thereafter the symbols are depicting fire: flames of consuming fire. The rainbow appeared as three-dimensional, burning lights flickering like a lamp or lighted candle and then as a furnace. And I could hear a buzzing sound that was comparable to raging fire.

○ **Flaming Rainbow:** Consequently, a flaming rainbow, a consuming fire, confirms God's presence and His intention. And the order of the burning lights also affirms the order in the way God cleanses sin. The rainbow that first depicted cleansing by water is now also depicting the pending cleansing of the earth by fire. God's intent could not be clearer or the warning more sincere. It reaffirms God's displeasure and how He will cleanse the world from sin. But it is also a token of God's mercy, a promise of love and faithfulness, salvation and redemption. And it is an offer of reconciliation if we would turn away from sin, repent, and return to Christ for grace.

○ **Coincidences**: What also are unique to this sacred vision are the coincidences and divine interventions that indicate confirmation. God is twice confirming His prophecy as divine truth—all of it being so harmoniously aligned with the Bible. But the coincidences (double event) also confirm that these things will soon come to pass.

○ **Emerging Rainbow**: It was an emerging rainbow, the kind that is perched upon a cloud. The emerging rainbow is the symbol of an emerging event, up and coming, and confirming what will soon come to pass. It points to the emerging/beginning of the tribulation, a period of testing and trial, both for me personally and for the world at large. But it points also to fulfillment of the covenant and is a symbol of pending deliverance because it points to the coming of the Lord.

- **Three Colors of the Rainbow**: The rainbow in nature has more than three colors. In the sacred vision, there were only three colors: green, red, and blue, the reflections of precious gemstones. The rainbow is always associated with precious gemstones in Scripture (as we see in the other appearances of this symbol in Scripture above) and is indicating how precious the covenant is to God. The precious nature of the covenant is confirmed by God's continuous mindfulness of it and by the fact that it is established in heaven, a prominent part of His throne and kingdom. It is precious to God because it is a symbol of cleansing from sin.
- The fact that there were merely three colors brings us essential messages that will be illuminated in a subsequent volume.

CHAPTER 27

FLAMES OF FIRE—SYMBOL OF THE FURNACE

The fire conveys the presence of the Godhead, according to Scripture. "For our God is a consuming fire" (Hebrews 12:29). In Ezekiel 1:4, the presence of God is described as "a fire infolding itself." In Exodus 3:2, the angel of the Lord appeared in a flame of fire.

The letter of Paul, Silvanus, and Timotheus to the Thessalonians describes Christ's coming in flames of fire: "The Lord Jesus shall be revealed from heaven with his mighty angels, in flaming fire taking vengeance on them that know not God, and that obey not the gospel of our Lord Jesus Christ" (2 Thessalonians 1:7–8).

Christ, Our Perfect Sacrifice

The fire points to sacrifice. Sacrifice is made complete by fire, and this symbol points to Christ, our great sacrifice. He is our fire and by whom the new covenant is secure and complete. Through His sacrifice, we are made perfect and acceptable to God and confirmed into covenant with God.

Holy Spirit

On the day of Pentecost the disciples were together. "And suddenly there came a sound from heaven as of a rushing mighty wind ... And there appeared unto them cloven tongues like as of fire, and it sat upon each of them" (Acts 2:2–3). The fire is a symbol of the indwelling Holy Spirit. The Lord Jesus sent the fire of the Holy Spirit to empower them to preach the gospel.

But they were mocked. Peter explains to the people who were mocking that those who are speaking in tongues were not drunk but that this was the fulfillment of prophecy by the prophet Joel. For it says,

> And it shall come to pass in the last days, saith God, I will pour out of my Spirit upon all flesh: and your sons and your daughters shall prophesy, and your young men shall see visions, and your old men shall dream dreams: And on my servants and on my handmaidens I will pour out in those days of my Spirit; and they shall prophesy. (Acts 2:17–18).

This symbol of fire confirms this prophecy, which has been fulfilled, and is an indicator of the time in which we live, "the last days".

Presence of the Angels

The fire is a symbol of the presence of the angels of God, which is revealed in the words of this beautiful psalm:

> Who coverest thyself with light as with a garment: who stretchest out the heavens like a curtain: Who layeth the beams of his chambers in the waters: who maketh the clouds his chariot: who walketh upon the wings of the wind: who maketh his angels spirits; his ministers a flaming fire. (Psalm 104:2–4).

Days after the sacred vision I had been much discomforted because of this great mystery which I did not understand. Thoughts of what has occurred were never far from my mind. And as I was sitting at home one evening suddenly, there appeared in the distance of two feet away from me, a cluster of sparks of fire. This needed no waiting for interpretation; I knew right away that this was the presence of an angel of the Lord. The message of the angel was comfort and peace because thereafter, my discomfort was taken away, and I was happy again.

The comforter is the Holy Spirit who would reveal the mystery and teach me the interpretation. Jesus said, "But the Comforter, which is the Holy Ghost, whom the Father will send in my name, he shall teach you all things, and bring all things to your remembrance, whatsoever I have said unto you. Peace I leave with you, my peace I give unto you: not as the world giveth, give I unto you. Let not your heart be troubled, neither let it be afraid" (John 14:26-27).

Purification

Flames of fire represent divine cleansing and purification under grace. Job, in his agony, said, "But He knoweth the way that I take: when he hath tried me, I shall come forth as gold (Job 23:10). By fire of afflictions, all the impurities of sin are separated out, just as gold is purified. This refers to a life purified through the blood of Christ. But purification takes place in the soul, although it is beneficial also to the body.

Work and Reward

Fire represents work and reward. A soul that has been purified becomes serviceable to God. The book of Corinthians tells us,

> Now if any man build upon this foundation (Christ) gold, silver, precious stones, wood, hay, stubble: Every man's work shall be made manifest: for the day shall declare it,

because it shall be revealed by fire; and the fire shall try every man's work of what sort it is. If any man's work abide which he hath built thereupon, he shall receive a reward. If any man's work shall be burned, he shall suffer loss: but he himself shall be saved; yet so as by fire. (1 Corinthians 3:12–15)

Fire of Tribulation

Fire is the way God brings judgment and the fire of Christ gives us righteousness. Jesus said, "I am come to send fire on the earth; and what will I, if it be already kindled?" (Luke 12:49). The fire speaks of the refining power of the gospel as the Holy Spirit is poured out during the time of the tribulation and the gospel purges the world in preparation for Christ's return. The fire separates and creates division. As said in the gospel,

Suppose ye that I am come to give peace on earth? I tell you, Nay; but rather division: For from henceforth there shall be five in one house divided, three against two, and two against three. Father shall be divided against the son, and the son against the father; the mother against the daughter, and the daughter against the mother; the mother in law against her daughter in law, and the daughter in law against her mother in law (Luke 12:51–53)

This is the effect of the refining fire that separates out the gold from its impurities in the spiritual furnace. This spiritual symbolism is manifested as such that even families will be divided. Those who are for Christ will draw closer to Him and those who are against Christ will hold a firmer position against Him. This is the rise in righteous indignation, as many will not want to hear even the name of Jesus or the gospel. And they are offended and fight against those who do. We now observe this prophecy fulfilled, with deep division in the world.

Testing and Trial

Fire is symbolic of testing and trial, but fire also speaks of mercy and faith made perfect by the revelation of God's assurances. God shows great care and mercy and is constantly available when we are tested. In Isaiah 43:2, we read, "When thou passeth through the waters, I will be with thee; and through the rivers, they shall not overflow thee; when thou walkest through the fire, thou shalt not be burned; neither shall the flame kindle upon thee."

It points also to God's faithfulness in time of testing. In the book of Daniel, when King Nebuchadnezzar commanded that Shadrach, Meshach, and Abednego be put into the fiery furnace because they refused to serve his gods, he commanded that the fire of the furnace be heated seven times hotter than it would normally be heated. But God was with them in the furnace, and though they were in the middle of the fire, they were not burnt. The fire had no power, so not even their hair or clothing was singed. They did not even smell of smoke (Daniel 3:13–23).

Although the fire of our affliction takes hold upon the soul, it does not have the power to consume it and we do not show the effect of our afflictions. But this is not because we are of ourselves stoic, or because we are strong. It is the strength of Christ and the power of His protection. This level of protection is still available to us today, but only by faith through grace of Jesus Christ.

Holiness

"And I will bring the third part through the fire, and will refine them as silver is refined, and will try them as gold is tried: they shall call on my name, and I will hear them: I will say, It is my people: and they shall say, The LORD is my God" (Zechariah 13:9). They are consecrated, separated unto God, and God writes His name upon them and owns them as His. Fire is the symbol of the holiness of God.

Furnace of Affliction

The furnace of God's fire points to refinement by afflictions and God's deliverance. In Deuteronomy 4:20, Israel is reminded of God's faithfulness to them in bringing them out of the furnace of afflictions in Egypt. "But the LORD hath taken you, and brought you forth out of the iron furnace, even out of Egypt, to be unto him a people of inheritance, as ye are this day." Again, we read in Isaiah 48:10, "Behold, I have refined thee, but not with silver; I have chosen thee in the furnace of affliction."

Divine Justice

Jesus sent messengers to the Samaritans to prepare for Him, but when Jesus arrived, the Samaritans did not welcome Him. "And when his disciples James and John saw this, they said, Lord, wilt thou that we command fire to come down from heaven, and consume them, even as Elias did?" But Jesus said he had not "come to destroy men's lives but to save them". (Luke 9:52–54, 56). Fire is hereby symbolizing divine justice.

Judgment

The furnace also means pending judgment. In the destruction of Sodom and Gomorrah, it was said that "the smoke of the country went up as the smoke of a furnace" (Genesis 19:28). We read also in Matthew 13:49–50, that the furnace is associated with judgment. Jesus tells us in one of His many parables when He was explaining that the kingdom of heaven is like a net cast into the sea, which gathers everything. When it is full, it is drawn to shore where the good is gathered into vessels and the bad is cast away. Verses 49 and 50 tell us, "So shall it be at the end of the world; the angels shall come forth, and sever the wicked from among the just, and shall cast them into the furnace of fire: there shall be wailing and gnashing of teeth." In Revelation 9:2, the smoke of the bottomless pit is also described as "the smoke of a great furnace." The furnace of burning light is a symbol of the pending consummation.

Ratification

Fire is the way God confirmed His covenant with Abraham. God requested Abram (as his name was before God changed it) to take a heifer and a female goat, a ram, a turtledove, and a young pigeon and cut them into halves, laying the pieces one against the other, except that the birds were not to be divided. And as Abram waited upon God, the fowls came to eat the carcasses, and Abram, in great faith, drove them away. Then in the evening when Abram fell asleep waiting upon God, a smoking furnace and a burning lamp passed between the pieces, and God confirmed His covenant with Abraham. (Genesis 15). Fire depicts the ratification of the holy covenant. The symbols of the lamp and the furnace in the sacred vision are invoking the ratification of the covenant God made with Abraham through the promised son, Isaac. This covenant points us to Christ.

Trinity of God in Christ

The flames went up three times, symbolizing the presence of the Trinity of Persons in Christ, who is our Judge. It is depicting the cooperative involvement of the three persons of God in Christ in the cleansing of sin.

CHAPTER 28

SYMBOL OF THE LAMP/ LIGHTED CANDLE

Guidance and Direction

The flames flickered like a lamp or lighted candle. The lamp is a symbol of direction and guidance. It denotes a pathway of affliction and suffering, where our forefathers have gone before. It also means following in the way of Christ, the way of the cross. This pathway of suffering is the way of redemption and grace. Christ provides cleansing to the soul from sin as we travel the pathway of life.

The Gospel

The oil that keeps the lamps burning represents the gospel. The lamp points to the gospel, and by this symbol, God is also confirming His Word. "Thy word is a lamp unto my feet, and a light unto my path" (Psalm 119:105). God's Word enlightens us, provides us a pathway, and guides us in the way we should go. God promises to make this a plain path and to order our steps to make them secure. God will remove obstacles, enemies, and evil that prevent us from carrying out the duty that He has set for us.

The candle and the lamp are symbols of enlightenment through the gospel. "For thou wilt light my candle: the LORD my God will enlighten my darkness" (Psalm 18:28). Job also speaks of this candle and this enlightenment of the Lord: "When his candle shined upon my head, and when by his light I walked through darkness" (Job 29:3). "For thou art my lamp, O LORD: and the LORD will lighten my darkness" (2 Samuel 22:29).

Service

Our Lord said, "Ye are the light of the world. A city that is set on an hill cannot be hid. Neither do men light a candle, and put it under a bushel, but on a candlestick; and it giveth light unto all that are in the house" (Matthew 5:14–15).

And this flickering of the fire like a lighted candle means service to God and to others. God does not give knowledge to be hidden so that others may not benefit by it. Instead, God scatters the seed of the gospel so that it accomplishes all that is intended. And the gospel gives light that all may see. We are to use the blessings that God has given us for the benefit of others. The lamp and the candle are symbols of service.

Anointing and Consecration

The lamp and candle are symbols of anointing and consecration, being sanctified and blessed by God for work. Christ prepares us for His service by bestowing upon us all the blessings of grace. Christ gives us the skill by preparing us in wisdom and understanding and by His Holy Spirit in the knowledge of the gospel. And we are prepared by Christ for the covenant relationship, and for His coming.

Covenant Confirmation

This special symbol appeared in God's confirmation of His covenant with Abraham. The burning lamp came between the pieces of Abram's sacrifice. God is hereby evoking this covenant confirmation.

193

Similarly, in our time, God is replicating this ratification as evidenced by the same symbols appearing in the sacred vision.

God established Abraham as the "father of many nations." All those who are of faith are also blessed with him and are therefore brought into the covenant God made with him. This also is pointed to the new covenant of grace of Jesus Christ. The law is a lamp that points us to Christ.

A burning lamp is a symbol of "a perpetual incense before the LORD " (Exodus 30:8). And this is representing the covenant.

Heir to the Covenant

When God made the covenant with Abram, He promised him by saying, "And I will establish my covenant between me and thee and thy seed after thee in their generations for an everlasting covenant, to be a God unto thee, and to thy seed after thee" (Genesis 17:7). By this promise, the spiritual seed (the descendants) of Abraham are successors to the covenant and are heirs to the heavenly inheritance. These successors are of the faith and grace of Jesus Christ.

Duty of a Watchman

Preparation: The lamp denotes the duty of a watchman, to be aware of the times and be of warning to others. This is a symbol that makes us aware of our need for preparation. In the parable of the ten virgins, they that were foolish took their lamps, but no oil with them. The wise took oil in vessels with their lamps. The bridegroom was delayed and they all fell asleep. When they awoke, the foolish virgins had no oil and their lamps had gone out. The wise virgins did not have enough to share. When the foolish virgins went to buy oil, in came the bridegroom. The foolish virgins were left out of the marriage ceremony; the door was shut. Here they all had potential access to the marriage, for they were virgins awaiting the bridegroom, yet some were foolish. This is a symbol of those who believe they are waiting for Christ (the Bridegroom) and have potential for redemption and access to heaven (the marriage supper of the Lamb), because of His shed blood, yet have no lamp and no light, for they are in spiritual darkness.

This is the circumstance of those who know that the Bridegroom is coming, yet they are unprepared. They have no oil—the oil of wisdom and understanding that gives quickening, and that comes through preparation in the gospel. This is the condition of those who are focused upon the world and have hearts set upon the things of the world. This distracts from the focus of sincere preparation in the gospel as we wait for Christ. "While the bridegroom tarried, they all slumbered and slept" (Matthew 25:5).

Preparation comes from having the gift of understanding and is a sure sign of grace. For all those who are of grace Christ will lose none. We are prepared for Christ through the spirit of wisdom and understanding that comes from the power of the spirit of the gospel of Christ.

Prophecy

Both the lamp and the candle have end-of-time symbolism. In Revelation 8:10, at the sound of the third angel, "there fell a great star from heaven, burning as it were a lamp, and it fell upon the third part of the rivers, and upon the fountains of waters."

The candle also denotes time limitation. For there is a limited time within which a candle can burn. There will be a time when the candle will shine no more and a time when it will be no longer needed. There will be no need for the candle in heaven. "And there shall be no night there; and they need no candle, neither light of the sun; for the Lord God giveth them light: and they shall reign for ever and ever" (Revelation 22:5).

Blue—The Third Flame

The flames of the rainbow were green, red, and blue. In contrast to the two earlier parts of the sacred vision—the two raindrops and the blood, the seal of Christ, which appeared as shadows reflecting from gemstones—this time, when the three colors converged into the formation of the rainbow, the colors were no longer shadows. They had transformed into three-dimensional layers of flaming fire. The fire was bright, and the colors were as the lights reflecting out of the purest diamond.

As mentioned, each of these three colors represents a stage in the process of the sacred vision, and consequently each is also representing the three stages of grace. Altogether, they reveal another aspect of covenant confirmation and point to the work of the Holy Trinity in the covenant.

The special meaning is threefold mercy: restoration, replenishment, and recreation of the soul from sin. First, the color green points to the recreation and replenishment by the water of Christ. Second, the color red points to the cleansing, restoration and reconciliation by the blood of Jesus Christ. We have dealt with the green and the red, and now let us look at the interpretation of the color blue.

Holiness

Blue, the final color in the flaming rainbow, was the appearance of light reflecting from the purest sapphire. The fact that blue is the final color is particularly significant. It is a symbol of holiness and righteousness, the fruit of God's work.

In Numbers 15:38, the Jews were commanded to make "fringes in the borders of their garments throughout their generations, and that they put upon the fringe of the borders a ribbon of blue" so that it should serve as a reminder to keep the commandments and be holy.

Garments of Righteousness and Grace

Blue, purple, and scarlet were often worn or used together in the Old Testament. "Moreover, thou shall make the tabernacle with ten curtains of fine twined linen, and blue, and purple, and scarlet: with cherubims of cunning work" (Exodus 26:1). The priest wore blue. They made the "ephod of gold, of blue, and of purple, of scarlet and fine twined linen, with cunning work" (Exodus 28:6). The Bible speaks of embroidery, fine linen and needlework. These are symbols of garments of righteousness and grace. They are symbols of God's work upon the soul, depicting delicate and careful attention, diligence, refinement and beauty. God's work upon the soul is a delight and He adorns His people with the beauty of grace.

Heaven

Although these three colors are symbols of grace, blue (the color of the heavens) points to heaven, our final rest and inheritance under grace. This color is a symbol that confirms our eternal condition, future status and association, and our place of abode. "God will create a new heaven and a new earth where righteousness will be eternal."

The three colors are the reflection of precious gemstones, and this is a special revelation and confirmation of heaven. For we know that heaven is made of all manner of precious stones. This is confirmed in the vision of John the Apostle. In the spirit, John saw a vision of

> that great city, the holy Jerusalem, descending out of heaven from God, having the glory of God: and her light was like unto a stone most precious, even like a jasper stone, clear as crystal … And the foundations of the wall of the city were garnished with all manner of precious stones. The first foundation was jasper; the second, sapphire; the third, a chalcedony; the fourth, an emerald; the fifth, sardonyx;

the sixth sardius; the seventh chrysolite; the eighth, beryl; the ninth, a topaz; the tenth, a chrysoprasus; the eleventh, a jacinth; the twelfth, an amethyst. (Revelation 21:10–11, 19–20)

The reflection of gemstones in the sacred vision provides incontestable proof of the presence of God, and the precious gemstones point to heaven. These symbols in general portray a glimpse into heaven, and the reflection of the gemstones confirms just that. Gemstones are symbols of eternity.

Heaven, having foundations of precious stones, signifies how precious God is and all that surrounds Him. The precious stones also signify how precious the covenant is to God and how precious to Him are those who are His. God confirms this by assigning a precious stone to each of the twelve tribes of Israel. This is a symbol that points to God's covenanted people, the spiritual Israel, of every nation. "And they shall be mine, saith the LORD of hosts, in that day when I make up my jewels; and I will spare them, as a man spareth his own son that serveth him" (Malachi 3:17).

Light—The Seventh and Final Symbol

The sacred vision ended with a clear, tiny light as the light reflecting out of the purest diamond. It emerged from the flames of fire and lingered for a couple of seconds after all the other symbols had disappeared.

The light is a symbol of Jesus Christ, the light of the world. It is the glory of God who dwells in light "and in whom there is no darkness at all" (1 John 1:5). Jesus said, "I am the light of the world; he that followeth me shall not walk in darkness, but shall have the light of life" (John 8:12). The light is also a symbol of the resurrection and of everlasting life. It is evidence of the power of the Holy Spirit.

Such a great honor Christ has bestowed upon His people by grace. Our Lord refers to His people as "the light of the world." And these words are particularly beautiful so that our Lord says to His people, "Let your light so shine before men, that they may see your good works, and glorify your Father which is in heaven" (Matthew 5:16).

The meaning of light is typical of that of the lamp. The Word of God is not only our lamp but also our light. Here again, this symbol is reaffirming the gospel of Jesus Christ. "For the commandment is a lamp; and the law is light; and reproofs of instruction are the way of life" (Proverbs 6:23). The light of the Word of God directs us to the truth of the will of God and points us in the way of Jesus Christ.

Thus, the symbol of light is reaffirming spiritual understanding, enlightenment in the wisdom, and knowledge of God. And the light is guidance. God is again reaffirming answered prayer for wisdom and understanding, for the knowledge of Him.

The light is grace, and so light represents the way of grace through perfection in righteousness that Christ gives us on the day of redemption. The Scriptures say, "But the path of the just is as the shining light, that shineth more and more unto the perfect day" (Proverbs 4:18). It was a white light, a symbol of Christ's righteousness; "without spot or blemish."

Safety

Light is a symbol of salvation, safety, and protection as we learn from the words of this beautiful psalm: "The Lord is my light and my salvation; whom shall I fear?" (Psalm 27).

Christ, Our Deliverer

This symbol declares Christ as the Deliver who will come. The light that emerged at the end of the raging fire of the furnace is the light of grace. This is the light of Christ, the light of the resurrection. And the light of believers. "Light denotes deliverance out of the furnace," says Matthew Henry (Abraham, 1994: 43).[vi]

Job, in the agony of his afflictions, speaks much of light, as he longed for the light and the end of his afflictions. This symbol speaks of deliverance out of affliction and suffering. It is also the symbol of renewal and means transformation of heart, mind, soul, and spirit. It is a symbol of rest.

Fellowship

Light also means fellowship. "But if we walk in the light, as he is in the light, we have fellowship one with another, and the blood of Jesus Christ his Son cleanseth us from all sin" (1 John 1:7). There is fellowship is walking in grace with those who are of grace; otherwise, there is no fellowship, only conflict.

Glory of God

Inter alia, light is a symbol of joy, happiness, and honor. The Lord sets His glory upon us. For He says, "Arise, shine; for thy light is come, and the glory of the LORD is risen upon thee" (Isaiah 60:1). The greater spiritual meaning of light is discussed in detail in a later volume in this series.

CHAPTER 29

THE SYMBOLS—NUMBERS SEVEN AND EIGHT

The Seven Symbols of March 15

When I add the major symbols of March 15—the water (two symbols), the blood, the furnace, the lamp/candle, the flaming rainbow, and the light—this amounts to seven major symbols altogether that were revealed on March 15.

Seven

The book of the Revelation of John speaks much of this number. It speaks of "seven angels which stood before God" (Revelation 8:2); "seven golden candlesticks" (Revelation 1:12); "seven lamps of fire burning before the throne, which are the seven Spirits of God" (Revelation 4:5); the book with "seven seals" (Revelation 5:5); and "seven stars" and "seven churches" (Revelation 1:20).

These seven symbols represent a complete and final message—a message of warning against corruption and violence. But it also represents a message to the church because it is a message that speaks of preparation.

Seven Priests

Coincidentally, it was ten years after the sacred vision that I decided to recall and count the number of priests I had met with as

God provided the opportunities. They were seven only. The first two initial meetings I had sought, but all of the others thereafter became available as God guided me.

I met with one priest at the United Church of Christ, two at Metropolitan AME church, two at St. Mary's, and two at Grace Church—seven priests and four churches. I was stunned when I realized that the number was seven. When I became aware of the numbers and their symbolism, I understood that there was significant spiritual correlation.

The seven meetings with the seven priests denote spiritual work. Seven is completion, and four also represents completion. And the two numbers represent a complete message to the churches. The Bible says, "And this gospel of the kingdom shall be preached in all the world for a witness unto all nations; and then shall the end come" (Matthew 24:14). The number seven is highly associated with end-of-time prophecy. Seven is a symbol of wholeness, fullness, totality, and comprehensiveness. Thus, the seven messages represent fullness and completion; a final message and warning that must be shared for the benefit of all. This represents spreading to the whole world the complete message of the gospel of Jesus Christ.

Consequently, my meetings were not for the purpose that the priests would assist me. Instead, it represents that God had given me a message to deliver to the church regarding the spreading of the gospel. I delivered to each the news of what God had done, and thus, it represents that I had a message to bring to the church. Although neither they nor I understood.

The meetings are symbols of my work as spiritual messenger because of the message that I brought. And after delivering the messages, God Himself rewarded me for my service with the knowledge, wisdom, and understanding that I was seeking when I came to meet with the priests. This is the reason why very soon after meeting with each of them, I was rewarded with leaps of new knowledge regarding the interpretation of the sacred vision. The leaps of new spiritual understanding represent reward for work completed and of which God is pleased.

The priests represent those that prepare others in holiness, those that preach the gospel. Thus, the message is one of preparation and represents that Christ is preparing the church.

Tribulation

The number seven also points to the time of tribulation, as seven is associated with tribulation. It is associated with Daniel's vision of the seventy weeks. "Seventy weeks are determined upon thy people and upon thy holy city, to finish the transgression, and to make an end of sins, and to make reconciliation for iniquity, and to bring in everlasting righteousness, and to seal up the vision and prophecy, and to anoint the most Holy" (Daniel 9:24).

Thus, seven relates to the milestones of the tribulation. There are seven days in a week, and weeks are associated with the timeline of prophecy and events leading up to the return of our Lord, as we observe in the book of Daniel. The weeks represent prophetic clusters of years in the timeline of prophecy, though not in sequence. And the final weeks correspond to our current time, the periods that constitute the final tribulation.

Tribulation is a time of preparation. And Christ will be preparing many. "These are they which came out of great tribulation, and have washed their robes, and made them white in the blood of the Lamb" (Revelation 7:14). The white robes are robes of righteousness, and it is a time when many will put on the righteousness of Christ. Thus, this is the work of the church, to support and to prepare. For many will be "purified and made white and tried."

Seven also represents the completion of God's work of redemption and grace. And it is symbolic of rest, sanctification, and holiness. In the book of Exodus, God said, "For in six days the LORD made heaven and earth, and on the seventh day he rested, and was refreshed" (Exodus 31:17). It points to the new covenant Sabbath and is related to the confirmation of the covenant. Because it represents completion, it is an everlasting symbol of rest from labor and from affliction. God's rest is a symbol of grace.

The symbol seven is particularly significant as it relates to afflictions, testing, and trial. And it is associated with afflictions mixed with mercy. There were seven years of plenty throughout the land of Egypt and then seven years of famine. The famine was so great that the years of plenty were forgotten (Genesis 41:29–30).

Seven is also symbolic of the seven seals of Christ in the book of the Revelation, which, when they are opened, have a great effect upon the earth. The seventh seal relates to a brief period of silence in heaven and denotes rest (Revelation 8:1).

Timing

Seven is also highly associated with timing of events and with waiting, faith, patience, hope, and deliverance. Elijah went up to the top of Mount Carmel and prayed to God for rain. He sent his servant to look toward the sea to determine if there was rain, but there was nothing. He told them to go seven times, and on the seventh time "there was a great rain" (1 Kings 18:44–45).

God appeared to Noah seven days before the rain began. The Scriptures say, "And it came to pass after seven days, that the waters of the flood were upon the earth" (Genesis 7:10). God revealed to him that it was time to prepare to enter the ark.

And Noah, after the flood, waited in the ark for the earth to dry out. He sent forth a raven, and then a dove, but the earth was not yet fully dried out. He waited seven days and again sent forth a dove, and it came back with an olive leaf so Noah knew that the waters were abated. Then he stayed another seven days and sent forth the dove, which returned not, so Noah knew that the waters were dried up. The ark rested on the earth on the seventeenth day of the seventh month. On the twenty-seventh day of the second month, the earth dried (Genesis 8:7–14).

The Lord instructed Joshua that "seven priests shall bear before the ark (of the covenant) seven trumpets of rams' horns." They marched around the city seven days, and on the seventh day, they marched around the city seven times. And on the seventh time, when the priests blew the trumpets, the people shouted, the wall fell down flat, and they took the city of Jericho (Joshua 6:4, 16–20).

Jacob offered to serve Rachel's father seven years for the opportunity to marry her, but they seemed like a few days because he loved her so much (Genesis 29:20).

The number seven confirms divine providence and divine intention. Ezekiel in Telabib waited seven days for the word of the Lord to come to him. At the end of seven days, God appointed him a watchman to take notice of God's displeasure and His intention and bring warning to Israel. The Lord told him, "Yet if thou warn the wicked, and he turn not from his wickedness, nor from his wicked way, he shall die in his iniquity; but thou hast delivered thy soul. (Ezekiel 3:19). God always provides warnings before He acts in judgment. It is a testament to His mercy.

Purification

The number seven is also a symbol of purification. It is a symbol widely used in the Old Testament relating to sin offerings and as a symbol of purification. In sin offerings, the priest would dip his finger in the blood and sprinkle it seven times before the Lord. And it was sprinkled upon the altar seven times to sanctify them (Leviticus 4:6, 8:11). The priest also would dip his right finger in the oil and sprinkle it seven times before the Lord (Leviticus 14:16). The altar was purged seven days to purify it and for consecration and cleansing (Ezekiel 43:26, 44:26).

Forgiveness of Sins

Peter the apostle asked Jesus how often should his brother sin against him and he forgive him. "Till seven times?" he asked. But Jesus said to him, "I say not unto thee, until seven times: but, seventy times seven" (Matthew 18:21–22). Forgiveness must be absolute and indefinite in the number of times, such that we forget the wrongs that are done to us and we lose track of how many times we have forgiven. The seven symbols represent sins forgiven through the blood of Jesus Christ, sins that are no more counted against us or remembered.

Eight Symbols Altogether

The addition of the first symbol of March 6 (the shield/head of gold) brings the number of major symbols to eight. Eight represents the eight major covenant confirmations in the Bible. These covenant confirmations all point to Christ and are fulfilled in Him. Therefore, this sacred vision represents the fulfillment of all things in Christ, through the new covenant of grace. The eight covenant confirmations are parts of a single covenant, and the eight occasions represent its gradual revelation.

Eight is a symbol of safety. In the covenant with Noah, there were eight persons God kept safe in the ark: Noah, his wife, his three sons, and their wives. This symbol represents three multiples of two (two times two times two equals eight), and represents both mankind and God together. And this is the essence of salvation. It means chosen, set apart for mercy and safety.

In the covenant with Abram, every male child was circumcised at the age of eight days old. Here again the number eight means chosen of God. Eight is a symbol of the holy covenant. "I have made a covenant with my chosen" (Psalm 89:3).

The Scriptures assert that when "eight days were accomplished for the circumcising of the child, his name was called JESUS, which was so named of the angel before he was conceived in the womb" (Luke 2:21).

Putting the Symbols All Together

Imagine my excitement and astonishment as God guided me through these discoveries, one by one and increment by increment. I could feel His presence, giving me "the desire (of) the sincere milk of the word" that helped me to grow. I could taste the goodness of the Lord as I enjoyed His gentle guidance.

Now I am able to decipher all the symbols and their initial meaning, by the guidance of the Holy Spirit, I felt I had segments of covenant knowledge. But I began to wonder how all of this would come together so that I could understand the inclusive aspects of what God is saying.

As I pondered, God continued to enlighten me. I recognized that this was just the beginning, that there was much more yet to come. As it turned out, this was merely the first layer of divine knowledge.

The Divine Process

The ability to comprehend the interpretation is in itself a miracle. Although the interpretation is from the Bible, unless the Lord had quickened me and given me knowledge and enlightenment, I would not have the understanding or the wisdom to decipher any of this. Except by the power of the Holy Spirit, I would never have been able to grasp the simplest interpretation. That is to say that this is not evidence of my own scholarship, nor was there anywhere I could look for cohesive knowledge of the sacred vision. And this affirms that deeper spiritual knowledge is not gained by worldly scholarship but by the Holy Spirit in communion with our spirit.

Consequently, the next stage of my deeper spiritual understanding would be by a harmonious process of personal experiences paralleled with the communion of the Holy Spirit and through prayer and diligence in God's Word. In other words, as I studied the Word of God, the knowledge I was gaining was also revealing what I was experiencing in daily life. I learned incrementally the spiritual aspects of life, by the timing and the power of the Holy Spirit.

It was a divine process of transformation by His Spirit from sin to grace. I began to understand what sin is from a spiritual perspective, and by so doing also understood grace. I gained confidence, my steps became secure, and I was enabled to walk with certainty. It was a journey with many milestones, with much learned at every juncture along the way.

This is how God answered my prayer for perfect faith and trust, divine wisdom and guidance, and deeper spiritual understanding. And life became a parable as I walked with God. My faith became strong as I learned to wait for God's guidance, depend upon Him, and submit to His will. This is how the light of deeper understanding continually appeared, and grew brighter, and the barriers to faith were removed.

CHAPTER 30

THE HOLY COVENANT—
AN OVERVIEW

L et us encapsulate what we have discussed by taking an overview of the holy covenant, and the remaining volumes will illuminate the symbolism from a deeper layer of spiritual knowledge.

We have established comprehensively that the sacred vision is saying that God is confirming His holy covenant and sealing His people. The word *covenant* (in secular terms) means "a mutual agreement between two or more people to do or refrain from doing certain acts ... in *ENGLISH LAW,* a promise or contract under seal" (*Shorter Oxford Dictionary: On Historical Principles* (6th Edition), Vol. 1 (2007): 544).[vii]

There are several words that can be used to describe the basic meaning of a covenant, such as a pledge, binding mutual agreement, promise, treaty, vow, oath, bond, surety, guarantee, arrangement, an understanding, and an alliance. It is a commitment, an obligation, entered into by two or more persons.

When we make a secular covenant, it is based upon a specific transaction or activity of our life, is effective for a prescribed period of time or until the obligations have been fulfilled, and is dependent upon the ability and willingness of the parties involved to carry out their duties as prescribed.

A covenant may be conditional or unconditional. A conditional covenant means that achievement of the predetermined set of benefits is contingent upon the willingness or the ability of the individuals/parties involved fulfilling their agreed obligations. And there are mandatory consequences if there is non-compliance. An unconditional covenant, on the other hand, means that there are no mandatory consequences if there is non-compliance by either party. And there is no effect upon the agreed benefits because the benefits ascribed are not dependent on the willingness and ability of the parties to carry out their obligations. The benefits depend totally on the goodwill and favor of the other.

The holy covenant is enormously different from the secular covenant and far more complex in every respect, though both are established upon these basic precepts. It is distinctively diverse in scope and complexity because of its structure of sacred principles that bind the divine and perfect nature of God with His creation. This makes the holy covenant uniquely dissimilar from anything else imaginable.

In simplistic terms, the holy covenant is a solemn vow initiated by God whereby "God promises to be our God and we promise to be His people". It is founded upon the principle that God gave man of Himself by the power of the Holy Spirit, in the beginning of creation, and has established man as a people for Himself to be owned by Him in a personal, everlasting, and harmonious relationship.

God and mankind coming together in a holy bond of love, as one, is the essential principle of the covenant. This spiritual principle is reflected in the natural sense through the coming together of male and female, the bridegroom and the bride, in the holy bond of love and marriage, but under principles of grace. They are different, and this difference presupposes incompleteness one without the other, and they must come together in order to be complete as one, inseparable in agreement and covenant. God is divine, and mankind is human, yet in order for there to be a covenant, both must come together in an inseparable and eternal bond. Christ is the Bridegroom and the congregation of the redeemed is His spiritual bride.

It behooves us to accept that our relationship to God is not left to chance but established in the beginning for divine and everlasting communion. Neither is His creation left on its own but established upon divine principles that are firm, secure, and everlasting.

The order that establishes human life and the systems of nature that regulate it are designed by the power of God through divine commands that are established in the creation and the covenant. The holy covenant establishes and confirms the order and ordinances of all life. Within it the rule, guidelines, and design for the divine relationship are established. And all is originated within the eternal nature of Jesus Christ, because the holy covenant is founded upon Him.

The Holy Covenant Is Revealed in Creation through Christ

These are some of the last great words of King David: "Although my house be not so with God; yet he hath made with me an everlasting covenant, ordered in all things, and sure: for this is all my salvation, and all my desire" (2 Samuel 23:5). Without Christ, there is no other God, and no other Savior. For all that pertains to salvation and eternal life are ordained in Him and by Him. The Scriptures declare, "The same was in the beginning with God. All things were made by him; and without him was not anything made that was made" (John 1:2–3).

How God Deals with Creation

There are heavenly and spiritual as well as natural and physical aspects of the holy covenant that are revealed in the beginning when God created the heavens and the earth. In other words, God deals with all of His creation by way of the holy covenant, and inherent in the act of creation is the covenant.

The parties to the holy covenant in the beginning under the status of grace are the Trinity of Persons: God the Father, God the Son and God the Holy Spirit, and all mankind through the first man, Adam. The whole world is brought into covenant because God put all under the dominion of mankind through Adam. So all of creation is established for covenant relationship and inclusion as mankind's inheritance.

The covenant relationship is made possible in the beginning because all was created under the status of grace, in goodness and righteousness. Jesus is the foundation for all the goodness ascribed to man and nature in the beginning, and therefore upon Him all creation is established. Consequently, in the beginning, mankind is joined together in harmony with God through the goodness and righteousness of Jesus Christ. When God declared upon creation that it was good, this goodness attributed to mankind was not of them but founded upon Christ "before the foundation of the world."

Consequently, through Jesus Christ, the holy covenant is established upon grace, and all of creation is founded upon grace. It is established in irrevocability, immutability based upon the bond of divine love that is founded upon the eternal nature of Christ. This is the essential foundation for the unmerited favor of God under grace in the beginning.

Through Christ are all the blessings of creation freely given to man. For this is not dependent upon the willingness or ability of man or any obligation placed upon him in the beginning, but all freely given under his dominion based upon the goodwill and favor of God through the eternal Spirit of Jesus Christ.

Covenant Established before the Foundation of the Earth

The covenant is eternal and established to fulfill the divine purpose of eternity. It is spiritual, established to fulfill the purpose of the soul. This is duly confirmed and revealed to us in these words:

> Blessed be the God and Father of our Lord Jesus Christ, who hath blessed us with all spiritual blessings in heavenly places in Christ: According as he hath chosen us in him before the foundation of the world, that we should be holy and without blame before him in love: Having predestined us unto the adoption of children by Jesus Christ to himself, according to the good pleasure of his will. (Ephesians 1:3–5)

Through Jesus Christ, mankind was blessed as children of God because we were created based upon the likeness of Christ. Jesus is God of the universe, the God of all people. His goodness was attributed to man. And all of creation having been established in goodness, was created with the divine intention of grace and eternity.

Therefore, Christ is the "Lamb slain from the foundation of the world" (Revelation 13:8). In eternity past, Christ had already covered our sins and declared that we were good. Therefore, in the beginning of creation we were established as good. By this, we know that the crucifixion of Christ, in the flesh, is confirmation of the eternal covenant established before the world was created.

"The Lamb slain from the foundation of the world" means that the covenant of grace foreordained in Christ and sealed by His blood in latter days is accomplished in eternity, and sealed in creation, and is as secure as the foundation of the earth. It says that the benefits of grace of the holy covenant had already been accomplished in eternity before it had been revealed in time, in the natural and physical.

What this means is that eternity does not need to wait to see whether an action ordained by God will indeed come to pass. Eternity is superior to time, and time must catch up with eternity. For instance, prophecy speaks of what is yet to come to pass in the flesh, whereas the prophet has seen those same events because they have already occurred in the spirit. In other words, by the gift of God, the prophet is blessed to see what has occurred in eternity but is yet to be revealed in time. Consequently, the prophet is able to see into the future those things that are yet to come to pass in the flesh but which have been accomplished in eternity.

For this reason, the true prophet of God speaks of things that will surely come to pass because he speaks of the providence of God. And what has been accomplished in the spirit is secure. Whereas the false prophet speaks based upon his own wicked imagination, and his prophecy will fail because it is not founded upon the spirit of grace and is not of God.

But, God the Creator of all, has all power over the order, timing, providence, and rule of the course of nature. Therefore, only God knows the future, and only God knows His intention and purpose until He has, by mercy, revealed such knowledge to man.

Thus, the holy covenant sealed by "the blood of the Lamb (Christ our sacrifice) that was slain before the foundation of the world" is established in eternity, reconfirmed in Eden, accomplished in the flesh in the latter days by the crucifixion of Christ, and continues forever. Therefore, "Christ suffered for us before the foundation of the world."

The Scriptures tell us, "For then must he often have suffered since the foundation of the world: but now once in the end of the world hath he appeared to put away sin by the sacrifice of himself" (Hebrews 9:26). Thus, the covenant of grace established before the earth was created is the authority for the government of mankind and nature in the beginning of creation.

Accordingly, Christ is "Savior of the world." He has established grace in creation and made it available to all the generations of Adam. In the book of John, "And we have seen and do testify that the Father sent the Son to be the Saviour of the world" (1 John 4:14). He has from eternity made the benefits of grace available to all people, because all are created according to the goodness of Christ. For when the first man was created, he was declared good, and through him is the original intention of God toward mankind.

Covenant of Grace Is Rejected

Although grace is made available to all people, it is not accessible; mankind, because of sin has rejected grace. And man must be restored to the original condition of goodness, through Christ, "the author and finisher," the one who established the covenant in the beginning.

This is the divine order and method established in the covenant from before the world was created. Mankind does not regain, or revert to goodness after sin, without Christ, for in the beginning mankind did not have goodness without Christ. Therefore, mankind must be reconciled to God by the method of Christ, by divine wisdom, autonomy, authority, and eternal method, and by design of the Father for access to grace.

Yet although mankind, in the condition of sin inherited as descendants of Adam, have rejected grace, Christ did not suffer in vain. Although Christ had already duly fulfilled the requirements of grace from eternity and made this available to all, His suffering was not in vain.

The Scriptures tell us, "But God commendeth his love toward us, in that, while we were yet sinners, Christ died for us" (Romans 5:8). God is not surprised by sin, and therefore Christ did not die in vain. God who knew everything, before the "foundation of the world" and the heart of every creature before it existed yet died for us.

And God has predestinated in the covenant of grace all those who by the quickening of Christ and the mercy of God would be redeemed and adopted from under sin and restored to grace. He knew those who would accept grace and who would reject in all generations.

God, who foreknew, has chosen His people by the grace that was made available in eternity through Christ. The Scriptures affirm by these words: "Who hath saved us, and called us with an holy calling, not according to our works, but according to his own purpose and grace, which was given us in Christ before the world began" (2 Timothy 1:9).

God initiated the covenant and named a people for Himself, having confirmed it all in Christ before the world was formed. For there is not a covenant without the specific parties being named therein. Likewise, it is with God who has named His people in the holy covenant, in the Lamb's Book of Life, from before the world was created.

Thus, the covenant established in Christ bears the names of those that are party to the inheritance by grace. They are given spiritual dominion through the inheritance given to Adam in the beginning under grace. And though all have inherited the nature of sin through Adam, under grace we are chosen, returned to agreement with God, and given the gift of eternal life through Jesus Christ.

Christ Is Revealed in Creation

In order for the soul to return to grace after sin, it must be recreated. Consequently, the divine methodology of creation of the world is synonymous with the work of Christ in recreating the soul after sin. Therefore, the foundation of the world is created based upon the mystery of Christ and His work of redemption. Thus, when God was creating mankind and all that is placed under their dominion God was also establishing the ordinances of the holy covenant.

Therefore, in the beginning, the Scriptures declare, "And the earth was without form, and void; and darkness was upon the face of the deep" (Genesis 1:2). This is identical to the soul that has been corrupted by sin and is in the state of spiritual darkness. It has lost its goodness and is without form. The soul that has rejected Christ has rejected the covenant. There is a void and emptiness—the soul has no light or life if it is without Christ. It exists in a condition of darkness that is symbolic of the spiritual grave where the soul under sin is relegated. "This chaos represents the state of an unregenerate, graceless soul. There is disorder, confusion, and every evil work; It is empty of all good, for it is without God." (Abraham, 1994: 1, 2).[viii]

Central Theme of the Holy Bible

The holy covenant is revealed in Genesis and is the central theme of the Holy Bible. In fact, the fundamental purpose of the Bible is the covenant. For all that God says and does is based upon His covenant. It overarches every doctrine that is required for an understanding of grace and righteousness. The covenant is all-encompassing of the Old Testament as well as the New Testament.

It is sufficient to say that the books of the Bible are all the articles of the holy covenant. There are knowledge, guidance, and instruction regarding our duty in the divine relationship in each of its pages. It is the foundation of everything that God wants us to know regarding the holy covenant. Within it is the purpose, motivation, intention, and providence of God.

Critical Knowledge

There is no greater spiritual knowledge than what is contained within the holy covenant, and there is nothing more important in all of creation.

The holy covenant is the authority that governs life and nature. Consequently, a sound understanding of the Holy Bible is an essential part of life. It is the most valuable aspect of human knowledge and ought to be an essential part of everyone's life. For it is this sacred knowledge that establishes and guides our relationship with God. This is where we learn of God, His love, and mercy. And this is how God is able to commune with our spirit and facilitate us in His will.

Many of us are unaware of the holy covenant and do not know that it exists—and that it has personal significance for each of us. There is critical lack of understanding regarding the essential truth that our lives are guided by the covenant and that it is the superior spiritual authority of God in His dealings with His creation. There is no escaping from this basic truth that the covenant is interwoven in every aspect of life.

Thus, the holy covenant is not given the prominence it deserves, whereas God never forgets it; "he will ever be mindful of his covenant" (Psalm 111:5). God has established within it the principles that we live by and that guide the natural course of life. But also within it are principles and duties that we must each uphold. And so it is written, "Be ye mindful always of his covenant; the word which he commanded to a thousand generations" (1 Chronicles 16:15).

How can a person have a relationship with God without an awareness of the covenant (what guides the relationship) and what is expected from us in the relationship? And how can we uphold our part of the vow without knowing what that vow is and what its essential responsibilities and duties are?

It is impossible to be of grace and yet not know the covenant. The lack of this spiritual knowledge is a barrier to faith and grace. How can two be in a relationship unless they are both in agreement? We must understand what is in the agreement in order to agree in covenant with God. For the Scripture declares, "Can two walk together, except they be agreed?" (Amos 3:3).

Strangers to the Holy Covenant

Just as we would, if we do not know someone or have a personal relationship with him or her, describe that person as a stranger, likewise we are strangers to the holy covenant if we do not hold it in memory or do not know of it. And we are strangers to God if we are not aware that we need a personal relationship with Him that is guided by the covenant. And if we do not see ourselves as a personal stakeholder and party to it, we have rejected and turned away from it.

Strangers to the holy covenant are strangers to Christ, and we are without covering for our sins. What the Bible says regarding strangers to the covenant is this: "That at that time ye were without Christ, being aliens from the commonwealth of Israel, and strangers from the covenants of promise, having no hope, and without God in the world" (Ephesians 2:12). This is speaking of strangers from the commonwealth of the redeemed under grace.

Yet the Scriptures say, "But now in Christ Jesus ye who sometimes were far off are made nigh by the blood of Christ" (Ephesians 2:13). When we are in agreement with God in covenant, we are no longer in estrangement, our sins have been removed, and we have been brought back into reconciliation by the blood of Jesus Christ.

What Does It Mean to Be Covenanted?

Pledged to God is what it means to be covenanted. It means to be in agreement with God by the enablement of the Holy Spirit of Christ, sealed to Him and pledged as His own forever. It is agreement in a special bond of love—a divine belonging whereby God vows to be our God and we vow to be His own forever.

A covenanted life is consecration to God and sanctification. It is preparation by Christ in repentance, redemption by His calling and grace, conformity of the soul to His image, and transformation in mind and heart to live in harmony with God. We are enabled by the eternal Spirit of Christ to delight in God, to see Him as merciful, to acknowledge His love, and to submit to His will in a manner that was never before possible until Christ gave us quickening. A covenanted life is a life prepared by Christ.

To be covenanted means to grow continually in the knowledge of Christ. This knowledge of Christ means much more than professing Christianity. It is spiritual knowledge based upon a personal and passionate love of God—a passion given to us by the gift of grace through Jesus Christ. It is a life based primarily upon the love of God and love of fellow man. We acknowledge the mercy of God toward us and we are ever mindful of that. And in turn, we want to spread His love and mercy to others. We acknowledge that God has forgiven our sins, although we have much offended Him. Likewise, this engenders our hearts to forgive and to love, to show compassion to those who have offended us. It engenders an obedient heart and a life of peace and contentment that are gifts to us under grace.

Under grace, God gives us the spiritual awareness and the wisdom and deeper spiritual understanding that enable us to see His greatness in a manner that is more powerful than before. For God said, "And I will establish my covenant with the; and thou shalt know that I am the LORD" (Ezekiel 16:62). God opens our eyes and causes us to see the work of His hands and His glory in everything and everywhere as never before. And it is magnificent!

Being covenanted means living under the special care and protection of God in both flesh and spirit. The soul prospers under the care of Christ and abundance of blessings and favor of grace. A covenanted life encompasses all that is required for restoration, regeneration, reconciliation, and spiritual rest. For this is evidence of grace.

Thanksgiving

Praise and thanksgiving are essential to a covenanted life. Our thanks to God say that we acknowledge how wonderful and majestic God is and how excellent is His mercy. For thanksgiving is an acknowledgement and recognition of the precious and priceless treasure that is the gift of grace. It demonstrates that we are grateful and that we know how much we need and depend upon Christ. And it is acknowledgement of God's promises; therefore, it is a demonstration of faith. It says that we are grateful for the unimaginable blessings that await us in eternity.

When I became covenanted, it became evident how essential it is in every situation to give praise and thanks to God. I described earlier how on that sacred evening on March 15, 1996, by the guidance of the Holy Spirit, I had been reading Daniel's prayer of thanksgiving while I had no knowledge of the mercy and immeasurable kindness that awaited me. But God facilitated me in holiness, by causing me to uphold my duty and give Him thanks.

Thanksgiving encourages the favor and mercy of God. It is in itself a blessing to us when we are able to give God thanks in every situation. Abraham gave thanks to God at each step along His journey, even in the midst of his trials and hardships. And God blessed him in material things and gave him special protection from harm physically and spiritually. God likewise will bless us more than we are able to imagine when we give Him thanks.

Types of the Covenant Confirmations

The following types of inclusive covenants introduce important principles regarding what it means to be covenanted. These concepts are initiated here, and details will be illuminated during the course of the remaining volumes. Types of covenants God made include the covenant of salt, covenant of peace, and covenant of priesthood.

Covenant of Salt: The covenant God made with King David and his descendants is described as a covenant of salt (2 Chronicles 13:5). All meat offerings were commanded to be seasoned with salt, as we read in the book of Leviticus. "And every oblation of thy meat offering shalt thou season with salt; neither shalt thou suffer the salt of the covenant of thy God to be lacking from thy meat offering: with all thine offerings thou shalt offer salt" (Leviticus 2:13).

The meat is a symbol of sacrifice and the salt is a symbol that represents cleansing, purging, purification, and removal of sins. It means forgiveness and points us to the work of Christ. The purging of the salt denotes the covenant pledge to turn away from sin and points to the only one who can purge our sins. The sacrifice of animals cannot take away sins, and there is no forgiveness of sins through the law, but the salt that was a part of animal sacrifice under the law is a symbol that points to purification of sins through Christ. Therefore, the salt was never to be lacking from the offering.

Sacrifice offered without the pledge to turn away from sin and return to God is useless and is as the meat sacrifice that has no salt— tasteless and useless. God has no delight in it and sees no purpose in it. Therefore, the Scriptures tell us that "Salt is good: but if the salt have lost his saltness, wherewith will ye season it? Have salt in yourselves, and have peace one with another" (Mark 9:50).

We are a delight when we have salt within ourselves, just as salt is for seasoning and gives a good taste to the meat and makes it delightful. "Ye are the salt of the earth: but if the salt have lost his savour, wherewith shall it be salted? It is thenceforth good for nothing, but to be cast out, and to be trodden under foot of men" (Matthew 5:13). Taste is what makes salt what it is, and without taste, it has no purpose. It is as a person whose deeds God does not delight in. God delights in us when He sees us in alignment with Christ—someone that He can use for His service. This comes when we have turned away from sin and have pledged ourselves to God in an everlasting covenant.

Commingling Salt with Meat: The covenant of salt brings out an essential covenant concept that emphasizes the everlasting nature of the covenant. The salt, when mingled with the meat, can never again be separated from the meat but permeates and seasons it and becomes a part of it. The salt changes the meat in that it gives it a new and better taste. The salt transforms the meat into a source of delight. This good taste is a symbol of God's delight and is therefore a symbol of grace.

The salt is symbolic of the everlasting and irrevocable nature of the holy covenant. The salt, when mingled with the sacrifice, cannot be removed and once again cause the meat to become totally unsalted. So the salt brings to bear the essential covenant principle of irrevocability. Once done, it can never be undone. This is a picture of the covenant, which is everlasting.

This is symbolic of giving ourselves to the Lord in an everlasting covenant, as the salt when mingled with the sacrifice becomes an irreversible part of it and can never again be removed. And so, it is the delight of God when His people agree in covenant with Him to be forever His. The salt with the burnt offering, therefore, is not only a "sweet smelling savor" but also a good taste and a delight that God enjoys. The salt means that God takes pleasure in His people, accepts them, and takes them unto Himself as His own forever.

Covenant of Peace

The covenant of peace is the covenant God made with Phinehas, the grandson of Aaron, the priest. He appeased the jealousy of the Lord because of the immoral conduct of Israel. It is synonymous with the covenant of priesthood, as we read in the book of Numbers.

> Wherefore say, Behold, I give unto him my covenant of peace: And he shall have it, and his seed after him, even the covenant of an everlasting priesthood; because he was zealous for his God, and made an atonement for the children of Israel. (Numbers 25:12–13)

It was the work of the priest to offer the atonement for the people, reconciling them to God. Therefore, this is a covenant of peace. The Lord turned away His wrath, restored mercy, dwelled in Israel, and promised harmony, safety, and protection from evil and deliverance. The covenant of peace is a demonstration of agreement, oneness, and the divine bond of perfect love and marriage.

Covenant of Priesthood

The covenant of priesthood denotes that God is confirming a holy generation to carry on the work of the gospel. Thus, the holy priesthood also represents the everlasting nature of the covenant. It is testament to the perpetual nature of God's Word that must be conveyed to all generations. It is symbolic of the work of heaven, the generation of Christ, our great high priest.

This is the covenant of the Levites. God regarded them as a special, holy, and honored people. God commanded that they should be given no inheritance, as God Himself was their inheritance. God pledged Himself to them, giving them a heavenly inheritance—the greatest of all. Instead of an earthly inheritance, they were given the sacrifices of the Lord, and the priesthood as their inheritance, and they were given the tithe of Israel for their service in the tabernacle (Numbers 18:21). This covenant is a demonstration of the generational and perpetual nature of the covenant of grace.

The Eight Major Symbols

The eight major symbols that God revealed in the sacred vision represent the eight major covenant confirmations in the history of the Bible. We will discuss the greater spiritual meaning of each in the upcoming volumes. It is important to note that there are not eight separate covenants but one holy covenant with eight major confirmations. Each is building upon the prior, gradually revealing advancing aspects of God's relationship with man and His intentions regarding redemption and grace. Thus, the eight sacred symbols encompass these eight covenant confirmations and give us further incontestable proof of God:

1) Covenant in Eden
2) Covenant with Adam
3) Covenant with Noah
4) Covenant with Abraham
5) Covenant with Moses
6) Covenant with Israel
7) Covenant with David
8) New Covenant of grace of Jesus Christ.[ix]

CHAPTER 31

SUMMARY OF DIVINE DECLARATIONS IN THE SACRED VISION

God Provides Proof of Himself

In this modern-day covenant confirmation, God provides declarations that provide incontestable evidence of His presence and His covenant. And as testimony to the measure of seriousness of the message that is being revealed, God affirms with unquestionable certainty that the symbols and the sacred vision are divine.

In this regard, the symbolism provided are reflecting, replicating and mirroring His actions of the past. They reveal common links that provide proof of Him, and serve to validate what is now being revealed. By certain precise and purposeful deeds, God is authenticating His truths, and corroborating through the consistency and constancy of the symbolism that they are of Him.

In other words, the symbols and actions God has declared today are substantiated by those that were revealed to His prophets in ancient time. There can be seen, common links to the past that indisputably declare His handiwork, and reveal His divine presence.

These divine actions substantiate that God is the same always. The Scriptures affirm this. "Jesus Christ the same yesterday, and to day, and for ever." (Hebrews 13:8). Because the sacred vision proclaims God's consistency, and uniformity in His actions, it affirms this truth. And by the constancy that is revealed in the symbolism, God provides an incontestable approach to declaring the truth of the holy covenant, and authenticating His presence.

This is an immense mercy, a demonstration of His loving kindness toward us as God reassures us of His faithfulness, steadfastness, loyalty and dependability. And God seeks to prove Himself so that we may grow in faith and grace.

God Declares Proof of His Covenant

Consequently, in act of mercy, God declares the holy covenant by reaffirming each of the eight major confirmations of ancient time. And God does this by symbolism that gives evidence of His presence in each of the confirmations. Accordingly, God asserts and restates that He is a God to all those with whom these covenant confirmations were made.

This attests to the fact that it is same covenant that God is formally and officially reaffirming in our time. Consequently, God is presently evoking all the major ancient confirmations of the Bible.

In this regard, the symbolism that is presented in the sacred vision today is also present in each of the major confirmations of the past. And God's actions of past confirmations are brought together, converged in this modern-day occurrence.

As God brings them to mind, He calls our attention through symbols that replicate them and remind us of them. This is testament to the fact that God never forgets His covenant. He repeats it through confirmations continually throughout the history of the world. And, so it is now.

And God affirms Himself today by consistent actions throughout these covenants. He declares Himself as the God of the covenant. And God evokes all the promises of grace, the warnings and consequences that were revealed in these eight major covenant confirmations. This validates that there is one covenant and testifies that there is one God.

Accordingly, in evoking each of these eight major confirmations, God, through His consistent actions, declares that He is all of the following:

1. God of Eden

This declaration is assured by the symbol of light. Light was the first proclamation by God in creation. Therefore, this symbol evokes the actions of God in the beginning of creation when the covenant was established in Eden. It declares God as the God of Eden. "And God said, Let there be light: and there was light" (Genesis 1:3).

The symbol of light confirms Christ in Eden. "The same was in the beginning with God. All things were made by him; and without him was not any thing made that was made" (John 1:2–3). Jesus is the "light of the world" for He is the Creator. In Him, the holy covenant is ordained in Eden with all creation and is confirmed and made as secure as He established the foundations of the earth.

By the symbol of light, God is declaring that He is the true God; the God of our Lord, Jesus Christ, the Creator. By evoking this first covenant confirmation in Eden, God evokes all the covenant confirmations that follow.

God, the Creator: The declaration of God as the Creator is also demonstrated by His consistent action and method of approach to this modern-day confirmation. The symbols came from nothing that already exists in the natural world, but by the command of God's word through the power of His Holy Spirit. This action is evoking the powers of God in creation.

Consistent with creation, God spoke in the beginning and all that now exists appeared by the power of His word. The Scriptures tell us: "Through faith we understand that the worlds were framed by the word of God, so that things which are seen were not made of things which do appear." (Hebrew 11:3).

Similarly, the sudden appearance of the symbols in natural, physical form originated by the power of His word. And at that moment, the barriers between time and eternity, natural and spiritual were vanished.

Thus, the sudden emergence of the symbols of the covenant evokes the work of God in creation. They established that the covenant was evoked in creation through Christ. They are confirmation of creation by the word of God, and they indisputably declare God as the Creator. God is evoking the powers of creation to prove Himself to us. And this is pointing us to the resurrection, and the creation of the new heaven and earth.

2. God of Adam and Eve

The essential element of covenant confirmation is the holy bond of love. This modern-day covenant confirmation evokes this first bond of covenant love.

God is declaring Himself as the God of Adam and Eve. By evoking this covenant, God is reaffirming the first marriage of Adam and Eve. This first marriage is a symbol that points to the marriage of mankind to God under the status of grace in the beginning.

Under grace in Eden God established the bond of love in marriage with all mankind as descendants of Adam and Eve. Mankind was created in goodness and grace and fit for communion with God in the holy bond of love and marriage.

Although that covenant was subsequently broken because of sin, God is declaring His love for us. This modern-day covenant confirmation is essentially an offer to return to grace. It is a reminder of God's love, and an offer to mankind to return to Christ. Christ has provided the way of redemption. Consequently, the symbolism presented is depicting the marriage of Christ to the redeemed under conditions of grace.

Thus, in evoking this confirmation, the symbols God presented are reminding us of this essential bond of love that is the foundation of grace and the covenant. And God is evoking the many promises that were made with man in the beginning.

God is declaring that He is the God of Adam and Eve as a reminder of how it was in the beginning before there was sin. And God is calling us to return to our duty in the covenant, and to God, through the grace made available to us by Jesus Christ.

3. God of Noah

The symbols of the water, the raindrops, and the rainbow declare God as the God of Noah. These symbols evoke the covenant God confirmed with Noah, his generations of all people, and with nature.

The kind of symbolism presented in this modern-day confirmation points us back to the circumstances of this covenant. The corruption and violence of our time is spiritually comparable to the time of Noah in the eyes of the Lord. Accordingly, God particularly evokes this covenant confirmation.

Accordingly, the symbols presented affirm that this is a Noah-like covenant confirmation. They point us to this covenant confirmation as our frame of reference. Here God evokes His actions of the past as an indicator of His actions in the future. Essentially, they convey what God's message is.

The essential purpose of the covenant confirmation with Noah is that sin had overspread in the earth, and it focuses upon warnings against corruption and violence. The heart of God is grieving over the corruption and violence just as it was in time of Noah.

The covenant with Noah reveals how God cleanses sin. By evoking this covenant, God is revealing His intention to cleanse the world of sin by destroying sin. The water declares Christ as He who cleanses the world of sin, and the rainbow also symbolizes Christ who points us to the promises of grace.

The symbol of the rainbow is a sign and precursor to the action of God in the cleansing of sin. It is a token of the covenant that was established with Noah even before the rain began. Thus, this covenant is evoked as a precursor to destruction.

Just as God confirmed His covenant in time of Noah as a warning to all people against the great flood, God is likewise confirming His covenant as warning against the fire.

But also, thereafter there is the hope of grace—grace that comes by Jesus Christ. Our ark is Christ. Now is the time to come into the ark. The symbol of the rainbow also speaks of the return of mercy after the cleansing of sin. Thus, it points to the resurrection, through renewal and regeneration under the conditions of the return to grace for those whose ark is Jesus Christ.

The rainbow signifies the eternal nature of Christ, for it is established in Heaven, around the throne of God. By the consistent revelation of these symbols, God is declaring Himself as the God of Heaven. It testifies of God's eternal covenant.

And God is reaffirming the truth of His actions in days of old. God confirmed His covenant by the symbol of the rainbow. Likewise, in our time God confirms His covenant and is pointing us to the way it was then. This tells us that our Lord will come and that His coming is near.

God—Christ the Judge: The symbolism that evokes this covenant with Noah also declares Christ as our Judge. "For the Father judgeth no man, but hath committed all judgment unto the Son: That all men should honour the Son, even as they honour the Father. He that honoureth not the Son honoureth not the Father which hath sent him." (John 5:22–23). The flaming rainbow is a symbol of judgment by fire therefore, it declares Christ as our Judge. For in the time of Noah, judgment came by water but now is declared by fire. The purpose is to declare God's warning against the day when Christ will judge the world.

4. God of Abraham, Isaac, and Jacob

The covenant confirmation with Abraham is evoked by the symbols of the shield, furnace, lamp and lighted candle of the sacred vision as these are the symbols God similarly revealed in confirming His covenant with Abraham and his descendants. By this consistent action, God is declaring Himself as the God of Abraham, Isaac and Jacob.

In evoking this covenant, God is reminding us of all the promises of grace. In confirming His covenant with Abraham God imputed to him the faith and righteousness of the promised Messiah, Jesus Christ. God is declaring Himself as the God of grace, righteousness and mercy.

The symbols of the shield, furnace, lamp and lighted candle are reaffirmations of the covenant promises to Abraham specifically through his son Isaac. For it is through Isaac that the promises of grace would be fulfilled. This covenant confirmation is pointing us to Christ and declaring Christ as the way of grace and righteousness.

God, the Shield: This symbol of the shield declares God as protector of His people. The three layers of divine protection that was revealed, affirm His ultimate mercy as God evokes the powers of the Trinity on behalf of the redeemed. God is our shield, our armor and safeguard. He is a protector to shelter us from harm and to keep us from sin. He is a guard to us and that which concerns us, a defender to fight our cause, our support, advocate and champion to fight against those who fight against us. God is a shield to us when we are under the blessings of grace.

When God made covenant with Abraham, God greeted him saying, "Fear not, Abram: I am thy shield" (Genesis 15:1). God is evoking this covenant by consistently conveying the same greeting, now as it was then. And God is evoking the same benefits of grace that were promised to him.

5. God of Moses

By the consistency of His actions, God reminds us of Moses and affirms His association with him. By the symbol of fire God evokes the covenant made with him and consequently declares Himself as the God of Moses.

The flames of fire evoke Moses' vision of the burning bush. Though there were the natural flames of raging fire upon the pages of my Bible, the Bible was not burned or damaged in any way. Comparable to the vision God gave to Moses, the Scriptures say,

> And the angel of the LORD appeared unto him in a flame of fire out of the midst of a bush: and he looked, and, behold, the bush burned with fire, and the bush was not consumed. And Moses said, I will now turn aside, and see this great sight, why the bush is not burnt. (Exodus 3:2–3).

Because the modern-day covenant confirmation incorporates this symbolism, this attests that God is evoking the covenant made with Moses. The fire that did not consume declares the presence of the angel of God, the angel of the covenant. The constancy of God's actions is revealed in that the fire of God did not consume the bush or, as in my circumstances, the pages of my Bible. Only God has the power to reveal such. This symbol declares the holiness of God.

Because the symbols evoke this covenant, God is reminding us of the Law, the covenant delivered to Moses. And by the Law, God is pointing us to the blessings of grace by reaffirming His covenant with Abraham through Jesus Christ.

For God spoke to Moses out of the burning bush and evoked the covenant made with Abraham. The Scriptures tell us,

> When Moses saw it, he wondered at the sight: and as he drew near to behold it, the voice of the LORD came unto him, Saying, I am the God of thy fathers, the God of Abraham, and the God of Isaac, and the God of Jacob. Then Moses trembled, and durst not behold." (Acts 7:31–32).

The place where he stood was holy and this is a declaration of grace. The Law that God declared to Moses is established as a lamp to point us to Christ for the blessings of grace.

Moses was an advocate and mediator for Israel. By evoking this covenant confirmation God is pointing us to Christ and declaring Him as the mediator and advocate on behalf of them that are redeemed, the spiritual Israel under the blessings of grace.

6. God of Israel

In accordance with the symbol, March 15, the symbol of Purim, God calls to our attention the covenant confirmation with Israel. In other words, because Purim is evoked in connection with this covenant confirmation God is evoking the covenant made with Israel.

But it is pointing us not to the covenant God made with Israel when He brought them out of Egypt. God is pointing us to a better covenant, the New Covenant of grace in Jesus Christ. And God is again reminding us that Christ is the redeemer, the God of spiritual Israel under grace. The Bible says,

> Behold, the days come, saith the LORD, that I will make a new covenant with the house of Israel, and with the house of Judah: Not according to the covenant that I made with their fathers in the day that I took them by the hand to bring them out of the land of Egypt; which my covenant they brake, although I was an husband unto them saith the LORD. (Jeremiah 31:31–32).

God married to mankind in covenant under conditions of grace of Eden.

God, the Deliverer: By the revelation of the symbol of Purim God is proclaiming deliverance. And, God is declaring Himself as the deliverer who will come. God was the deliverer to Israel who kept them safe against the plot to destroy them and commanded this day to be held in sacred remembrance forever.

In ancient time, God was a deliverer to natural Israel. But, now God is evoking this symbolism, which declares that God is the deliverer to spiritual Israel under grace. These are those who are redeemed from "the four corners of the earth". The deliverer whose coming is imminent is Christ.

7. God of David

Each of these covenant confirmations, though of the Law, points us to Christ for the blessings of grace. The purpose of the modern-day confirmation is to remind us that grace is available to all people through Jesus Christ.

The promises of the kingdom of heaven are the essential objectives of this covenant confirmation with David. This covenant is symbolizing a precursor to grace and the coming of our Savior, Jesus Christ. By evoking this covenant, God is declaring Himself as the God of grace.

God is reminding us of the promises made to David through a sacred vision given to Nathan. God's promise to David is that he would establish unto him an everlasting throne and kingdom. For the Scriptures declare, "And thine house and thy kingdom shall be established for ever before thee: thy throne shall be established for ever." (2 Samuel 7:16). The throne and kingdom are symbols of grace. The natural throne and kingdom of David are pointing to the spiritual throne and kingdom of Jesus Christ.

In accordance with this covenant confirmation, God is declaring Himself as the God of David, the God of Heaven. The purpose of evoking this covenant is to remind us of His everlasting throne and kingdom. And God is attesting to the promises of heaven.

This is the last major covenant confirmation before the New Covenant of grace of Jesus Christ. It follows logically that God points to His throne and kingdom. This covenant confirmation is a precursor to Christ and, as such, it declares that "the kingdom of heaven is at hand." This covenant confirmation is pointing us to the coming Messiah.

8. God of our Lord, Savior and Redeemer, Jesus Christ

By the symbol of the blood, the seal of the covenant, God is evoking and reaffirming the new covenant of grace. It is a reminder that Christ has established a better covenant for us.

God, our Savior: And God is declaring Himself as the Godhead, Father of our Lord and Savior, Jesus Christ. This symbol declares Christ, as a reminder that Christ died for us. It establishes that all the work for the reestablishment of grace is complete in Jesus Christ. And His precious blood is available to all that believe and depend upon Him as covering for our sins.

God, our Redeemer: Blood declares Christ as our redeemer. All the symbols of the sacred vision declare the presence of Christ and indisputably affirm His existence. Their revelation declares His coming.

God Evokes the Holy Covenant

The eight symbols point us to eternity. And the eternal nature of the covenant is revealed by these eight symbols.

The eight symbols reveal Christ. Therefore, Christ is revealed as the only eternal and begotten Son of God.

Logically, the eight symbols correspond to the eight covenant confirmations. And God evokes each of them from creation in Eden to the present time by the cohesiveness, consistency and constancy of His divine actions. By bringing together the symbolism that evokes each in this single act of confirmation God reminds us that they are one. They are parts of a whole, affirming that there is one holy covenant with eight confirmations.

These confirmations with our forefathers gradually reveal the process of redemption from sin. Understandably, each confirmation points us to Christ. And God is reaffirming this truth by revealing the symbols collectively, presenting them jointly as one, and in a unique manner in our time.

By presenting them jointly, God has assembled them to show this process of redemption and grace as fulfilled and complete. And God is declaring the conclusion of the series of gradual revelations by the process of covenant confirmation. This maintains that the work of the covenant is complete in Jesus Christ.

Having brought them all together, this modern-day confirmation is revealed as a capstone confirmation. It is revealing a conclusion. And this conclusion is a symbol of consummation. Consistently, the raging fire that ended the sacred vision is also a symbol of the consummation.

But the light that emerged from the fire also proclaims the resurrection, new life and a new creation. Christ is the light in the beginning, the creator in Eden. He is the light in the end, the creator that is to come.

The covenant declares Christ, according to the Scriptures, "I am Alpha and Omega, the beginning and the end, the first and the last." (Revelation 22:13). And Christ is the blood in the beginning, "the Lamb that was slain before the foundation of the world", and Christ is the blood in the end that brings reconciliation and restoration to the world.

God Declares Himself by His Works

By many incontestable proofs, God reassures us. These common threads that are revealed by the symbolism link us to God's work in the past and declare the essence and substance of His Holy Spirit.

By the reliability of the symbolism, God gives us a solid foundation, a guarantee, confidence and security that His Word is true. By the following summary of these infallible proofs, God declares Himself:

God, the Almighty

By the trinity of the sets of symbols of the sacred vision, God declares the three Persons of God, and affirms that He is one God, the Holy Trinity, the Almighty.

God of the Bible

Through the visions of the word of God, God points to the Bible as His infallible word. God is affirming the promises of the gospel of Jesus Christ. And by this symbolism, God affirms that His word never changes. What God has done in the past is an indicator of what God will do in the future.

Among many others, God is declaring Himself as God of these great prophets: Samuel, Nathan, Gad, Solomon, Jehu, Elijah, Isaiah,

Shemaiah, Jeremiah, Hosea, Joel, Jonah, Micah, Zephaniah, Haggai, Zechariah, all of whom were blessed with visions of the word of God and also with the wisdom to know the interpretation.

And God is declaring that He is God of Ezekiel, who, in addition to visions of the word of God, was given symbolism that includes the rainbow, and the appearance of fire and lamps.

God also declares His association to John to whom He revealed prophecy of what would occur leading up to the end of time. And among the complexity of symbolism given to John also was the symbol of the rainbow in heaven.

And there were many great prophets to whom the Lord gave symbols in dreams and visions including Job, Joseph, and Jacob. God declared His great love.

God of the Disciples

Jesus taught His disciples heavenly knowledge by the use of parable—using symbols to convey spiritual meaning and to impart deeper spiritual understanding. The interpretation of this spiritual symbolism is conveyed by God by the use of parable. Likewise, God is hereby also using symbols and parable to convey spiritual knowledge, and is marking the fulfillment of the gospel. By this consistent action, Christ is revealing Himself by reaffirming His association with His twelve disciples and this serves to remind us of His time here on earth. It declares that He is coming again.

God of Daniel

Daniel's prayer of thanksgiving for the vision, the dream, and the interpretation God had ordained for Daniel. And God richly blessed him with skill of interpretation, wisdom and understanding.

Now, in revealing the sacred dream and vision, God evoked this prayer as a testament to His association with Daniel. And by this prayer God provided assurance, and a testament, that He would also give the skill of understanding and interpretation just as He had done for Daniel.

By the consistent action, God avows His blessings to Daniel, and declares Himself as the God of dreams and visions, the God of prophecy and the God of the blessings of wisdom and understanding. God replicates His actions as He proves Himself to us. And God is affirming that it is God who spoke, and God who also gave the interpretation.

By the constancy of His actions in acknowledging the prayer of Daniel, God is declaring Himself as the God of Daniel. God is pointing us to the prophecies given to Daniel—confirming the fulfillment of the prophecies regarding what would come to pass in the last days, which say that God would confirm His covenant.

God of Job

The symbol of the raindrops denotes the double blessings and double afflictions associated with a covenanted life. This was the measure of the blessings but also the calamities of Job. By revealing this symbolism, God remembers the circumstances of Job and acknowledges that He is the God of Job. As God remembers Job, He acknowledges the suffering and afflictions that are indicative of this current time of tribulation.

This is a reminder of the measure of suffering that the soul endures under covenant conditions, and the restoration that Christ bestows under conditions of grace. There is immeasurable mercy in this symbolism. This is a constant reminder that with the abundance of suffering there is the hope of deliverance and restoration.

God Declares His Holy Spirit

The shadows of the symbols denoting overshadowing are revealing the work of the Holy Spirit. Overshadowing denotes the grace and favor of God. God is revealing His good pleasure and favor toward us when we are His and when we are called to do the work of the kingdom of heaven.

By the symbol of overshadowing, God now replicates the divine action that was revealed on the following two occasions in ancient time.

God of the Blessed Mary

The Holy Spirit overshadowed Mary: The angel came to Mary announcing the great favor that God would bestow upon her. She would conceive of the Holy Ghost and bear a son who would be our Savior. The Scriptures tell us, "And the angel answered and said unto her, The Holy Ghost shall come upon thee, and the power of the Highest shall overshadow thee: therefore also that holy thing which shall be born of thee shall be called the Son of God." (Luke 1:35). In similar manner, the overshadowing of the Holy Spirit on that sacred night of March 15 is declaring an announcement. The replication of this divine action today is announcing the imminent coming of Christ, the Son of God, Savior and Deliverer.

God, Father of our Lord and Savior

God Declares His Only Begotten Son: At the transfiguration of Jesus, God declared His Son by the overshadowing of the Holy Spirit. Jesus was transfigured upon the mountain in the presence of Peter, James, and John. The Scriptures tell us that "a bright cloud overshadowed them: and behold a voice out of the cloud, which said,

This is my beloved Son, in whom I am well pleased; hear ye him."
(Matthew 17:5).

By the divine action of overshadowing God consistently declares His Holy Spirit. The Holy Spirit is declaring that our Savior would come into the world. And the Holy Spirit is declaring the glory of the resurrection. God will transform His people from sin to the blessings and the glory of grace. It declares God's favor to us, His ownership of us, His pleasure when He calls us to be of service, and the honor that He places upon us to have us do the work of His Kingdom.

This summarizes some of the declarations that God is providing through the sacred symbols of the vision. In confirming His actions God seeks to put at rest any uncertainties and doubts. And this is the great mercy of God that He is facilitating the blessing of faith.

And this calls our attention to the level of seriousness, sincerity and earnestness by which God calls upon each of us to prepare.

CHAPTER 32

HOW NEAR IS GOD?

Symbols—O. J. Simpson Trial, Barbara Walters and 20/20

I often wondered why God would make a secular television program like *20/20* to be a part of such a powerful spiritual revelation of covenant confirmation. Initially, the connection between the two seemed farfetched and mind-boggling.

As we go about our lives, it is difficult to imagine that the mundane things we do can have a parallel spiritual impact. And it is not easy to hold in memory that the way we live can either shed light upon the world or create darkness. It is challenging to conceive of the numerous ways in which we can touch the life of another from day to day. But this is how the soul makes its transactions and incurs its debt.

With each of our encounters, the soul has made a trade. This is why life is as an accounting system that takes place in the soul. The spiritual debts and the payments must equal each other and the books must balance. For this is the system of divine justice. And when we pray, "Forgive us our debts, as we forgive our debtors," we ought to know that this is not only natural, but more importantly, it is spiritual.

All of us are a part of God's divine plan. We are all part of a spiritual process that parallels our natural life. God can use the things we do and say to speak to us and to others in ways that are hard for us to imagine, and by His providence, this brings about a spiritual process that takes place in the soul.

It began with a television program and a conversation on the subject of violence. The divine providence would have me to be present on March 15, 1996, to watch the details of the television program *20/20* with host Barbara Walters. As I watched the analysis of the infamous trial of O. J. Simpson, I never could have envisioned that an eternal process was on the verge of unfolding and that my life would change forever. And it remains enormously astounding that at that moment, heavenly eyes were affixed upon this worldly event, as it was now the time for the accomplishment of a heavenly mission.

Divine Plan to Call the World's Attention

The period of the O. J. Simpson murder trial was an extraordinary and uncanny time. I sometimes watched the program *20/20*, but did not have an avid interest in the O. J. Simpson murder trial. Nevertheless, I could sense from the world's reaction that it was a strange time. There seemed to be a peculiar difference, both from the level of media coverage and the level of worldwide public interest. Consequently, it was dubbed, "the trial of the century". Media coverage galvanized the whole world around the issue of domestic violence. This was why, after watching the program, I was interested in discussing the details.

The conversation progressed from discussing the trial to violence all around the world in general. And it was just seconds after this conversation, and as I was engaged in my nightly Bible reading that the heavenly symbols of covenant confirmation appeared across the pages of my Bible. God, the director of the prophetic conversation and a silent listener, has seconded the words, revealing that His wrath will follow this level of violence and corruption that has overspread the earth. The same divine action as it was in the time of Noah is the divine plan that is for today. And this extreme revelation of divine openness serves to forewarn us of what is to come.

The Divine Purpose to Shed Light

The manner in which the events unfolded clearly emphasizes a divine purpose. What is evident by the sequence of events is that God would use the program to enable me in a much broader scope of conversation with regard to violence. By divine guidance I was speaking, indeed prophetically as I foretold where this was leading us, although I was very unaware that it was truly prophetic.

This affirms the presence of God in everything, and that God is everywhere beholding all that is occurring in the world. The Scriptures say, "They are the eyes of the LORD, which run to and fro through the whole earth" (Zechariah 4:10). "The eyes of the LORD are in every place, beholding the evil and the good" (Proverbs 15:3). The series of events are convincing that God is engaged with the world, observing the evil and the good.

God would use the O. J. Simpson trial and the program *20/20* as symbols to convey a spiritual message, and shed light upon the world regarding the issues pertaining to corruption and violence. And God would inform of the consequences that are to come.

A Heavenly Focus upon Corruption and Violence

The work of the media is to shed light upon what is going on in the world. It should not be surprising that likewise God would use this worldly symbol, the program *20/20,* and my conversation about violence, to shed light upon what is in His heart, and to bring to our attention what He is seeking to say. There is an essential spiritual message for each of us, and it is clear—it speaks of corruption and violence.

The circumstances speak to us of a divine warning. Just as in the time of Noah, God reacted with grief and anger at the level of corruption and violence, similarly it is now. For the Scriptures declare,

> The earth also was corrupt before God, and the earth was
> filled with violence. And God looked upon the earth, and,
> behold, it was corrupt: for all flesh had corrupted his way
> upon the earth. And God said unto Noah, The end of all
> flesh is come before me; for the earth is filled with violence
> through them; and, behold, I will destroy them with the
> earth. (Genesis 6:11–13)

As the prophetic conversation compared the violence of our time with the time of Noah, we have much reason to ponder regarding how God feels in His heart regarding violence and how God intends to deal with it in the future. In fact, in these similar circumstances God is reminding us of similar consequences, and is evoking the evidence of what occurred then. God confirmed His covenant then and likewise He is now.

This infamous duo—corruption and violence—causes this divine action, not only because it is spread worldwide but also because the evil is so deeply rooted within the heart and has permeated the imagination and creativity of mankind. The Scriptures say, "And God saw that the wickedness of man was great in the earth, and that every imagination of the thoughts of his heart was only evil continually" (Genesis 6:5).

Likewise is it today. We can see no end in sight to the creativity of imagination in evil and ways to shed blood and to destroy. In fact, corruption and violence constitute major aspects of the world's entertainment, the source of enjoyment, a so-called escape from real life. In the raw and vile manner in which the violence occurs, it would appear that all shame is gone from the earth. Whereas in the beginning of creation there was shame because of sin, now all shame is lost.

We have become numb and callous to violence, because it is everywhere. We see no need to cringe at the sight of another human being tortured, decapitated, or blown to bits (in entertainment or in life). We fool ourselves that this does not affect us, even though it is being fed into the soul. And this is a symbol that speaks to God.

It is so even among children. What is enormously disturbing is that little children are often the victims of the horrific decomposition in society. And there are children who themselves feel the need to commit such violence upon each other. At such an early age as we now see mass violence committed by children, this bears the signs of a corrupted imagination where there ought to be some measure of natural simplicity left in the world.

The measure of youth violence has terrifying spiritual symbolism with the youth cutting off the youth. It speaks of a world that is corrupting its future—and it speaks of the future that is cutting off itself. When even the youth is corrupted, it says to God that "all flesh has corrupted his way."

When children cut off abruptly, the lives of young children in mass shootings, before they have a chance to grow and strive; these are spiritual symbols of finality. This is an affront to God and the covenant. This goes against every doctrine of the covenant. And this speaks to us of enormous consequences.

And the corruption that we see in all the major pillars of society is even in the church and places of prayer. And there is much opposition and resistance as God seeks to cleanse these places in preparation for His return.

There's all of this, even as God watches.

Reasons why God Sheds Light—Light Exposes

Corruption and violence brings much darkness upon the world. Light exposes what is in the darkness and redirects our attention. As God sheds His light, secrets that were once hidden in the darkness are brought to light.

That light that is being shed upon the world can be seen through the many revelations that expose—by means of scandal, betrayal, gossip, etc., and news broadcasts that uncover the inner secrets of the world.

As sin is exposed and brought to the world's attention by natural means, God is shedding spiritual light to enable us to be mindful of our sins, so that we can be redirected from sin and turn to the light, Jesus Christ.

The shedding of light upon corruption and violence is revelation of the mercy of God. As the light exposes, it calls our attention to the things God wants us to address. We are able to bring them out from the hiding place and confront them, so that they can be purged and washed away. The light of Christ cleanses us from sin.

Consequently, what is occurring has spiritual symbolism that speaks to each of us. It is an opportunity for us to examine our own lives. It is a spiritual opportunity for all people to awaken, to know that all is not well and that there is need to return to our duty to God. It says that secret sins that are hidden deep within the soul, (and have not been cleansed by Christ), will be exposed before God on the day of His coming, when the light of Christ is revealed. By the mercy of God, we are awakened out of the darkness of spiritual slumber by the light, and are called to repentance and forgiveness so that Christ may make us ready.

As the media sheds light on the trial of O.J. Simpson, God is pointing us to a much broader spiritual mission, as He puts the spotlight on a world of corruption and violence. And God spreads the divine message of warning by reminding us of the last time He confirmed His covenant with the symbol of the rainbow.

The Spiritual Symbols and Their Meaning

There is much spiritual symbolism in this cohesive series of events that relate to the O.J. Simpson murder trial and the program *20/20*.

And there is a greater spiritual correlation that is being revealed. Let us focus on the initial layer of interpretation, and in the following volumes, we will continue to examine this message.

Program *20/20:* There are two major observations that reveal the same message. First, the media with great fervor spread the details of the trial around the world, and there was avid worldwide interest. Second, the program was used by the divine providence as the impetus for my conversation that spread from country to country and from continent to continent.

One point is common. It relates to the divine intention that light must be shed to expose a world of corruption and violence. The two actions represent that God is confirming His divine purpose and intention. He spreads it from the program to the conversation and expands it from a single issue to a much greater worldwide issue.

What God is revealing is that there is a message of warning that must be spread to the world. It says that God is observing and acknowledging the overspreading of corruption and violence.

The anger that God feels when He speaks of corruption and violence represents that this is, without any doubt, a divine warning that must be echoed in every corner of the world, from country to country and continent to continent. And God is bringing our collective attention to this divine warning.

O. J. Simpson Murder Trial: Consequently, the trial of O.J. Simpson is much bigger that it seems. It has spiritual correlation that makes it far greater than a trial for the murder of two persons.

The O. J. Simpson murder trial is another earthly symbol pointing to a spiritual message. This event is a spiritual symbol of corruption and violence that God is using to focus our attention on the message of warning.

Thus, it is well known as a worldwide phenomenon, a common denominator among us, a symbol that points to the greater problem of corruption and violence throughout the world. And just as the trial was the focal point of worldwide attention, corruption and violence is the focal point of God's spiritual message and conveys His intention.

It has universal appeal. And God has established it as a universal spiritual symbol of corruption and violence to convey an important spiritual message to the world. Therefore, God points to it through coincidence; enabling a heightened awareness to gain our attention by divine providence and intervention.

Thus, the mysterious link between the trial and the powerful revelation of the covenant confirmation represents the spiritual correlation that God has established. Therefore, by God's providence there became a fervent worldwide interest as never seen before in a case of trial for murder. And God watched along with us as the details of it spread from country to country and from continent to continent, just as my conversation on that sacred night. It is determined by divine providence for the purpose of a spiritual instrument that God would use to focus our attention around the matters of corruption and violence.

Symbol of Tribulation

Thus, the so-called "trial of the century" has parallel spiritual correlation that God is revealing. The trial is a symbol that marks the beginning of the tribulation in Bible prophecy.

Tribulation signifies trouble, trial, suffering, pain, distress, misery and problems. The trial as a worldwide phenomenon is a symbol that marks this spiritual milestone. It is symbolic of "time of trouble" and "time of trial."

The Scriptures describe the tribulation as a time of spiritual trial when "many shall be purified and made white, and tried" (Daniel 12:10). And it says, "there shall be a time of trouble, such as never was since there was a nation even to that same time" (Daniel 12:1). The natural trial of O. J. Simpson is a symbol that points to the greater spiritual trial for the world that is indicative of the tribulation period. It marks a milestone in prophecy.

The tribulation period is a time when corruption will be exposed. Therefore, it would be much increased as information that sheds light upon it is increased. This increase in information is foretold in the book of Daniel, which says, "many shall run to and fro, and knowledge shall be increased" (Daniel 12:4). Running to and fro is a symbol of restlessness, confusion, and instability of morals, beliefs, ideology and behavior.

Consequently, it marks the rise of spiritual indignation when many manifest resentment and righteous anger, being cross and expressing much fury and offense to the things of God. This anger and resentment is a symbol that conveys a world at enmity with God. A world at enmity with God is reflected in a world also much at enmity among itself.

And so it is a time of turmoil and distress, for individuals as well as the greater political, economic, and other systems that rule the world. And there seems to be no viable solutions, despite all the resources in the world. Thus, we have much turmoil brought about by divisions and the result is the blight that takes hold when there is no peace.

The increasing corruption and violence are indicators of the tribulation that is both natural and spiritual. We will have peace when we are first at peace with God.

Trinity of Divine Warnings

There is a trinity of divine messages of warning. In order to interpret the messages we must look at the victims. They are the symbols that point us to what God is seeking to say. There are the woman and the man who were the victims in the trial, and there are the victims referenced in the conversation that include the millions of victims of violence, corruption, injustice, oppression and strife around the world.

First, the symbol of the woman represents the family, and this is a message of warning regarding violence, corruption, deceit, jealousy and strife within the family.

Second, the symbol of the man represents our neighbor. And this is a message of warning regarding violence, hatred, covetousness, envy, jealousy, revenge and strife against our neighbor. We are called to brotherly love.

Third, the victims around the world are symbols that expand this message and make it grand, comprehensive, all-inclusive, and complete. This speaks to us of violence and corruption in the wider society, within and among nations through wars, unrest and strife, injustice and oppression. The increasing corruption and violence are precursors to divine consequences. This third and all-encompassing warning makes it final as God directs it and overspreads it to every continent.

These constitute a trinity of divine messages and initial warnings that God is revealing by the symbol of the trial. There is much more.

God is in Time of Grief

"And it repented the LORD that he had made man on the earth, and it grieved him at his heart" (Genesis 6:6). Likewise, it is now. This says that God is now in time of grief just as it was in time of Noah. The grief in the earth is reflective of the grief in heaven as God grieves along with us.

Spilled blood cries to God. When Cain killed Abel, God asked him, "What hast thou done? The voice of thy brother's blood crieth unto me from the ground. And now art thou cursed from the earth, which hath opened her mouth to receive thy brother's blood from thy hand" (Genesis 4:10–11). The earth from whence mankind is created cries to God when it receives spilled blood. It was never meant to be this way.

Divine justice dictates that spilled blood cries to God for justice and vengeance. The perfect justice of God affirms this. And God said to Cain, "When thou tillest the ground, it shall not henceforth yield unto thee her strength; a fugitive and a vagabond shalt thou be in the earth" (Genesis 4:12). We also read in the book of Revelation, at the opening of the fifth seal, "the souls of them that were slain for the word of God, and for the testimony which they held ... cried with a loud voice, saying, How long, O Lord, holy and true, dost thou not judge and avenge our blood on them that dwell on the earth?" (Revelation 6:9–10).

The justice that is required by the measure of spilled blood, which we see in the earth, tells us that this violence is a precursor to judgment. It tells us that God cannot violate His own laws of justice by refraining forever to act according to the cries for justice. God is merciful and long-suffering, but has a day and time appointed when He will judge.

The fact that God revealed Himself with such extreme degree of divine openness exposes the measure of grief and anger that is within His heart, just as it was in the time of Noah. For it would require this level of manifestation, as never since ancient time, to bring these warnings, and direct our collective attention to the corruption and violence, as "nation rise up against nation, and kingdom against kingdom," just as it is foretold in the prophecies of the Bible.

Divine Presence

So how near is God? I am continually reminded that God is everywhere, involved in all the details, a silent listener in every conversation. For the evidence is clear.

At this point, we should not ask whether God does exist, whether He sees the violence, or whether He knows of our distress. Know that God is present, observing all of the details, and is aware (before we are) of what is hidden deep within our hearts.

But God is long-suffering in that He waits upon us, although divine justice represents that sin brings consequences. He gives us the opportunity to awaken, as God sheds light upon the world, that this may enable us to return to our duty and to repent.

Seven years later, there were the attacks of September 11, 2001—another momentous spiritual milestone of the tribulation. This and other numerous acts of violence that are in the news, God continues to declare that His eyes have seen by revealing prophecy—some years in advance including the Sandy Hook School shootings that God revealed while I was in evening prayer in September 1995. This is another milestone in the timeline of the tribulation. And God's eyes are beholding the scandals of the church, the corruption and deceit of spiritually dark places of prayer, and the violence that is both within and against places of religion—also affirmed by prophetic revelation through prayer. The kind of prophetic revelations that I receive of the Lord, and the fact that they are numerous, affirms that they are expressions of God's state of grief. And as I watch the news on television, I am mindful that the eyes of the Lord are in every place.

In fact, God reveals even those circumstances that do not reach the wider attention of the media. This is the degree to which God is watching us and is observing every detail.

God is Merciful and Long-suffering

Though we ignore and reject Him, Christ does not change His redemptive love. His primary focus is to redeem us. His wish is that none should perish. God is merciful and willing to forgive. The Scriptures bring us that divine assurance.

> As many as I love, I rebuke and chasten: be zealous therefore, and repent. Behold, I stand at the door, and knock: if any man hear my voice, and open the door, I will

come in to him, and will sup with him, and he with me.
To him that overcometh will I grant to sit with me in my
throne, even as I also overcame, and am set down with my
Father in his throne. (Revelation 3:19–21)

This door is what opens our hearts.

We are living in a time of enormous spiritual outpouring, yet
there is enormous spiritual darkness in a world that remains unaware
and is oblivious to the work of grace that is occurring in these last
days. The Scriptures say,

For as in the days that were before the flood they were
eating and drinking, marrying and giving in marriage,
until the day that Noe entered into the ark. And knew not
until the flood came, and took them all away; so shall also
the coming of the Son of man be. (Matthew 24:38–39)

That is not to say that life should not continue its natural course.
Of course not! However, this is warning that the care and distractions
of daily living can keep us spiritually unaware and cause us to lose
sight of spiritual preparation. As we focus on the temporal, we ought
not to forget the spiritual and eternal, for this is the primary reason
we exist.

Let us all do our part for the cause of peace, one person and one
day at a time. We are reminded that God can use any of us. We don't
have to be "good enough," by the false standards of the world.

In fact, those who are much hated, despised, scorned, and
disregarded as the least among us are those that God uses. Actually,
God uses us even without our knowledge as in the circumstances
of Barbara Walters and her team that produced the *20/20* television
program on that sacred evening on March 15, 1996. God has the
power to make us fit to do whatever He has for us to do.

CHAPTER 33

AN IMMEASURABLE MERCY

The fact that I am able to write this first volume is declaration of a miracle. For it is not by my own efforts, understanding, or scholarship, nor is it by Bible study. And it is not by seminary, for I am not a theologian, but by the merciful and patient guidance of God, who gives the gift of spiritual skills by the power of His Holy Spirit.

I never would have thought that the symbols could mean this much. In fact, my understanding remained minuscule until I began to write. And as I sat at the computer with just a few pages of notes on the desk in front of me, God committed His Word to my memory and flourished my understanding. I could hardly type fast enough to keep pace with the knowledge that God was revealing. I never could have imagined that, a few years later, the interpretation would blossom into volumes.

And God taught me how to surrender everything in faith while knowing that God would guide me into truth and keep it safely written upon my heart. Consequently, I had no need to look here and there for the knowledge that should come only from God.

God has consecrated my life and caused me to know true silence. And so I wrote in complete silence from everything else but quiet prayer. I learned that, in silence and with patience, God communes with us. God is able to reach us in quietness and give us spiritual understanding when we are silent. Every word of this book was written by prayer, and in quietness, in the posture of listening to God. And this symbol says to God that I hunger for every word that

He would say. I learned that silence is a medicine for the body and a pathway to the soul.

The Precious Name of Jesus

It seems redundant to say that God is real and that He answers prayer. For everyone who had doubted before should know that by now. God has affirmed Himself on numerous occasions in the course of this interpretation and has openly conveyed His spiritual presence. The words of the book of Jeremiah are faithful and true: "And ye shall seek me, and find me, when ye shall search for me with all your heart" (Jeremiah 29:13). This prayer is where it began for me.

Psalm 37 says, "Delight thyself also in the LORD: and he shall give thee the desires of thine heart. Commit thy way unto the LORD; trust also in him; and he shall bring it to pass" (Psalm 37:4). Jesus said, "And whatsoever ye shall ask in my name, that will I do, that the Father may be glorified in the Son. If ye shall ask any thing in my name, I will do it" (John 14:13–14). And the Scriptures say, "And this is the confidence that we have in him, that, if we ask any thing according to his will, he heareth us" (1 John 5:14).

I want everyone to know that there is immense power available to us in the name of Jesus and great power on the pages of the Bible. Anyone can call upon the name of Jesus, without regard to who you are, what you have done, or to what religion or group you belong.

Life-Study Fellowship is a nondenominational organization, and it is remarkable that this is where God would direct me for prayer. This symbol represents that God does not favor one religious denomination over the other in His call for us to return. But it is clear that the only way of salvation is by the precious blood of Jesus Christ. It is His desire that all would return to Him and be saved by the power of His cleansing blood. There being no preference affirms that Christ is declaring a message of mercy to all people.

There is no other God but Jesus, and no other way of grace, so call upon Jesus. God is present and available in places of faithful prayer according to His will. He is mindful of each of us and hears us individually. For this assurance rests upon the covenant. And there is no other book like the Bible if it is uncorrupted by the intervention of error, so choose wisely and by prayer. The same words that brought creation into being are available to each of us, and God is faithful.

No Greater Blessing

There is no greater blessing than knowing, by the gift of the revelation of God, of the surety of one's redemption. It is far greater than a human heart and mind can fully comprehend. And there is nothing we will ever be able to do to deserve it. For it is not because I prayed, but rather it is Christ who ordained the prayers and the purpose. "Who hath saved us, and called us with an holy calling, not according to our works, but according to his own purpose and grace, which was given us in Christ Jesus before the world began" (2 Timothy 1:9). And the Scriptures say, "Having made known unto us the mystery of his will, according to his good pleasure which he had purposed in himself" (Ephesians 1:9).

I am not overtly, or exceedingly religious, but I do love God passionately and desire to know Him and to please Him. Thus, I am devoted to divine reverence and am deeply and devoutly mindful of the majesty of God. The gifts that enable us in the love of God are available to each of us through Jesus Christ.

Nevertheless, redemption is not an easy road but one that is encrusted by deep and prolonged suffering, in double measure, just as the blessings of the covenant are promised in double measure. It is a road that our forefathers have gone before us and it will be the same for us. A covenanted life involves periods of clustered difficulties, troubles, and afflictions. It includes successive periods of misfortune, misery, injustice, disappointments, persecutions, and hardships that come in strange and deeply burdensome ways, from multiple sources at once, and in a manner that is beyond our control. There is hatred without reason and scorn without a purpose. These conditions converge to test and try our faith so that it becomes strong.

A covenanted life is not for the faint of heart. We read in the Bible of the anguish of Job and the afflictions he endured. God allowed Satan to test and try Job's faith. "And the LORD said unto Satan, Behold, all that he hath is in thy power; only upon himself put not forth thine hand" (Job 1:12). And Satan destroyed his health, wealth, and children.

At the same time, we must have compassion for those who afflict us, and we must pray for them, love and forgive them, and wish the best for them. For they do not know what they do, and are unaware that they are part of a spiritual process. Testing and trial comes from the spirit of Satan through them just as the affliction of Job was the work of Satan. It is unfortunate that they are used in this manner. And while they afflict, they believe they are doing God a favor and that it is justified. They do not know that it is a false god that they please. Without repentance, there will sure be personal consequences.

But this work of evil God uses for good. And God allows the furnace of afflictions by measure, as much as we are able, and sets limits upon them. His protection and mercy are always available.

I often wondered why God would reveal Himself in this manner. However, the answer became clear when my afflictions began. The sacred vision enabled me to have perfect faith that I was in the midst of a spiritual work and that God was also in the middle of the fire. If I had not known, I would not have endured. My afflicters would have caused me to be no longer on this earth. Job wished he had died at birth. This is the way it is when the soul is in anguish. (An illumination of this kind of suffering is detailed in a later volume.)

Indeed, we should not expect it to be easy, for the Bible says "these are they that have come out of great tribulation ..." And God promised to "wipe away every tear from our eyes."

Nevertheless, I am able to testify that if we use our suffering wisely, it is for good. The sorrow of suffering facilitates our repentance and strengthens our faith. And with this suffering comes the blessing of wisdom and deeper spiritual understanding. Through it all, I have come to know the love of God.

Consequently, I choose not to dwell on my suffering because I have benefitted greatly. When we have come to know the love of God, all is well and all is complete. Every need is supplied, all hopes have been accomplished, and wishes fulfilled, every act of hate is an occasion of forgiveness, a time of suffering is an opportunity for strength, through injustice is the knowledge of the justice of God, in disappointment is a time of faith, in pain is the expectation of deliverance, and in tribulation is a way for patience. When we understand more, we are also able to love more. When God gives us understanding, God also gives us peace that surpasses our own comprehension. And there is no fear if we walk with God.

Bibliography

Abraham, A. Kenneth (ed.) *The KJV Matthew Henry Study Bible.* USA: World Bible Publishers, Inc., 1994.

English, E. Schuyler, and Bishop Bower, Marian et al (ed.). *Pilgrim Edition of the Holy Bible, Authorized King James Version.* New York: Oxford University Press, Inc., 1952.

FAITH Magazine, the official magazine of Life-Study Fellowship, World Headquarters, Noroton, Connecticut, published by Life-Study Fellowship Foundation, Inc.

Shorter Oxford English Dictionary on Historical Principles. Edited by Angus Stevenson et al. Sixth Edition. Vol. 1. New York: Oxford University Press, 2007.

The Holy Bible, Authorized King James Version Personal Gift Edition. Wheaton, Illinois: Tyndale House Publishers, Inc., 1976, 1979.

References

i.   *Prayer for Deeper Spiritual Understanding!* Life Study Fellowship, Noroton, Connecticut.

ii.   *Prayer May I Always Hear the Voice of the Lord Answering My Prayers!* Life Study Fellowship, Noroton, Connecticut.

iii.   *Prayer that I May Walk Close To Thee, My Lord!* Life Study Fellowship, Noroton, Connecticut.

iv.   See reference (ii) above.

v.   English, Schuyler and Bishop Bower, Marian et al (ed.). *Pilgrim Edition of the Holy Bible, Authorized King James Version.* New York: Oxford University Press, Inc., 1952, p. 1,708.

vi.   Abraham, A. Kenneth (ed.). *The KJV Matthew Henry Study Bible.* USA: World Bible Publishers. Inc., 1994, p. 43.

vii.   "covenant, n." *Shorter Oxford Dictionary: On Historical Principles.* Angus Stevenson et al (ed.). Sixth Edition, Vol. 1. New York: Oxford University Press. 2007, p. 544

viii.   Abraham, A. Kenneth (ed.). *KJV Matthew Henry Study Bible.* USA: World Bible Publishers. Inc, 1994, p. 1, 2.

ix.   English, Schuyler and Bishop Bower, Marian et al (ed.). *Pilgrim Edition of the Holy Bible, Authorized King James Version.* New York: Oxford University Press, Inc. 1952, p. 1,685.

INDEX

A

Abraham x, 30, 31, 53, 66, 86, 93,
109, 110, 112, 129, 135, 171, 191,
193, 194, 200, 217, 221, 225, 232,
233, 234, 261, 263
Afflictions 3, 66, 106, 108, 156, 157,
158, 163, 164, 187, 189, 190, 200,
204, 240, 258, 259
Almighty v, 4, 52, 116, 125, 132, 172,
238
ancient languages 47
ancient times 11, 37, 43, 51, 53, 69,
117, 178
armour of God 108
astonishing 14, 18, 22, 34, 114
atonement 11, 168, 169, 223, 224

B

baptism 11, 12, 125, 160
baptized 4, 121, 158
Barbara Walters 15, 16, 243, 244, 255
beloved condition 67
blessings 7, 47, 48, 65, 66, 88, 93, 105,
109, 111, 147, 151, 157, 158, 168,
193, 212, 213, 220, 221, 233, 234,
235, 240, 242, 258
blood v, 11, 31, 37, 55, 79, 100, 116,
117, 125, 137, 140, 144, 153, 166,
167, 168, 169, 170, 171, 172, 173,
174, 187, 195, 196, 200, 201, 203,
205, 206, 213, 214, 219, 236, 238,
246, 252, 253, 257
blue 20, 27, 87, 184, 196, 197
burning light 20, 21, 183, 191

C

candle 12, 21, 141, 183, 192, 193, 195,
201, 232
christened 4

Christopher Darden 15
clouds 20, 164, 165, 186
code of creation 139, 141, 147, 148
coincidences 8, 9, 10, 12, 15, 18, 34,
35, 96, 98, 110, 111, 112, 155,
174, 183
coincidences, double 9, 155
Cokesbury Bookstore 28, 29, 30
Colors 19, 20, 27, 184, 196, 197
commandments 39, 53, 54, 145, 146,
196
communed 10, 41, 52, 59, 66, 98
communion 10, 18, 47, 68, 83, 84, 86,
87, 91, 92, 93, 134, 164, 208, 211,
229
consecration 36, 37, 40, 161, 193, 206,
219
consummation 191, 237
corruption 16, 17, 22, 175, 177, 179,
180, 182, 201, 230, 244, 245,
246, 247, 248, 249, 250, 251,
252, 253, 254
Covenant v, ix, x, 25, 27, 40, 48, 52,
53, 56, 57, 61, 66, 74, 76, 78, 82,
83, 86, 92, 93, 95, 99, 108, 109,
110, 111, 112, 115, 116, 117, 118,
120, 123, 125, 128, 129, 132, 135,
139, 140, 141, 142, 143, 144, 145,
146, 147, 148, 149, 151, 152, 153,
154, 156, 157, 158, 159, 160, 163,
166, 167, 168, 169, 171, 172, 173,
174, 175, 176, 177, 178, 179, 180,
181, 183, 184, 185, 191, 193, 194,
196, 198, 204, 205, 206, 207,
209, 210, 211, 212, 213, 214, 215,
216, 217, 218, 219, 220, 221, 222,
223, 224, 225, 226, 227, 228,
229, 230, 231, 232, 233, 234, 235,
236, 237, 238, 240, 243, 244,
246, 247, 248, 250, 258, 263
covenant communion 92

covenant, confirming 53, 110, 115, 159, 209, 231, 232
covenanted life v, ix, 40, 84, 219, 220, 240, 258, 259
Covenant of grace v, x, 83, 116, 123, 153, 157, 167, 194, 206, 213, 214, 215, 224, 225, 234, 236
covenant of peace 221, 223, 224
covenant of priesthood 221, 223, 224
covenant of salt 221, 222
Covenant portion 76, 156
crucifixion 11, 12, 213, 214
curses 56, 149, 151

D

Daniel's prayer 14, 15, 17, 105, 110, 166, 221, 239
deeper spiritual understanding ix, 5, 10, 25, 32, 33, 36, 42, 44, 45, 50, 51, 65, 83, 84, 85, 86, 87, 89, 91, 96, 106, 113, 122, 123, 133, 208, 220, 239, 260, 263
deliverer 114, 116, 167, 199, 235, 241
diamond 20, 21, 196, 198
discerned 13, 43
distance 128, 187
divine intervention 8, 13, 14, 22, 23, 36, 46, 72, 76, 96, 105, 129, 155, 183
divine justice 149, 150, 151, 152, 153, 190, 243, 253, 254
divine presence 68, 110, 119, 226, 253
divine providences 8, 9, 15, 34, 98, 111, 119
divine wisdom 5, 67, 83, 84, 208, 215
double coincidences 9, 155
dreams 13, 64, 85, 186, 239, 240
duty of a watchman 194

E

Easter 11, 12, 24, 93
eight 117, 201, 206, 207, 224, 225, 227, 228, 237
emerald 19, 20, 155, 162, 163, 176, 197

enlightenment ix, 24, 25, 32, 48, 50, 83, 121, 122, 123, 128, 133, 134, 160, 171, 192, 193, 199, 207
equilibrium 151, 152, 153
eternal life v, 35, 50, 90, 93, 99, 132, 138, 150, 162, 167, 211, 216
extreme intervention 22
eyes open 97, 121, 122, 123, 124, 171, 220

F

faith 4, 5, 12, 23, 28, 32, 34, 36, 37, 39, 40, 41, 42, 46, 47, 50, 59, 63, 66, 67, 85, 86, 94, 97, 99, 107, 108, 109, 126, 129, 131, 134, 146, 152, 158, 163, 164, 171, 174, 177, 189, 191, 194, 204, 208, 218, 221, 227, 229, 232, 242, 256, 259, 260, 261
faithful 52, 118, 128, 257, 258
Faith Magazine 4, 5, 261
fasting 11, 12, 23, 57
fellowship 4, 5, 6, 44, 74, 86, 119, 200, 257, 261, 263
fire 17, 20, 21, 22, 61, 63, 92, 107, 149, 175, 181, 182, 183, 185, 186, 187, 188, 189, 190, 191, 193, 196, 198, 199, 201, 231, 232, 233, 237, 239, 259
First fruits 157
five 28, 71, 72, 80, 145, 146, 188
flame of fire 20, 21, 185, 233
flaming rainbow 21, 182, 183, 196, 201, 232
foundation of Christ 107
four 61, 62, 71, 117, 118, 129, 137, 144, 148, 149, 173, 174, 202, 235
furnace 21, 63, 92, 107, 183, 185, 188, 189, 190, 191, 199, 200, 201, 232, 259

G

Genocide and ethnic cleansing 16
God of Moses 21, 233
God, presence of 9, 23, 44, 68, 105, 108, 119, 132, 164, 185, 198, 245

God's heart 17, 73, 172, 180
God the creator 214
gold 13, 14, 105, 106, 107, 108, 109, 187, 188, 189, 197, 206
gold, head of 13, 14, 105, 108, 109, 206
Good Friday 11, 12
gospel 31, 47, 48, 50, 52, 53, 64, 66, 70, 83, 84, 108, 110, 121, 124, 136, 155, 160, 171, 174, 181, 185, 186, 188, 192, 193, 195, 199, 202, 203, 224, 238, 239
green v, 19, 20, 27, 38, 58, 155, 162, 163, 184, 196
grief 22, 38, 49, 180, 245, 252, 253, 254
guidance 5, 6, 7, 9, 10, 32, 33, 35, 40, 42, 43, 47, 85, 87, 112, 124, 125, 134, 158, 164, 192, 199, 207, 208, 217, 221, 245, 256

H

healing 126, 161, 163
heaven 3, 16, 23, 25, 39, 58, 61, 62, 64, 65, 75, 85, 91, 92, 93, 97, 105, 106, 113, 116, 117, 120, 122, 128, 129, 130, 131, 133, 137, 138, 145, 146, 149, 150, 151, 152, 158, 163, 164, 171, 172, 173, 174, 176, 182, 184, 185, 186, 190, 191, 195, 197, 198, 199, 204, 211, 224, 229, 231, 235, 236, 239, 241, 252
heavenly access 119, 120, 122
heir 194
hieroglyphic inscription 26
holiness 37, 50, 70, 95, 100, 161, 189, 190, 196, 203, 221, 233
Holy Saturday 11, 12
Holy Spirit 6, 10, 14, 18, 23, 25, 32, 33, 34, 36, 38, 40, 43, 44, 46, 47, 48, 50, 51, 52, 64, 65, 67, 70, 71, 74, 75, 83, 84, 85, 87, 97, 98, 100, 106, 111, 116, 119, 120, 121, 122, 125, 126, 130, 132, 133, 134, 141, 157, 160, 164, 172, 174, 178, 179, 185, 186, 187, 188, 193, 198,

207, 208, 210, 212, 219, 221, 228, 238, 241, 242, 256
Holy Trinity 36, 132, 134, 196, 238
holy week 11, 24
humility 23, 88

I

Illumination x, 9, 27, 48, 259
instruments 32, 108, 134, 145
intervention v, 8, 9, 12, 13, 14, 15, 22, 23, 26, 36, 46, 72, 74, 76, 77, 96, 98, 105, 116, 129, 155, 174, 183, 250, 258
Israel 53, 54, 56, 57, 59, 62, 63, 87, 88, 92, 116, 117, 124, 142, 156, 158, 161, 164, 170, 177, 190, 198, 205, 219, 223, 224, 225, 234, 235
Israeli-Palestinian conflict 16
Israel, natural 117, 235
Israel, spiritual 116, 198, 234, 235

J

jewels 19, 198
judge 87, 144, 191, 231, 232, 253
judgment 40, 54, 57, 58, 59, 65, 69, 73, 87, 89, 122, 137, 138, 170, 177, 188, 190, 205, 231, 232, 253
justice 87, 88, 149, 150, 151, 152, 153, 157, 170, 182, 190, 243, 253, 254, 260
justification 77, 146, 170

K

Kingdom 5, 32, 39, 57, 75, 85, 88, 106, 108, 115, 117, 122, 126, 134, 136, 141, 146, 161, 176, 181, 184, 191, 202, 235, 236, 241, 242, 253
knowledge ix, x, 3, 5, 6, 7, 8, 9, 10, 13, 17, 25, 26, 28, 32, 33, 38, 41, 43, 44, 45, 46, 47, 48, 50, 52, 61, 64, 65, 67, 68, 76, 79, 82, 83, 85, 86, 87, 88, 90, 91, 92, 94, 95, 96, 99, 100, 106, 111, 112, 113, 119, 120, 121, 123, 133, 134, 139, 142, 144, 155, 159, 164, 178, 193, 199, 202, 203, 207, 208, 209, 214, 217,

218, 220, 221, 239, 251, 255, 256, 260

L

Lamb 162, 172, 195, 203, 213, 214, 216, 238
lamp 21, 92, 108, 183, 191, 192, 193, 194, 195, 199, 201, 232, 234, 239
Lent 11, 12, 23, 93, 114
Life Study Fellowship 5, 263
light 5, 12, 14, 20, 21, 43, 60, 63, 64, 65, 70, 75, 83, 92, 121, 122, 123, 124, 130, 139, 148, 149, 160, 164, 183, 186, 191, 192, 193, 195, 196, 197, 198, 199, 200, 201, 208, 216, 228, 237, 238, 243, 245, 247, 248, 249, 251, 254

M

March 13, 15, 16, 105, 110, 114, 115, 116, 117, 201, 206, 221, 234, 241, 244, 255
mediator 125, 167, 234
mercy x, 7, 8, 38, 49, 51, 57, 58, 59, 60, 65, 66, 76, 78, 81, 82, 86, 93, 100, 101, 109, 114, 129, 130, 153, 158, 159, 162, 164, 170, 171, 173, 183, 189, 196, 204, 205, 206, 214, 215, 217, 220, 221, 224, 227, 231, 232, 240, 242, 248, 256, 257, 259
miraculous event 15, 18
movement 20, 127, 130, 166, 171, 172, 174
mysteries of the kingdom 85

N

natural 8, 41, 64, 68, 74, 82, 85, 97, 98, 100, 111, 117, 120, 121, 125, 135, 139, 140, 141, 146, 150, 151, 153, 158, 159, 176, 210, 211, 213, 218, 228, 229, 233, 235, 236, 243, 247, 248, 250, 251, 255
nature v, ix, 13, 20, 25, 67, 69, 73, 77, 84, 88, 132, 135, 139, 140, 146, 147, 148, 149, 152, 153, 162, 172, 175, 179, 184, 210, 211, 212, 214,

216, 217, 222, 223, 224, 230, 231, 237
new birth 84, 141, 157, 160
Noah x, 16, 17, 66, 114, 129, 159, 171, 175, 177, 178, 179, 180, 181, 182, 204, 205, 206, 225, 230, 231, 232, 244, 245, 246, 252, 253
Noah's ark 114
nondenominational 4, 257

O

O. J. Simpson murder trial 15, 244, 249
old testament 8, 52, 53, 60, 91, 94, 161, 168, 197, 205, 217
omnipotent 4
omnipresent 4
overcome 13, 130, 131
overshadowing 125, 126, 164, 241, 242

P

parable 111, 112, 113, 136, 137, 151, 159, 190, 194, 208, 239
Pharaoh 155, 156
posture of penitence 23
precious jewels 19
preparation 9, 10, 12, 49, 50, 65, 68, 96, 97, 100, 107, 110, 117, 118, 119, 120, 121, 122, 146, 156, 158, 160, 180, 188, 194, 195, 201, 203, 219, 247, 255
Program 20/20 15, 244, 245, 248, 249
promise 22, 23, 25, 40, 53, 59, 63, 66, 85, 128, 129, 179, 182, 183, 192, 194, 209, 210, 219, 221, 227, 230, 231, 232, 235, 236, 238
prophecy 22, 51, 62, 64, 67, 85, 91, 113, 137, 155, 160, 173, 176, 179, 182, 183, 186, 189, 195, 202, 203, 213, 214, 239, 240, 250, 251, 254
protection 29, 36, 56, 57, 66, 71, 74, 76, 78, 81, 89, 93, 108, 109, 114, 116, 117, 125, 159, 170, 189, 199, 220, 221, 224, 232, 259
providence v, 8, 9, 12, 14, 15, 17, 23, 26, 34, 42, 43, 59, 64, 74, 76, 94,

97, 98, 105, 111, 119, 129, 135,
205, 214, 217, 243, 244, 249, 250
Purim 114, 115, 116, 117, 234, 235

Q

Questions 3, 4, 25, 27, 99
quickening 33, 52, 68, 84, 85, 100,
111, 120, 121, 123, 124, 174, 195,
215, 219

R

rainbow 17, 20, 21, 22, 25, 27, 61, 62,
162, 172, 175, 176, 179, 180, 181,
182, 183, 184, 196, 201, 230, 231,
232, 239, 248
rainbow, emerging 20, 183
raindrops 19, 139, 155, 157, 158, 160,
162, 183, 196, 230, 240
ratification 167, 191, 194
reconciliation 39, 86, 116, 130, 169,
183, 196, 203, 219, 220, 238
redeem 39, 254
redemption v, 12, 37, 65, 82, 85, 93,
99, 105, 106, 107, 118, 124, 128,
146, 165, 168, 170, 172, 174, 183,
192, 195, 199, 203, 216, 219, 225,
230, 237, 258
redirected life 34, 36
regeneration 84, 134, 141, 162, 163,
220, 231
repentance 11, 39, 128, 144, 146, 219,
248, 259, 260
rest 7, 39, 100, 107, 115, 127, 130, 163,
197, 200, 203, 204, 220, 242, 258
resurrection 11, 12, 60, 93, 106, 130,
138, 160, 174, 198, 200, 229, 231,
237, 242
reward 39, 41, 44, 45, 53, 107, 109,
110, 150, 151, 152, 187, 188, 203
righteousness v, 38, 40, 65, 70, 86, 88,
95, 100, 109, 122, 123, 124, 128,
133, 145, 149, 152, 153, 156, 161,
162, 167, 170, 174, 182, 188, 196,
197, 199, 203, 212, 217, 232
ruby 20, 166

S

sacred dream 13, 14, 15, 43, 240
sacred moment 18
sacred symbolism 62, 96
sacred visions, the effects 64, 67, 68
safety 66, 109, 114, 115, 125, 159, 170,
173, 199, 206, 224
Salvation 25, 33, 72, 75, 94, 109, 130,
136, 159, 170, 181, 183, 199, 206,
211, 257
Sanctification 37, 50, 66, 161, 169,
203, 219
sapphire 20, 175, 196, 197
savior 11, 91, 126, 160, 166, 211, 214,
235, 236, 241, 242
scarlet v, 20, 87, 166, 168, 169, 170,
174, 197
seal 116, 117, 119, 137, 167, 171, 172,
173, 174, 176, 178, 196, 201, 203,
204, 209, 236, 253
sealing of the 144,000 173
secret treasure 61, 64, 67, 85, 86, 173
service 12, 24, 37, 49, 65, 72, 73, 74,
86, 87, 95, 109, 121, 134, 145,
146, 193, 202, 222, 224, 242
service of light 12
seven candlesticks 201
seven priests 201, 202, 205
seven stars 201
seventh symbol 198
shield of God 105
sixteen 5, 117, 118
skill 51, 52, 67, 83, 85, 142, 193, 239,
240, 256
smitten by God 73
Solomon 54, 55, 56, 87, 88, 108, 174,
238
soul ix, 33, 38, 39, 70, 83, 84, 85, 86,
89, 90, 94, 98, 99, 100, 106, 107,
111, 119, 121, 123, 124, 125, 126,
128, 130, 133, 134, 143, 144, 150,
158, 160, 161, 162, 163, 168, 169,
173, 174, 187, 189, 192, 196, 197,
200, 205, 212, 216, 217, 219, 220,
240, 243, 247, 248, 253, 257, 259
spaces 19, 127, 128, 139, 146
special hands 30

spiritual alignment 8, 9, 10, 15, 18, 27, 41, 98, 111, 112
spiritual awareness 8, 10, 220
spiritual bond 6
spiritual gifts 5, 68, 83, 87, 88, 94, 106, 121, 123, 125
spiritual knowledge ix, 8, 9, 10, 25, 28, 32, 41, 44, 47, 48, 52, 67, 82, 85, 91, 100, 111, 112, 113, 120, 133, 134, 139, 208, 209, 217, 218, 220, 239
spiritual milestones 41, 82, 250, 254
spiritual preparation 68, 110, 119, 158, 255
spiritual understanding ix, 5, 10, 25, 27, 32, 33, 36, 42, 44, 45, 48, 50, 51, 65, 83, 84, 85, 86, 87, 89, 91, 96, 106, 113, 122, 123, 133, 199, 203, 208, 220, 239, 256, 260, 263
Stations of the cross 12
submission 23, 88
suddenness 96, 178
suffering 11, 16, 48, 69, 71, 73, 90, 99, 107, 131, 163, 192, 200, 215, 240, 250, 253, 254, 258, 259, 260
Supernatural 64, 68, 97, 98
symbols v, ix, x, 11, 18, 19, 20, 21, 22, 23, 25, 27, 33, 36, 37, 42, 45, 60, 61, 62, 64, 91, 92, 93, 94, 96, 97, 98, 99, 100, 101, 103, 110, 111, 112, 122, 125, 127, 128, 130, 132, 133, 134, 139, 146, 149, 151, 152, 153, 155, 164, 167, 168, 172, 175, 176, 177, 178, 182, 183, 191, 192, 193, 194, 197, 198, 201, 202, 206, 207, 224, 225, 226, 227, 228, 229, 230, 231, 232, 234, 236, 237, 238, 239, 241, 242, 243, 244, 245, 247, 248, 251, 252, 256
symbols, consecrated 94
symbols, divine 19
symbols, universal 101

T

testimony 66, 159, 160, 226, 253
testing 67, 106, 107, 118, 128, 157, 158, 183, 189, 204, 259

thanksgiving 14, 15, 17, 18, 43, 105, 110, 166, 220, 221, 239
three 12, 15, 18, 19, 20, 21, 29, 31, 33, 54, 55, 58, 61, 62, 63, 72, 75, 81, 127, 128, 132, 133, 134, 137, 138, 139, 143, 145, 146, 150, 167, 171, 175, 183, 184, 188, 191, 196, 197, 206, 232, 238
time x, 1, 3, 4, 6, 7, 9, 10, 11, 12, 13, 15, 16, 17, 20, 21, 22, 23, 24, 25, 26, 28, 29, 30, 31, 34, 35, 36, 37, 38, 41, 43, 46, 47, 49, 51, 53, 57, 58, 60, 62, 64, 66, 67, 69, 71, 72, 73, 74, 76, 79, 80, 96, 99, 101, 105, 108, 109, 113, 114, 115, 116, 117, 118, 119, 120, 125, 126, 127, 128, 130, 136, 137, 138, 145, 151, 158, 161, 168, 172, 173, 176, 177, 178, 179, 180, 181, 182, 186, 188, 189, 191, 194, 195, 196, 202, 203, 204, 205, 206, 209, 213, 214, 219, 226, 227, 229, 230, 231, 232, 235, 237, 239, 240, 241, 244, 245, 246, 248, 250, 251, 252, 253, 255, 259, 260
trance 13, 62, 80
transfiguration 63, 164, 241
trial 15, 16, 106, 107, 118, 128, 131, 157, 163, 183, 189, 204, 221, 243, 244, 245, 248, 249, 250, 251, 252, 259
tribulation 107, 108, 116, 118, 127, 128, 131, 136, 137, 163, 177, 183, 188, 203, 240, 250, 251, 254, 260
two 8, 9, 15, 19, 35, 62, 72, 75, 76, 77, 80, 110, 111, 112, 115, 117, 118, 125, 128, 139, 140, 141, 142, 143, 144, 145, 146, 147, 148, 150, 151, 155, 156, 157, 158, 159, 160, 162, 167, 170, 187, 188, 196, 201, 202, 206, 209, 218, 241, 243, 249
two births 141
two bodies 140, 141
two, code of creation 139, 141, 147, 148

U

unbelief 39

understanding ix, 5, 9, 10, 13, 15, 25, 27, 28, 29, 32, 33, 35, 36, 38, 39, 41, 42, 43, 44, 45, 47, 48, 50, 51, 52, 65, 66, 68, 83, 84, 85, 86, 87, 88, 89, 90, 91, 93, 96, 98, 99, 100, 106, 113, 121, 122, 123, 124, 128, 133, 134, 144, 154, 158, 160, 174, 193, 195, 199, 202, 203, 207, 208, 209, 217, 218, 220, 239, 240, 256, 260, 263

unity 74, 86, 92, 144, 153

untouched 21

unwise 39

V

Violence 15, 16, 17, 22, 117, 175, 177, 179, 180, 181, 182, 201, 230, 244, 245, 246, 247, 248, 249, 250, 251, 252, 253, 254

Violence around the world 22

vision x, 13, 14, 17, 19, 21, 27, 29, 31, 33, 34, 44, 46, 47, 48, 49, 50, 51, 52, 53, 59, 60, 61, 62, 64, 65, 66, 67, 68, 69, 70, 79, 80, 83, 85, 94, 97, 105, 106, 109, 110, 114, 116, 118, 119, 121, 122, 129, 132, 133, 135, 139, 146, 154, 155, 162, 166, 171, 173, 175, 176, 177, 182, 183, 184, 186, 191, 194, 196, 197, 198, 201, 203, 206, 208, 209, 224, 226, 227, 232, 233, 236, 237, 238, 239, 240, 242, 259

visions, sacred 33, 44, 46, 47, 51, 52, 62, 64, 65, 66, 67, 68, 70, 83, 97, 106, 175

visions, written word 46, 47, 48, 51, 52

vocation of a messenger 45

W

walk according to the flesh 159

walk according to the spirit 159

warnings 24, 56, 180, 205, 227, 230, 251, 252, 253

watchman 57, 194, 205

white light 21, 199

wisdom ix, 5, 7, 32, 33, 36, 38, 42, 44, 45, 47, 50, 51, 52, 65, 67, 68, 73, 83, 84, 85, 86, 87, 88, 89, 90, 91, 98, 106, 113, 122, 123, 127, 133, 134, 142, 144, 154, 158, 159, 160, 193, 195, 199, 202, 207, 208, 215, 220, 239, 240, 260

word of God 9, 46, 47, 48, 50, 51, 52, 53, 56, 65, 69, 84, 91, 97, 98, 108, 112, 119, 127, 136, 176, 178, 199, 208, 229, 238, 239, 253

work v, 5, 28, 30, 32, 35, 37, 38, 44, 45, 46, 49, 51, 57, 59, 70, 74, 75, 76, 77, 78, 80, 87, 88, 97, 101, 105, 106, 107, 111, 112, 118, 120, 122, 123, 128, 134, 135, 136, 137, 141, 143, 145, 146, 151, 152, 154, 157, 158, 159, 160, 162, 168, 177, 181, 182, 187, 188, 193, 196, 197, 199, 202, 203, 216, 217, 220, 222, 224, 229, 236, 237, 238, 241, 242, 245, 255, 258, 259

271